TOWN AND COUNTRY IN BRAZIL

MARVIN HARRIS received his B.A. and Ph.D. from Columbia University and has taught at Columbia since 1952, where he is professor of anthropology. He served as chairman of the department from 1963 to 1966. Besides *Town and Country in Brazil*, he is the author of *Minorities in the New World* (with Charles Wagley) (1958); *Patterns of Race in the Americas* (1964); *The Nature of Cultural Things* (1964); and *The Rise of Anthropological Theory* (1968).

COLUMBIA UNIVERSITY CONTRIBUTIONS TO ANTHROPOLOGY

MARVIN HARRIS

Minas Velhas

TOWN and
COUNTRY in BRAZIL

The Norton Library NEW YORK
W · W · NORTON & COMPANY · INC ·

Originally published 1956

First published in the Norton Library 1971
by arrangement with Columbia University Press

SBN 393 00573 9

PRINTED IN THE UNITED STATES OF AMERICA

1 2 3 4 5 6 7 8 9 0

ACKNOWLEDGMENTS

THE FIELD WORK upon which this study is based was carried out as part of the Columbia University–Bahia State Community Study Project from July, 1950, to June, 1951. Columbia University, the Secretaria de Educacão of the state of Bahia, Brazil, and the Fundacao Para O Desenvolvimento da Ciencia na Bahia are the organizations chiefly responsible for sponsoring and financing the Project. My participation was made possible through an Area Research Training Fellowship of the Social Science Research Council.

I am especially indebted to Professor Charles Wagley, Director of the Project, for his guidance before, during, and after the field work and for his invaluable advice in the writing of this study.

To Dr. Anizio Teixeira, former Secretary of Education of the state of Bahia, I am deeply indebted for the exceptionally high standards of intellectual and social cooperation which prevailed throughout my visit to Bahia. I also wish to thank Dr. Thales de Azevedo of the University of Bahia for his scientific counsel and warm friendship as well as for his work in proofreading the manuscript.

The research in Minas Velhas was carried out in coordination with three other community studies in other regions of the state of Bahia. I am much indebted for the cooperation of Dr. Harry Hutchinson, Benjamin Zimmerman, and Anthony Leeds, fellow anthropologists from Columbia University, who carried out these related studies.

To Dr. Eduardo Galvao, formerly of the Museu Nacional do Rio de Janeiro, I owe thanks especially for his help in establishing the early working contacts with the people of Minas Velhas. To the Brazilian students who were my co-workers in the field, Joseldeth Gomez, Maria Guerra, and Nilo Garcia, I am also greatly in-

ACKNOWLEDGMENTS

debted. Many valuable data included in this volume are
due to their efforts.

I also wish to express my gratitude to the directors and
staff of the Fundacao Para O Desenvolvimento de Bahia
whose individual kindnesses are too numerous to mention. But most profoundly of all, I am indebted to my
friends who live in the beautiful little town where this
study was made.

MARVIN HARRIS

Columbia University
January, 1956

CONTENTS

Introduction   3

1. Setting   6

2. Economics   44

3. Class and Race   96

4. The Family and the Individual   147

5. Government and Politics   179

6. Religion   208

7. Folk Belief   242

   Conclusions   274

   References Cited   291

   Index   293

MAPS AND ILLUSTRATIONS

Minas Velhas and Vicinity   7

The Town of Minas Velhas   31

A Blacksmith's Forge   50

A Brass-Smith's Lathe   51

Class Structure of Minas Velhas   97

TABLES

1. Population and Number of Domiciles
   per Village 25
2. Distribution of Occupations 47
3. Monthly Industrial Exports from Minas Velhas 61
4. Occupations of Urban Émigrés 92
5. Population of Minas Velhas
   per Sex and Age Group 93
6. Urban Sample 107
7. Average Value of Property 107
8. Range and Distribution of Property 108
9. Monthly Cash Income per Head of Family 108
10. Percentage of Income Used for Food 109
11. Types of Dwellings 109
12. Housing 110
13. Distribution of Occupations 110
14. Years of School 111
15. Highest Grade Completed 111
16. Literacy 112
17. Relative Racial Attributes 120
18. Relative Racial Rank 121
19. Relative Rank as Seen by Each Racial Group 122
20. Actual Distribution of Racial Types
    per Economic Group 136
21. Ideal Distribution of Racial Types
    per Economic Group 136
22. Number of Individuals per Household
    in Minas Velhas 148
23. Godchildren per Head of Household 154

TABLES

24. Occupational Preferences
                                of Urban School Children   175
25. Expenditures of the County of Minas Velhas
                                          for 1949-50   180
26. Receipts of the County of Minas Velhas   183
27. State Bureaucracy in Minas Velhas   193
28. Church Attendance by Sex and Class per Year   212
29. Household Patrons   225
30. Minimum and Maximum Expenses
                              for a Typical Festa   235
31. Sources of Income for a Typical Festa   236
32. Fears of School Children   269

TOWN AND COUNTRY IN BRAZIL

INTRODUCTION

WITH its population density of 15.9 people per square mile, Brazil has long been characterized as a rural nation. According to T. Lynn Smith, "Quantitatively and qualitatively Brazil's population is among the most rural in the world. No other fact is of greater importance than this for one who would understand Brazil and the Brazilians." [1] As further evidence of this condition, the opinion of the Brazilian sociologist Oliveira Vianna is often cited:

From the first days of our history we have been an agricultural and pastoral people. . . . Urbanism is a modern element in our social evolution. All of our history is that of an agricultural people, is the history of a society of farmers and herdsmen. In the country our race was formed and in it were molded the intimate forces of our civilization. The dynamism of our history in the colonial period came from the countryside. The admirable stability of our society in the Imperial period was based on the country. [2]

The use of the terms "rural" and "urban" as applied to Brazil, however, is usually far from clear. Although in most Brazilian census figures, as T. Lynn Smith points out, inhabitants of county seats, no matter how small, have been classified as urban, most students have considered all small towns and villages of less than five thousand inhabitants as rural. The fact is that no attempt has been made to define what is meant by "rural" and "urban" in the specific context of Brazilian culture patterns. Can Brazilian settlements be considered rural largely on the basis of size, degree of isolation, and level of technology, as Smith seems to propose?

With less than fifty million people spread throughout its enormous territory, with relatively few important focal points

[1] T. L. Smith and Alexander Marchant, *Brazil*, p. 153.
[2] *Ibid.*

of urban and industrial cultural influences, with a high proportion of the population engaged directly in agriculture and collecting activities, and with systems of transportation and communication still in a rudimentary form, it should be evident that the degree of rurality in Brazil is very high.[3]

In the central and northern portions of the Eastern Brazilian Highlands, there are many communities of less than two thousand people, strikingly isolated from the nation's metropolitan centers, with a retarded level of technological development and a world view which is essentially nonscientific, but which nonetheless present a large number of conspicuously urban features. Whatever the opinion of social scientists may be, the inhabitants of these towns feel themselves to be profoundly different from their country neighbors who live nearby in villages and on farms.

The Eastern Highlands were the first portions of the Brazilian interior to be settled by any substantial number of people. The discovery of gold and diamonds early in the eighteenth century provided the reason for the bulk of this settlement. With respect to the settlement of the interior of the three important states of Sao Paulo, Minas Gerais, and Bahia, the early founding of a number of sophisticated, nonagricultural urban centers based upon mining is of paramount importance. As the geographer Pierre Deffontaines has indicated:

Mining creates a form of urban civilization: the miners were founders of towns; the mining mountain might be defined as an empty countryside dotted with towns. . . . In Brazil, as in many other regions, the mining civilization was a purely urban one. Between the centers was a desolate country; under the demands of the mines, the primitive forest was rapidly destroyed, the bare soil where ferruginous concretions of the laterite characteristically appeared, supported no pasturage; cultivation for the most part was impossible.[4]

[3] *Ibid.*, p. 154.
[4] Pierre Deffontaines, "Mountain Settlement in the Central Brazilian Plateau, *Geographical Review*, XXVII (1937), 412.

If Brazil is to be best understood as a rural nation, many of its rural areas cannot be understood at all except in relation to hundreds of deeply entrenched urban nuclei which, like Minas Velhas, got their start in the halycon days of the mining boom.

These urban centers were on the whole premature. If one considers the agricultural potential and the population density of the surrounding countryside, they were like an abundance of leaven amid a shortage of flour. Flung westward on a wave of prosperity that quickly retreated and left them stranded in the most unlikely places, they have waited for two centuries for the new Brazilian frontier to catch up with them.

In this early westward jump lies the chief difference between the changing frontiers of the United States and Brazil:

The United States . . . showed a fairly orderly westerly advance decade by decade with no bad breaks until 1849 when the gold rush to California carried the margin of humanity in one great leap to the rim of the western ocean. . . . But in Brazil as early as 1700, gold broke the frontier into a thousand fragments and scattered humanity over the boundless face of nature.[5]

Having pushed on too far too quickly, the Brazilian frontiersman in the mining region has been as much the sophisticated, conservative city dweller looking back to the comforts of the east as the rough and ready man with the axe seeking to carve out a new empire in the west.

[5] Roy Nash, *The Conquest of Brazil*, p. 327.

SETTING

MINAS VELHAS (Old Mines) is a small county seat located in the midst of the mountains of central Bahia. The town has a very lonely setting. It is three thousand feet above sea level and surrounded on all sides by rugged hills and escarpments. Only a few people in Salvador, the state capital, have ever heard of it. Minas Velhas has, in fact, little that would recommend it to their interest. The town has no automobiles, electricity, movies, telephones, steel, or concrete. It is one of those increasingly rare places still immune to the penetrations of Coca Cola. The nearest railroad approaches no closer than a stop called Bromado, fifty miles away. From this point the rest of the journey has to be made by truck and horseback.

The ride by truck is a hot and turbulent affair. If you are lucky, and the place beside the driver is not already taken, you may sit inside the cab. Otherwise you must join the crowd of men, women, and children perched precariously on top of the cargo. It is best to find something solid to hold onto for the road is full of pits, rocks, and treacherous sand. The driver, with great skill and effort, manages to keep the truck moving most of the time. His cargo of kerosene, farm tools, cloth, and wheat flour is firmly lashed down, but the passengers are expected to fend for themselves. There is a saying among the truck drivers who frequent this part of the country that the best cargo is a human cargo: "You don't have to lift them on and off, and they hold on by themselves."

About once or twice a week you may find a truck that is going directly from Bromado to Minas Velhas. It is more likely, however, that you can find one leaving before then for Vila Nova (New Town), the next closest town. A few miles outside of Vila Nova there rises a towering blue-green escarpment stretching north and

MINAS VELHAS AND VICINITY

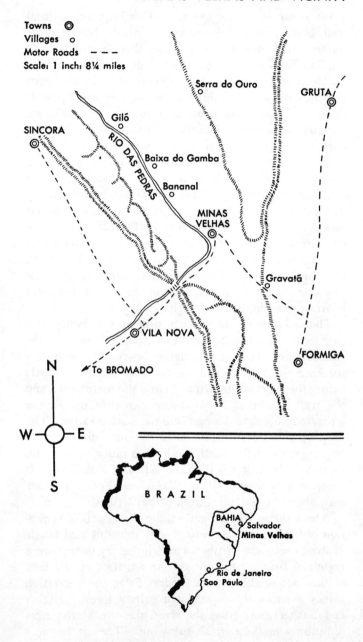

Towns ◎
Villages ○
Motor Roads − − −
Scale: 1 inch: 8¼ miles

Serra do Ouro

GRUTA

Giló

SINCORA

RIO DAS PEDRAS

Baixa do Gamba

Bananal

MINAS
VELHAS

Gravatá

VILA NOVA

FORMIGA

To BROMADO

N
W ─○─ E
S

BRAZIL

BAHIA
Salvador
Minas Velhas

Rio de Janeiro
Sao Paulo

south as far as the eye can see. This imposing natural wall is part of a subcontinental divide between the waters which flow to the sea and those which flow to the Sao Francisco River. On top of the ridge and invisible from below lies Minas Velhas. Until three years ago the only way to complete the journey was by horse or mule. Now there is a motor road. But trucks are few and far between; the most reliable way is still on the back of an animal—preferably a mule that is familiar with the precipitous stone-lined trail up the mountain. This trail, or *ladeira* as it is called because of its similarity to a flight of stairs, climbs almost straight up the wall of the escarpment adjacent to the spectacular Rio das Pedras Falls. The Rio das Pedras runs along a deep trough in the top of the escarpment. It veers past Minas Velhas and plunges into the valley of Vila Nova in a series of rapids and cataracts, creating the best east-west passage for miles. One of the falls at this point is over three hundred feet high.

The Vila Nova or western side of the escarpment culminates in a six-thousand-foot peak; on the east, the maximum elevation is but slightly lower. On both sides the escarpment drops off steeply into valleys. Shortly before the entrance to Minas Velhas the motor road and the trail combine. Beyond the city they once more separate in order to descend into the eastern valley. The drop on this side presents much the same difficulties as the other; the valley itself, however, is much smaller and more heavily dissected than the valley of Vila Nova. It contains two towns, Gruta (Cave) and Formiga (Ant), each about fifteen miles from Minas Velhas.

Where there is no irrigation, the characteristic vegetation of both valleys is *caatinga*—the spine-infested tangle of trees, cacti, and shrubs for which the dry northeastern region of Brazil is so famous. As you start up the trail at the foot of the Rio das Pedras Falls, the vegetation briefly assumes the aspect of a gallery forest. Higher and farther away from the river, the size of the trees diminishes and the brush thins out. The air becomes perceptibly cooler, and stretches of desertlike barrenness suddenly appear. At the top of the trail you have entered the *gerais*—the vegetation zone characteristic of the higher elevations of Bahia.

The *gerais* is a lonely, wind-swept empire of sparse grass and stunted trees. Between the gullied slopes of the escarpment lie vast barren plains inhabited chiefly by termites whose spherical nests perched on ruined boulders and twisted trees are everywhere visible in awe-inspiring multitudes. A bewildering variety of small shrubs and cacti grow here. Ancient rock crumbles at the touch. Upturned layers of fossil-bearing slate crop out of the hillsides. Gneiss veined with quartzite appears at the rivers. In the hills, scattered about in unverified quantities, are amethyst and topaz. There are iron lodes, traces of platinum, bauxite, and tin. Blocks of crystal are abundant and two hundred years ago gold was abundant, too.

At a distance of half a mile from the small stone wall which marks the entrance to Minas Velhas, the *gerais* still keeps its biggest secret. There is no gradual thickening of houses, no visible farm, no concentration of cattle, no evidence of converging pedestrian or vehicular traffic. A heavy silence, broken only by the wind and the cries of parakeets and canaries, hangs over the last leg of the journey. The empty white sand road in the midst of the apparently empty hills makes a turn and one sees the buildings already close at hand. The isolation is profound and perplexing.

As he stepped off the train at Bromado, covered from head to foot with fine red dust as a result of his journey, the traveler was ready to believe that he had arrived at a point close to the limits of civilization. The scattered few peasant villages between Bromado and Vila Nova confirmed this opinion. The streets were deserted, the adobe houses crumbling and unpainted. Along the road groups of wide-eyed naked children peered out of the doorways of thatch-roofed huts. Flocks of goats scattered wildly before the oncoming truck. At the sound of the motor, horses and mules reared up, got away from their drivers, and charged off into the underbrush. The people looked hungry and the land looked parched. Now and then barefoot women in tattered dresses could be seen digging down into the dry river beds in search of water.

In Vila Nova it is different. Here there are energetic signs of commerce and agriculture. Irrigated by the waters of the Rio das Pedras, green rice waves in the fields. Large groves of coconut palms provide welcome shade. Vila Nova is in the midst of a boom. All day long the air is filled with the creaking of oxcarts bringing sacks of rice and corn to the water-driven mills that hum in the distance. Trucks arrive and depart at the rate of two or three a day. At night a diesel motor lights the streets and a few of the houses. True, the power is shut off at eleven, the light is feeble, and the motor is constantly breaking down; but it is electricity and the townspeople are proud of it. They say their town is growing: land has doubled in value, fifteen new buildings are going up at once, and a hospital and secondary school are almost ready. Two bars proudly advertise that they sell refrigerated *Guarana* and Coca Cola. The pensions are crowded with traveling salesmen who can be seen at the windows in the morning brushing their teeth and rinsing the water from their mouths onto the sidewalk. Vila Nova is a raw, bustling, uncomfortable town—the typical bizarre mixture of old and new expected at a frontier. But what kind of a town can lie beyond, still more remote, up there on that unlikely spot on top of a mountain?

The people of Vila Nova are not very encouraging. "What do you want to go up there for?" the pension owner asks. "Stay with us. We've got electricity and coconuts. Plenty of fresh fruit and pork. There's always something doing here."

"Minas Velhas is the deadest place in the world," the barkeep says. "There hasn't been any progress up there for two hundred years. If you like cold beer, you'd

better stay with us.   There's only one bar in Minas
Velhas and it doesn't do enough business to make a
refrigerator worth while."

"They live in a terrible state of backwardness," says
the owner of a well-stocked hardware store.   "Business is
awful.   It's a sad place—very cold and no activity at all."

Provisioned with no further information, the visitor is
in for a surprise as he rounds the last bend in the sandy
road and sees Minas Velhas for the first time.   The
prospect is one of long, neat rows of houses, most of them
freshly whitewashed and all of them roofed with tile.
Decorative bands and friezes ornament the walls.   Level,
well-made sidewalks paved with slate line the clean
streets.   A big four-room schoolhouse stands near the
entrance to the town.   School children dressed uniformly
in white blouses and navy-blue skirts stop to watch you
approach.   Some of them are carrying small briefcases.
Passing over a stone bridge that spans a small stream
channeled by retaining walls, you come to the spacious
main square.   A well-proportioned stone church, freshly
painted in white with blue trimmings and a large gold
crest on the façade, shines brightly in the sunlight.   In
front of the church there is a wide circular flower bed,
geometrically interlaced with level walks.   Standing on
the apron at the center of this garden, attired in well-
pressed suits, white shirts, neckties, and hats, are a group
of the townspeople.   Before they turned to look at you,
they had been watching a workman going among the
flowers with a watering can.

The journey to Minas Velhas is a long and arduous
one.   Yet it is not long before you begin to suspect that
you have not gone so far after all.   Automobiles, refrigerators, tractors, movies, and electric lights are indeed
far behind.   The mountains have kept them out.   But
they have not kept the city out.   The city is here despite the absence of steel and concrete.   In fact it has
been here a long time, rich in an urban ethos, distinct
from the peasantry—complicated, sophisticated, specialized.

HISTORICAL BACKGROUND

Stretching parallel to the Atlantic coast from central Minas Gerais to northern Bahia in a belt thirty to one hundred and fifty miles wide is the range of scarps and mountains known as the Serra do Espinhaco. From this region during the eighteenth century came the mineral wealth that made Brazil for a time the largest producer of diamonds and gold in the world. Here the primordial form of settlement, as in the case of Minas Velhas, was profoundly urban in character.

The discovery of gold contributed immensely to the settlement of the Brazilian interior, and possibly half the towns in east-central Brazil owe their origin to mining.[1] Until the rush which took place during the early eighteenth century, the highlands were empty. Even the Indian population had been sparse in this region. In a few decades, however, some of the most opulent cities in Brazil, perhaps in all South America, were established right in the middle of this rugged wilderness. The most famous of these was called Vila Rica (Rich Town, now known as Ouro Preto, Black Gold), which according to Robert Southey, the English poet, was "the richest place in the world, if gold alone were riches." [2] At its maximum the population of Vila Rica has been estimated at 100,000.[3] It was a city built hastily but on a pretentious scale, with a remarkable amount of urban improvements. Some of the best wood and stone sculpture in America was done here as in other cities of Minas Gerais by "Aleijadinho," famous throughout Brazil as the "little cripple." So impressive are the delicately worked baroque churches, graceful public fountains, paved streets, well-proportioned stone houses, and the fine statuary, that Vila Rica has been declared a national monument and is now preserved for the future as a museum city.

[1] Fernando de Azevedo, A Cultura Brasileiro, p. 44.
[2] Robert Southey, History of Brazil, III, 803.
[3] Pedro Calmon, Historia do Brasil, p. 93.

The quantity of gold removed from the Brazilian highlands and transported to Europe during the years from 1690 to 1770 was great enough to have affected the course of European history. During this period more than 44 percent of the gold produced in the world was mined in Brazil.[4] Even so seemingly remote a phenomenon as the rise of English industrial capitalism is to a significant degree associated with the sudden expansion of the world supply of hard cash created by the Brazilian bonanza. In 1703 the treaty of Methuen was concluded between England and Portugal by which the Portuguese agreed to kill their nascent textile industry in exchange for an English agreement to import Portuguese wines. This treaty eliminated the only significant competitor of the English textile industry—the basis of England's first great industrial expansion. It also committed Portugal to a foreign trade deficit—a situation which she was able to face with equanimity because of the seemingly endless stream of wealth that poured into her coffers from across the sea.

Trade with Portugal became of great importance . . . at the beginning of the eighteenth century after the discovery of rich gold and diamond fields in Brazil. The Methuen Treaty of 1703 bound Portugal to England in such close relations that Portugese gold almost all went to the London market. "We gain a greater balance from Portugal than from any other country whatever," wrote a contemporary observer. "By the treaty we have increased our exports thither from about £300,000 to near £1,500,000." In the eighty years from 1700 to 1780 this favorable balance of trade together with other means of getting Portuguese gold such as colonial investments by Englishmen in Brazil, brought perhaps £120,000,000 of gold into England.[5]

The Portuguese star, made of Brazilian gold and encrusted with Brazilian diamonds, rapidly ascended to a glittering but ephemeral zenith. Many of Lisbon's great palaces, monuments, and museums were built at this

[4] Preston James, *Latin America*, p. 367.
[5] George Young, *Portugal Old and Young*, p. 188.

time. In pomp and splendor the court of Don John V came to rival that of Louis XIV. Portugal's equivalent of the Palace of Versailles dates from this period:

The monastery-palace-barracks of Mafra took thirteen years to build during which fifteen to fifty thousand workman were employed; it has 860 rooms, and 5,000 doors; 10,000 men could drill on the roof; and it cost over 20,000,000 crowns.[6]

The discovery of gold had equally far-reaching consequences in Brazil. The demand for slave labor created by the mining enterprise itself, together with the rise of foreign production in the West Indies, contributed directly to the senescence of the Brazilian sugar plantation. Gold rapidly replaced sugar as the colony's chief source of wealth, belatedly fulfilling the original Portuguese dream of finding an El Dorado in the New World. The price of African slaves in the mining region rose beyond the ability of the sugar planters to pay. Many plantations were abandoned outright as the population moved en masse from the coast to the mountains with thousands of additional prospectors coming directly from Portugal. Rio de Janeiro, as the port city closest to the center of the mines, dates its florescence from this period.

Toward the end of the eighteenth century, the gold cycle drew to its unhappy close. The mines gradually dwindled into insignificance and with them the Portuguese Empire. In Brazil, the center of population moved back to the coast. The opulence of the Vila Ricas and Diamantinas became memories. Already in 1821, the English traveler John Mawe could write: "Vila Rica at the present day scarcely retains a shadow of its former splendor. Its inhabitants, with the exception of the shopkeepers, are void of employment."[7] In the typical Brazilian economic tradition, prosperity was succeeded by poverty, boom by bust. Sugar and gold were gone, coffee and rubber were yet to come.

But the ephemeral riches of the mines had wrought a

[6] *Ibid.*   [7] John Mawe, *Travels in the Interior of Brazil*, p. 250.

profound and enduring change on the Brazilian landscape. When the gold ran out, the mountains, in a
sense, once more became the Brazilian frontier—but a
frontier with a very special feature. Hundreds of towns
now lay scattered about in the hills like islands in the
midst of an ocean. Like the subject of our study, Minas
Velhas, the majority of these, if not prospering, are still
alive and on the map.

Most of the old mining towns, none more conspicuously than Minas Velhas, sprang up at sites deficient in
potential food-producing soils. In the early stages of
mining, the bulk of food and supplies had to be brought
in from remote places. Agriculture in the mountain
region was at best a secondary development, restricted
to the occasional enclaves of fertile soil in the river
valleys between the major escarpments. Optimum
farming or grazing conditions rarely coincided with the
sites of intensive mining, yet in all the mountains of
Bahia not a single real ghost town is to be found. There
are many former mining centers which today, like Minas
Velhas, are "cold and dreary places" in the eyes of
people living in more fortunate localities, but all of
them continue to be inhabited and to function as communities to some degree. By the time mining had
ceased to be feasible, the towns had become entrenched
distributing points, filled with merchant middlemen, the
scenes of small-scale industries, the homes of prelates
and schoolteachers, and, above all, the centers of enlarged and predatory governmental bureaucracies. The
end of the gold mining era definitely did not mark the
end of these towns, though it is frequently difficult to
explain why this is the case.

Wherever possible, the established urban centers
adapted to the disappearance of their original *raison
d'être* by evolving new basic economies. The old mining towns turned to handicrafts, cattle raising, coffee
growing, mixed farming, fireworks manufacture, or
whatever else the particular local environment would
permit. Some of them managed to continue mining

for gold and other precious and semiprecious minerals on a subsidiary basis. Most of these adaptations were makeshift and permitted little more than a marginal standard of living for the majority of people.

Minas Velhas was never as imposing a city as Vila Rica, yet in its prosperous days it was among the most important mining centers in the state. After the exploitation of the local mines ceased to be profitable, the people of Minas Velhas took to producing gold and silver jewelry, metal and leather harness parts, saddles, knives, and, more recently, shoes, boots, and sandals. At one time there were more than twenty goldsmiths in the town. Today there are over forty small workshops that turn out objects in brass, nickel, tin, gold, silver, iron, and leather.

The initial discoveries of gold centered in the present state of Minas Gerais. With the influx of a large number of prospectors and semiofficial exploring parties, the fields were rapidly extended to include portions of Matto Grosso, Goyaz, Sao Paulo, and Bahia.

It is known that a Paulistan adventurer by the name of Sebastiao Raposo was working rich fluvial deposits of gold before 1722 in the near vicinity of Minas Velhas.[8] Since it was to the best advantage of the earliest prospectors to guard their discoveries from the rest of the world, it is probable that the streams and hillsides around Minas Velhas were being worked several years earlier. Undoubtedly many of the early explorers in the area were led to traverse the western escarpment near the site of Minas Velhas while taking advantage of the natural passage provided by the Rio das Pedras. This passage, today linking Minas Velhas with Vila Nova, became an important highway during colonial times and was known for a hundred years as the Royal Highway. It became part of the main route between the gold fields of Minas Gerais, the cattle ranches of the Sao Francisco Valley, and the cities of the coast.

In 1725 Minas Velhas was designated a *vila* (town-

[8] Pandia Calogeras, *As Minas do Brasil e Sua Legislacao*, p. 71.

ship). This meant that the settlement was to be the
seat of a whole series of governmental functions including the maintenance of law and order and the collection
of taxes. Judges, officers, soldiers, tax collectors, and
clerks were part of the urban scene almost from the
start.

In 1726 the output from the local mines had become
important enough for a smelting house to be constructed
in order to facilitate the collection of the *quinto*—the 20
percent royal tax on crude gold (Edict of the Conselho
Ultramarino, May 3, 1726). It was in the smelting
down of gold into transportable bullion that the
knowledge of the goldsmith's art was introduced in
Minas Velhas—a skill which was destined later to be
widely disseminated among the townspeople and which
eventually gave birth to the other metallurgical crafts
that form the basis of the town's present-day economy.

A record of this royal tax for the year 1746-47 shows
that about thirty pounds of gold were collected. According to popular accounts, Sebastiao Raposo alone took
1,344 pounds out of the mines near town. Books of the
times in the municipal hall list large quantities of gold
in transit through the city. The accounts are signed in
an ink in which tiny flakes of gold and silver appear.

Throughout the area surrounding the town abundant
evidence of the magnitude of the old mining enterprise
still is furnished by rubble-strewn hillsides, deep rock
caves and tunnels, long canals, aqueducts, and stone
dams. Most of the mining being done presently consists of merely in the reworking of these excavations in
the hope that *os antigos* (the old ones) may have over-
looked something.

The golden age of Minas Velhas seems to have lasted
until the end of the eighteenth century. The German
naturalists Von Spix and Von Martius visited the town
in 1820 and observed that twenty years before, the mines
had still been yielding important riches.[9] But despite
the steadily decreasing importance of gold in the local

[9] J. Von Spix and K. Von Martius, *Atraves da Bahia*, p. 53.

economy, Minas Velhas continued to expand its bureaucratic functions until well into the first half of the nineteenth century. As a judicial center it was elevated to
higher categories in 1811 and again in 1832. A massive
jail and courthouse still standing today was built at this
time. Although little used now, scores of prisoners from
all over the interior used to be brought to trial and im-
prisoned in it.

Minas Velhas continues officially to be the seat of a
judicial district to this day, but the creation of new
legal centers within the area formerly controlled by the
town has reduced it to but a shadow of its former judicial importance. The same is true administratively. In
1746 Minas Velhas was the seat of an immense *municipio*
(county) that stretched eastward almost to the Bay of
Bahia and westward to the Sao Francisco River. The
area of its control has been sliced six times (in 1746,
1810, 1840, 1847, 1878, and 1921), and from the dis-
membered units no less than thirty-four new counties
have been established. Today the county of Minas
Velhas, of which the town of Minas Velhas continues to
be the *sede* (county seat) is one of the smallest in area
and population in the entire state, and from the standpoint of tax income, one of the poorest. The scope of
the city's religious functions has dwindled in the same
ratio. Once the seat controlling nine parishes, it now
controls but one. Government, however, still continues
to be big business in Minas Velhas. Over thirty different kinds of remunerative activities are still, as we shall
see, subsidized by municipal, state, and federal funds.

That there are no ghost towns in the mountain region
of Bahia is due in no small measure to the self-perpetu-
ating characteristics of the civil and religious bureaucracies. In a sense, the bureaucratic superstructure was
the real backbone of the old urban centers. It was a
type of indestructible seed capable of bearing fruit in
barren soils and of withstanding the ravishes of droughts,
depressions, and migrations. It could do this because
it derived its income from an area many times greater

than the economic sphere of influence of the town alone. In addition to state and federal subsidies, the bureaucracy could live off the agricultural enclaves more prosperous than the town itself. For this reason, for example, Vila Nova fought bitterly for fifty years to free itself from Minas Velhas's parasitic grasp. It was a sad day for the politicians of Minas Velhas when in 1921 the neighboring town finally became the seat of a new county. However, for many years the tax collectors, the clerks, the notaries, the judges, the soldiers, the road workers, the street cleaners, the lamplighters—the whole complex of services subsumed under the rubric of government—were fully capable of maintaining a trajectory tangent to the plunging line of the rest of the town's economic destiny. As long as Minas Velhas remained defined as an important political nucleus it could never be completely abandoned.

The story of Minas Velhas's decline is really the story of the rise of the rest of the state. The reasons for the town's early prominence proved to be ephemeral. New urban centers sprang up in more fertile regions. New roads were developed, and except for the occasional cattle herds that still make their way from the southwestern basin of the Sao Francisco River through Minas Velhas and on toward the coastal markets, the Royal Highway fell into disuse. All through the nineteenth century, traffic dwindled on this road. With the building of the first rail line about twenty years ago between Salvador and the southeastern portions of the state, the deathblow was administered; the line passed almost fifty miles to the south. What is still the most direct route for animal traffic has been almost as completely ignored by trucks as well. Today in order to reach Minas Velhas by automobile from Salvador, one must make an enormous detour to the south or north. The recently completed motor road, which follows the old Royal Highway up the escarpment only in the stretch between Vila Nova and Minas Velhas, entails a detour from the direct route of over one hundred and seventy-five miles on a trip from Salvador. This journey still takes anywhere from two to five days. As we have seen, the nearest approach by public transport leaves the traveler with fifty miles to be covered by truck, horse, or mule, depending on his luck.

In 1820, Von Spix and Von Martius estimated the population of Minas Velhas at nine hundred (they speak of a famine in 1810 in which hundreds were reported to have perished). It is doubtful, however, that the population was ever much greater than it is today (1,500). Externally, the physical signs of a real decadence are nowhere to be found; the town as a whole is in a relatively good state of repair. Except for one church abandoned before completion and another which was demolished, there are few genuine ruins visible. Actually the impression of decline is produced more in comparison with the changes which have taken place in other cities than by comparing Minas Velhas with its own past. It is true that gold mining has practically disappeared and that the level of commercial activity is greatly inferior to what it once was. But the concept of decadence when applied to living societies is extremely connotative. There is no way of comparing the contemporary over-all standard of living with that of the past, especially when the existence of slave labor during colonial times is taken into account.

Some of the luxuries associated with a prosperous leisure class have disappeared; most of them, however, have simply paled by comparison with modern standards of opulence such as electric lights, hot and cold running water, refrigerators, and automobiles. Rich families still have three or four servants; many people own more clothes than they need, have more to eat than they are hungry for, pamper children, horses, and dogs, have time for plenty of idle conversations, and need do no work.

The scale of luxury has vastly expanded since the time when such a life was aristocratic bliss. The decadence of Minas Velhas consists in the fact that the

social definition of poverty has almost caught up with
the old social definition of luxury. Rich and poor alike
in Minas Velhas are poorer today because there are more
things they want to buy and nothing additional to buy
them with.

The failure of Minas Velhas to keep pace with the
material progress of the twentieth century does not
affect its essential urbanism.[10] Poverty and technological
backwardness have not dimmed the distinction between
country dweller and city dweller except in the eyes of
the inhabitants of the great coastal metropolises, who
tend to lump all the people in the interior under the
same term—*sertanejo,* inhabitant of the backlands.
This catch-all category has never been justified. If there
is any single concept that is important to the way of life
of the people who live in Minas Velhas, it is precisely
that they live in a city, that they are the carriers of a
sophisticated and not a folk culture. This distinction
goes back a long way and continues in the present.

When Von Spix and Von Martius visited Minhas
Velhas in 1820, the contrast between city and country
was as valid then as it is now. They wrote: "Since the
climate does not favor agriculture, the exploitation of
the gold mines and commerce are the most important
activities of the townspeople, who are distinguished
from the rest of the population of the interior of Bahia
by their opulence and education." [11]

Finding this "opulence and education" on top of a
mountain in the midst of a wilderness greatly impressed
the two Germans. In another passage entitled "Classical
Education in the Bahian Interior," they used Minas

[10] "It is particularly important to call attention to the danger of
confusing urbanism with industrialism and modern capitalism. The
rise of cities in the modern world is undoubtedly not independent
of the emergence of modern power-driven machine technology, mass
production, and capitalistic enterprise. But different as the cities of
earlier epochs may have been by virtue of their development in a
pre-industrial and pre-capitalistic order from the great cities of
today, they were, nonetheless, cities." Louis Wirth, "Urbanism as
a Way of Life," *American Journal of Sociology,* XLIV (1938), 2.
[11] Von Spix and Von Martius, *Atraves da Bahia,* p. 58.

Velhas as proof that high European educational standards could be maintained in the tropics: "The Latin professor, a man of truly classical erudition, proved that the fruits of the spirit can also ripen in the much maligned tropical climate."

A contemporary local historian, himself devoted to eulogizing the "cultured tradition" of Minas Velhas, asserts that from very early times classes were given in Latin grammar, Portuguese, French, and philosophy.[12] The same source states that secondary instruction terminated about 1850. It has never been reinstated, but the concept of an elite tradition has been successfully maintained.

Not only do the townspeople consider themselves to be superior to their country neighbors, but they also claim a measure of superiority over the neighboring towns. Despite the low opinion of Minas Velhas tendered by the inhabitants of Vila Nova and the much lamented lack of technological progress, the town keeps its head up. "Minas Velhas is a beggar with jewels in her pocket," writes Sr. A. G., ". . . the cradle of civilization in the Bahian interior." Upper-class townspeople regard themselves as exemplars of courtesy and hospitality. They feel as Von Spix and Von Martius felt, that Minas Velhas is still readily distinguishable from the rest of the backlands by superior social know-how and a spirit of gentility.

An ever present aspect of this heritage is the attempt on the part of literate official and semiofficial spokesmen of Minas Velhas to distort the real picture of poverty and stagnation by glossing it over with invocations to superior social opulence. Shining verbalisms worthy of a highly organized chamber of commerce are considered the *noblesse oblige* of educated persons. The report made by the local representative of the Brazilian Institute of Geography and Statistics for the 1940 census is a good example: "The inhabitant of our county . . . is a man molded in the sentiments of honor, dignity,

[12] Thesis presented to the First Historical Congress in Bahia in 1950 by A. G.

and honesty; he is peace-loving and a hard worker . . . .
He has a lofty sentiment of the family which he respects
as something sacred . . . . He is given to arts and
letters." The most characteristic customs of the county
were described as "those of men civilized and educated
in the postulates of morality, religion, and society."

The history of Minas Velhas shows that its urbanism
has deep roots. The earliest inhabitants of the town-
site were sophisticated adventurers, not peasants. They
were the agents of an elaborate civilized tradition, who
looked upon the soil not as something to plant but
merely as an obstacle in their search for deeper and
more spectacular treasures. Using slave labor they sifted
the sands of the rivers and streams, built dams, aqueducts, and canals, dug tunnels deep into the hillsides.
They were joined by merchants who provided them
and their slaves with food and hardware brought in
from distant places. Subjects all of an autocratic and
predatory political state, they were joined as well by a
large bureaucratic task force that struggled with pens,
papers, seals, and swords to help keep Portugal from
going bankrupt. All together they founded a settlement
that tended to duplicate the contemporary urban ideal.
They started construction on a total of four churches
furnished with elaborate baroque ceilings and altars,
and expensive silver chalices, lanterns, and standards.
The settlement rapidly became the distributing and
administrative center of a large area; it grew to be not
only a city but a kind of capital, unrivaled for hundreds
of miles around. In the beginning the town fed as well
as clothed and equipped the workers in the rural areas;
only much later did the rural area begin to feed the
town. In the mining region, the city came first;
peasantry was a by-product of town life. The town
sprang up and gave birth, so to speak, to the country.

TOWN AND COUNTRY

As the traveler from Vila Nova arrives at the entrance
to Minas Velhas, he must get down from his horse or
out of his car in order to open a large swinging gate

which blocks the entrance to the city. If he arrives from the other direction, from Forno or Formiga, it is the same. Every trail leading in from the country has its own swinging gate also. These gates are all connected by a series of walls and fences. Together with the river and the back-yard walls of some of the houses, they form an interconnected system sealing the town off from the countryside. These barriers are designed to keep the few head of cattle which roam the *gerais,* unfenced and untethered, out of the streets, mainly to protect the municipal garden. If a line were to be drawn everywhere five hundred yards distant from the periphery of the enclosure, we would be demarcating 98 percent of the primary community. Within these limits live about fifteen hundred people in two hundred and seventy domiciles.

Beyond the five-hundred-yard line, extending in all directions except along the banks of the Rio das Pedras, there is a wide belt of uninhabited *gerais* from two to ten miles in width. The insularity of the houses, streets, pastures, and small farms of the urban site caused by this desolate expanse is the outstanding feature of Minas Velhas's settlement pattern.

The picture of an urban nucleus surrounded by a dependent farming population spread out evenly in concentric circles and eventually overlapping with similar rural groups dependent on a neighboring town is inapplicable. The rural populations which one encounters beyond the periphery of Minas Velhas at a distance of from two to twelve miles are spatially and socially distinct, not only from the town, but from each other as well. These rural groups take the form of clusters of farmhouses and villages surrounded to a limited depth by contiguous farms. The isolated farmhouse is the exception. Two of the villages consist of houses arranged regularly and closely enough to form streets. Not all of the houses are to be found on these streets; the rest are spread out at intervals of three hundred feet or so, with the heavier concentration forming the center of the settlement.

TABLE 1. POPULATION AND NUMBER OF DOMICILES PER VILLAGE

VILLAGE	DOMICILES	POPULATION
Serra do Ouro	115	585
Baixa do Gamba	46	202
Gravata	30	162
Gilo	29	149
Bananal	14	76
Brumadinho	14	67

The three largest villages have their own churches and their own cemeteries. All have different patron saints and three of them have annual celebrations including mass. Very few of the residents of the villages will normally attend mass on Sunday in Minas Velhas. The long walk is effectively discouraging. Serra de Ouro has Sunday services of its own conducted by a sacristan. Most of the baptisms, communions, and marriages of the villages are· performed *in sitio* when the priest from Minas Velhas makes his annual visit for the festival of the patron saint. The rural dead rest in their own cemeteries and are buried without the benefit of the priest. The people of Gilo, of Bananal, and of Brumadinho bury their dead in Baixa do Gamba. The three largest villages also have their own county primary schools, and there are no children from any of the villages registered in Minas Velhas.

There is a pronounced tendency for inbreeding to take place within these villages. When samples of the rural population are gathered in Minas Valhas for the weekly fair on Saturday, the townspeople claim to be able to identify the members of each village by their physical type. Serra de Ouro is widely known for its "pure white" population, with grey or blue eyes, straight to wavy, brown to light-brown hair, and reduced stature. (It is reputedly too cold where they live, right on top of a mountain, for them to grow very much.) Baixa do Gamba, on the other hand, is inhabited by a negroid group with very kinky hair and tall stature. According to the popular accounts, which more or less represent the actual facts, it is impossible to find a single Negro in Serra do Ouro or a single white in Baixa do Gamba. A group which was not studied because of its prohibitive distance from Minas Velhas contains a predominance of *caboclo* types—dark-brown skin, brown eyes, straight black hair, thin lips, and medium height. The physical homogeneity of these rural groups also permits identification even when the criteria are not so glaringly different from the normal cross section of the general population of the region. The bulk of the residents of the clusters usually consist of two or three families which present certain continuing characteristics readily apparent among themselves and to their intimates.

Almost without exception the people of the villages farm for their livelihood. They leave their houses in the morning and work in the surrounding fields, returning near nightfall. If their houses are close enough, they also return for lunch. They plant a variety of crops usually including beans, corn, and mandioca as the staples, with rice, sugar cane, coffee, pineapples, oranges, bananas, tomatoes, gourds, potatoes, watermelon, wheat, and quince of secondary interest. Surplus beyond the requirements of the household is sold to the nonfarming populations of the neighboring urban centers and to other farmers who have not planted a particular crop or enough of it. Sale takes place at the public fair in the neighboring towns on regularly recurring days. It is the established pattern for the producer himself to carry his produce to the town and make the sale either directly to the consumer or to a storekeeper. Because of the variety of crops, the average farmer generally has something to sell, though sometimes in almost minute quantities, at least every second week throughout the year.

Minas Velhas, Vila Nova, and Formiga have their fairs on Saturday. Forno has one on Sunday. The farmers from Serra do Ouro, Baixa do Gamba, Gravata, and Gilo have a choice of from two to three of these places to sell their products, taking distance as the primary consideration. The choice is actually based on several other factors, including, for example, habit and variations in prices. The fact is that while some of the farmers regularly go to the fair in only one particular town, many others attend the fair in two or three different places throughout the year. Representatives of the same village therefore may always be found in several different fairs on the same day. The realm of feasible market places, however, has definite spatial limitations. As long as it is the farmer himself who must transport the commodities and as long as his harvest is varied and seasonally broadcast, the transaction must take place at a distance which does not require more than a day of travel to go and return. The farming clusters, economically speaking, are bound to a group of fair towns but to no given one exclusively.

The phenomenon of the cluster-type settlement pattern of the rural population is correlated with the intermittent nature of the arable land. All along the escarpment soil conditions vary abruptly, changing from bare rock to sand to rich red clay in a matter of a few feet. The human habitations are confined to the sections of good soil and clearly show where such begin and end. This condition is true of the lands about Minas Velhas in all directions but one. The exception consists of the lands which margin the course of the Rio das Pedras, and the banks of the river constitute the only arable continuum leading out of Minas Velhas. The size of the river's flood plain is diminutive, however; where it is met by tributaries and broadens out are to be found the areas of most intensive farming—precisely at such sites as Baixa do Gamba and Gilo occupy.

Considering all of these factors—spatial, social, ethnic, and economic—it is clear that the population to be found outside of the urban periphery does not form part of the community in the same sense as does the population to be found within it. Yet the ties between the farming clusters and the town are vital to both.

When the farmer comes to market, he not only brings with him the foodstuff which will keep the townspeople alive for the coming week, but he also buys from the local merchants such things as kerosene, bushknives, hoes, medicines, cloth, thread, and *cachaca* (a crude rum, the most popular Brazilian alcoholic beverage), which are of great importance to the merchants' as well as the farmers' welfare. The primary focus of village life, in other words, lies within the village itself, but two or three secondary foci are to be distinguished in the towns in which the people of the villages go to market.

In the compound unit, the town definitely plays a dominant role. This is true because the distributive function takes place within the town—the farmer goes to the townspeople, not the townspeople to the farmer. It is also true socially since the townspeople consider themselves to be more sophisticated than the farmers— an opinion to which the majority of farmers readily acquiesce. The townspeople call the farmers *tabareus* (yokels), make jokes about their slowness and their manners, and refuse to dance in the same room with them. In the case of Minas Velhas, the dominance of the town is immeasurably strengthened by its being the center of political authority, the locus of an impressive and mostly self-interested bureaucracy which does not always bestow benefits as devotedly as it exacts tribute. It is very rare for a nonurbanite to become a member of the municipal council and correspondingly difficult for a rural group to get any help from county funds.

The level of commercial activity of a town is largely determined by the number of people who come in from the surrounding area to make purchases on the fair day. The more village satellites a town has, the better off it will be. But the economic relationship between the neighboring urban centers is perforce of a different order than the symbiotic one which exists between the urban centers and their village satellites. The urban centers, which are spatially as much neighbors to Minas

Velhas as some of the villages, are frankly competitive. The stores in all four towns—Minas Velhas, Vila Nova, Gruta, and Formiga—have the same commodities to sell. Each one, well within the range of some of the others' village satellites, duplicates the distributive function.

The economic rivalry born of this situation often extends to other spheres as well. Between Vila Nova and Minas Velhas a feeling of mutual hostility is outstanding. Residents of the two towns speak derisively of each other. Minas Velhas claims that the townspeople in the neighboring valley are perpetually ravaged by dust storms, are subject to unbearable heat, drink the water Minas Velhas throws away, have no time to be friendly, and do not know the elementary rules of hospitality. The residents of Vila Nova, on the other hand, laugh at Minas Velhas's *estado de atrazo terrivel* (terrible state of backwardness), its moribund commercial life, and its pitiful deficiency in *movimento* (general activity). They think that Minas Velhas is full of snobs and falsely *gran fino* (upper class).

Up until 1921 Vila Nova was a district of the county of Minas Velhas. In that year Vila Nova became the seat of a new county split off from what had been until then part of Minas Velhas. According to Sr. A. G.:

On this occasion the ancient and traditional county of Minas Velhas was subject to the greatest of injustices . . . . I am not referring to the creation of the new county . . . . The injustice lay in the manner in which the division was made . . . . Vila Nova got an area almost twice as large as that of Minas Velhas with six hundred more farms, twenty-six thousand inhabitants, while Minas Velhas was left with only thirteen thousand . . . . Minas Velhas lost its political importance because the size of its electorate was diminished. Such is human justice.

Antagonism between the two urban centers reached its bitterest extreme when Minas Velhas started to build the motor road that connects with the road that links Vila Nova to Brumado. For many years Vila Nova refused to participate in the enterprise, claiming that it

would never be possible for trucks to ascend the escarpment. It was to the obvious advantage of the merchants
of Vila Nova that their city should remain the terminal
point of the Brumado road and that their competitors
in Minas Velhas should have to buy and sell through
intermediaries in Vila Nova. For two years a few
hundred yards of the road within the county of Vila
Nova were deliberately left unfinished. This part of
the road served effectively as a road block, even though
the rest of the route had already been completed. The
most difficult part of the trip from Vila Nova to Minas
Velhas by automobile is still this stretch on perfectly
level terrain just outside of the town of Vila Nova.

With this quick excursion into the countryside and
to the neighboring towns, let us return to Minas Velhas
itself.

THE URBAN SCENE

In contrast to the neighboring towns and especially to
the rural villages, Minas Velhas gives an impression of
refreshing neatness. The majority of its houses have
been recently whitewashed; where its streets and squares
are unpaved, they are covered by grass and most of them
are bordered by sidewalks made of rectangular slate
slabs. The houses adjoin one another in long even rows
broken only by narrow alleys which lead from one street
to the other. The houses have one story, except for a
few "sobrados" which have two.

Architecturally, the city presents many details which
reflect the urban aspirations of both past and present
inhabitants. No feature is more impressive in this sense
than the habit of building the houses one next to the
other in long unbroken rows. Not only do the walls
adjoin, but each house is exactly on a line with its neighbor in relation to the sidewalk. A detached house, set
off at a considerable distance from the rest, is regarded
as a definite disadvantage. One man who moved outside the gate to a house surrounded by spacious grounds
now wants to move back to his old home crowded in

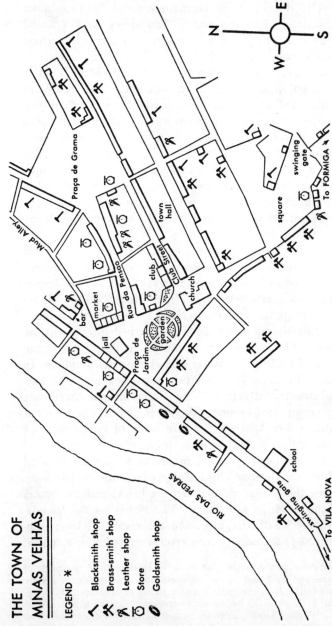

THE TOWN OF
MINAS VELHAS

LEGEND *

⊥ Blacksmith shop
⚒ Brass-smith shop
⚒ Leather shop
⚗ Store
𝒪 Goldsmith shop

Praça de Grama

Mud Alley

market

bar

jail

Praça de Jardim

Rua da Pensão

club

Club Street

garden

town hall

church

square

swinging gate

To FORMIGA

RIO DAS PEDRAS

school

swinging gate

To VILA NOVA

* Only principal installations have been indicated.

next to the others in the main square. "It's too quiet out there," he explained. "You don't hear a sound when you get up in the morning. I like it better where there's more *movimento*."

Whatever noise and bustle may be created by a neighbor's activities is more than welcome. The people of Minas Velhas are, in fact, passionately fond of this quality of life called *movimento*. At the fair or a religious *festa*, the *movimento* is at its best—a combination of shuffling feet, voices in debate, church bells ringing, a band playing, firecrackers going off, and people milling about in their best clothes. The average level of *movimento* is the factor which most distinguishes the city from the country and a good city from a mediocre one in the eyes of the people.

The great majority of the houses including the church have their outside woodwork—window frames, shutters, doors—painted the same color, a sky blue, so that despite the occasional deviations from plain whitewash to maroons, pinks, and greens for the outside walls, a pleasing color harmony has been maintained throughout the town. The blue is part of the urban Portuguese architectural tradition which is overwhelmingly dominant in Minas Velhas. This tradition furnished both the one- and two-story structure. The church and the courthouse are constructed of stone; the great majority of all other structures in Minas Velhas are made of sun-dried brick mounted on a shallow stone foundation.[13]

The adobe bricks used in Minas Velhas are of local fabrication. Stone chips are tapped into the joints between the bricks and between the bricks and the frames of the windows and doors. The stones for the foundation are small, irregular, and are cemented by a commercial preparation. In a typical town house a central

[13] In contrast, the majority of domiciles in the villages are made of wattle and daub and do not require a stone foundation. Poles are placed directly in the ground, and a wattle of branches is built up. Mud is then daubed among the interstices. This mode of construction is called *taipa*. Such wattle and daub walls crack easily and are considered inferior to those made of adobe.

roof beam is flanked by auxiliary beams, all of which rest directly on the walls. Posts are rarely used for supporting the roof, except in large structures. The roof covering of town buildings invariably consists of fire-baked tiles which are supported by a group of rough-hewn pole rafters that slope from the central beam over the auxiliary beams to the outer wall and usually slightly beyond to form eaves. Over these poles are laid crosspieces of light staves. The tiles are set down without fastening and remain in place by force of gravity alone. In the entire structure nails are used only to put hinges and locks in place.

Size and internal and external embellishments performed upon this basic pattern determine the quality of the structure. As part of the urban complex and the wide class differences, there is considerable variation in the houses. The number of rooms per house, for example, may range from two to twenty. Some houses have special rooms for kitchens; others do not. Floors may consist of hard-packed earth, or may be laid with square or hexagonal fire-baked tiles. The finest floors in Minas Velhas are considered to be those made of wooden planks. An important detail is whether or not the rooms have false ceilings below the roof tiles. Such ceilings may be made of heavy cloth or of wooden planks —the latter mode being preferred. The more windows a house has, the finer house it is, especially if the windows have glass panes. Some windows are elaborately latticed with diamond-shaped colonial designs. More common, however, are single- or double-piece wooden shutters. Outside and inside walls may be plastered or the brick left bare. Inside walls may be merely white-washed, or they may be painted. They may be white-washed a single color, or they may have decorative bands and lines near the floor and around windows and doors. Many houses have bright friezes of geometric or flower designs just below the eaves; other houses have such designs on their outside walls.

All these houses are examples of the same basic

architectural tradition. Within the last twenty years a radically new tradition which has almost replaced the colonial ideal of the beautiful house has infiltrated Minas Velhas. The new style involves raising the façade above the level of the roof tiles so that the latter become invisible from the street. The false front is called *platibanda* and is greatly admired as a symbol of modernity. Curved lines are traced in the plaster of the façade, faintly suggesting large irregular stone blocks. No important structural modifications are required, however, in order to produce these effects. The traditional front is easily converted to the new style. Only eight buildings to date boast the full *platibanda;* of these, four are domiciles. All of the latter are the result of remodeling.

Sharing two walls with the neighbors means that in houses of more than four or five rooms some of the rooms will be without windows. In such cases, light is provided by small glass panes set in the roof tiles. Ventilation poses no problem since the roof tiles fit so loosely that during a heavy rain a fine spray may be expected to make its entrance through the interstices. If anything, the problem facing the people of Minas Velhas is not how to get cool air in but how to keep it out. The houses are by and large admirably suited to a tropical temperature without too much rain. The adobe bricks make excellent insulators, and the high peaked roofs effectively protect the interior from the punishing rays of the sun. The only trouble is that Minas Velhas does not have a tropical climate. Minimum temperatures of 43° Fahrenheit have been recorded; maximum is about 86° Fahrenheit. Cool air falling through the roof tiles during the months of May through September frequently produces room temperatures of 59° Fahrenheit. This, together with the entrance of rain-spray, accounts for the high value which is placed on a room which has a ceiling below the tiles. The majority of townspeople simply suffer when confronted with these low temperatures. Those who can afford them dress in sweaters and heavy capes; those who cannot have only the recourse of gritting their teeth to keep them from chattering. The fireplace or any other indoor heating apparatus is unknown in the region. To make matters worse, there is a widespread fear that warming oneself by a fire is dangerous because of the cold drafts which one encounters upon leaving it. Hence people will normally not avail themselves of the heat which they might get even from cooking stoves, forges, or ovens. Occasionally, however, some old people will build a small fire on the floor of a vacant room and huddle around it. The situation is considerably worse in the village of Serra do Ouro, 900 feet higher than Minas Velhas, where even during the summer months night temperatures of 59° Fahrenheit are common.

The bona fide kitchen contains an adobe-brick cooking stove. A channel at the top extends the length of the stove and is covered by a sheet of iron. Small logs and branches are slid into the channel. The fire is started by igniting pieces of *candomba,* a highly inflammable plant found in the *gerais.* At the front of the stove there is an indentation hollowed out from the floor to the lip of the fire-bearing channel. Ashes are pushed out over the lip and fall to the floor. The top of the stove is paved with slate. No provision is made for disposal of smoke other than letting it escape between the roof tiles and the space between ceiling and walls. An oven is also part of the kitchen's standard equipment; it consists of a brick dome mounted on an adobe platform. The floor of the oven is paved with slate or floor tiles. A wood fire is burned on this floor; when the bricks are sufficiently hot, the fire is cleaned out and the material to be baked takes its place.

A number of the houses, however, characteristically lack the kitchen appendage. Cooking is done in one of the rooms which perhaps also serves as a bedroom or living room. The stove will consist of a wooden frame daubed over with mud to form a table resting on wooden legs. Loose adobe bricks and stones are manipulated on top of the table to form a channel in which the combustible is placed. Pots and pans are balanced precariously on top of the loose stones.

An outstanding feature of the urban scene is the back yard (*quintal*). Some of these extend fifty, one hundred and fifty, or more feet behind the house and are completely enclosed by high adobe-brick walls. The back yard is usually divided into two sections by a separating wall: a small inner part that blocks off the area formed by the kitchen appendage, and a larger section with a door at the rear which opens on the next street, on one of the streams, or on pasture land, as the case may be. The back yard is where the latrines are dug—when they are dug.

The majority of families use the back yard to supplement their food supply, planting fruit trees, corn, sugar cane, coffee, lettuce, tomatoes, and gourds, and stocking it with pigs and chickens. Wealthier families, however, devote a considerable portion of the back yard to growing flowers.

Just as there are good and bad houses in Minas Velhas, so are there good and bad streets. The farther from the main square, the poorer the house. The streets which lead to the principal square are the best streets even though the quality of the houses gets worse toward their extremities. The streets which do not lead directly to the principal square, regardless of their distance, are by and large the poorest streets and are inhabited by Minas Velhas's lower class. The worst street of all is called Beco da Lama (Mud Alley) and in the best urban tradition is tenanted mainly by prostitutes.

The situation in the village satellites is quite different. While house types vary, there are none that compare with the best houses in Minas Velhas and no such thing as good and bad streets. Similarly, it is only outside of the town that houses having thatch instead of tile for the roof are seen. Furthermore, while the tendency to build houses in adjoining fashion occasionally produces a small row, the village domiciles are characteristically detached from each other. Some villages have one or two small stores; the majority have none.   In addition, if there are any public buildings, they are either the church or a small schoolhouse.

A large part of the difference in the physical appearance between the town and the villages is due to the county government's conception of what a city ought to look like.   These conscious ideas play a key role in the perpetuation of the urban ethos.   For example, considerable attention has been paid to laying the sidewalks out smoothly and to uniform width.   Holes and hollows in the ground are regarded as abominations and are filled in and smoothed out with a great sense of satisfaction.   One of the jokes about the village of Serra do Ouro is that the streets have been made impassable by craters caused by wallowing pigs.   Much attention in Minas Velhas is also devoted to the problem of keeping the streets clean.   Two county workers are employed as street cleaners.   Squads of municipal workers can also be seen from time to time busily engaged in pulling out the grass which manages to grow between the stone flags of the one street which is paved (Rua da Ponte).   An old municipal ordinance prohibits the construction of palm-thatched houses within the city limits.   Another local law prohibits the raising of pigs.   This one is not enforced very rigidly, but a determined effort is made to keep them off the streets.

A special municipal employee has the obligation of catching stray pigs as well as other stray animals and impounding them in the municipal corral.   When the town garden was completed a couple of years ago, the pressure on the incumbent to perform his duty reached a new high.   The attempt to protect the garden from the various pigs, cattle, mules, and horses which occasionally escape from their corrals or wander in from the *gerais* has also led to the construction of the massive swinging gates found at every road and trail entrance to the city.

One of the characteristics of a folk as opposed to an urban community is the fact that in the folk community everyone knows everybody else. This is one of the features which is negatively correlated with the urbanism of Minas Velhas. Almost every adult in town knows at least the family name of every other adult in town. In order to find out where a particular family lives, all that is necessary is to stop the first passer-by and give the name and occupation of the family. You will then be told where the street is and whether the house is near the end or middle of the block. Anyone who lives nearby can then point out the exact house. In a gesture which almost seems as if it were an attempt to deny these facts, the municipal government has fitted each house with a blue and white metal plaque bearing the house's number in the city's official street plan. In addition, each important street is marked by a sign bearing the street's official name. These devices are of no functional importance in everyday life, and hence few people know the number of their house, while the streets they live on are known by names other than the official ones.

The town flower garden is also an excellent example of the official version of the urban spirit. Built at a cost of approximately $1,666 U.S.,[14] an amount equal to one quarter of the total receipts of the entire county for one year, it is the town's pride and joy. In order to water the plants, a well was dug directly at the center of the garden. The water is dumped into a nearby gasoline drum which serves as a reservoir into which two municipal gardeners dip their cans. The rather heroic effort of the two gardeners has failed to call forth the blooms which the official planners of the garden had envisaged. The progress of the garden is the subject of frequent informal conferences between the mayor and other prominent citizens whenever they happen to encounter each other near the site. It still lacks several benches included in the plans but for which the money has yet to be appropriated.

[14] On the official exchange, the U.S. dollar is stabilized at the rate of one dollar to eighteen cruzeiros. The unofficial, though legal, exchange was one dollar to thirty cruzeiros at the time of the field work.

On moonlit evenings and every Sunday afternoon the garden is the scene of the strictly urban pastime known as the "footing." This involves getting dressed up in one's best clothes and walking around the garden. Groups of young girls, arms interlocked, pace slowly round and round the paved walks. A few married couples also appear. Groups of men, including the town's higher-ups—men of position and wealth—station themselves at the edges of the walks and with eyes absently taking in the antics of the promenaders, converse for hours about politics, the need for a hydroelectric plant, and ways of improving the garden.

It goes almost without saying that none of these features are present in the satellite villages.

URBAN ACTIVITIES

With the first rays of the morning sun the city begins to stir; but nobody would think of going out on the street before the sky is well lightened. The first persons out are women and girls on their way to fetch water. Drinking water is taken from the rivers and streams as early as possible since later on the water is reputed to be dirtier owing to the actitvities of the laundresses and the passing of animals. It is carried on the head in kerosene cans and earthen jars. While one woman is out getting the water some other female member of the family is starting the fire. About the same time from various households one can hear the sound of coffee being crushed. This is done by pounding a heavy club into a hollowed-out log filled with the beans. Simultaneously men are out milking the cows in a few small corrals within the city. Boys carry the milk in bottles and pots to the houses which have requested it. In a little while the church bell rings for mass and a small group of women—not more than a dozen—can be seen on their way to answer the summons. Forges are soon ignited all over town, and the bellows laboriously begin to suck in air. The sound of hammering rings out from the many blacksmiths' workshops. The doors to the leatherwork shops are thrown open and the workers take their places at bench and table. The grinding, cutting, pasting, snipping, sewing, hammering, and filing of Minas Velhas's artisans begins early. Presently the storekeepers emerge carrying chairs—the symbol and vehicle of their profession—which they place in the early morning sunlight and proceed to use with a skill born of many years of practice, tipping back against the walls and stretching their legs in preparation for the generally lethargic day which lies ahead of them. From the poorer houses groups of women can be seen walking briskly out of town carrying bushknives and axes into the *gerais* in search of the ever receding supply of firewood. Soon the children, some in blue and white uniforms, start down Rua da Ponte toward the school. Then to the river and streams the women come with their wash. They squat down in the water in twos and threes, drawing their skirts tightly around their laps, and proceed to slap and pound the dirty clothes. The day's gossip is slapped and pounded with equal thoroughness by their tongues. When the clothes are clean, they are spread out on the rocks or hung from barbed-wire fences to dry. At midday the church bell rings once, the storekeepers rise from their chairs and disappear into their houses, the children troop back from the school, the forges are banked, the workshops are closed, and the washerwomen return to their homes. A few thirsty souls appear at the town's only bar for a pre-lunch shot of *cachaca*. Lunch is eaten quickly—in ten minutes some of the storekeepers have resumed their vigil. Some people sleep; others return immediately to the work they had started in the morning. Only a few prosperous and leisure-filled individuals, like Sr. Luiz Morais, the president of the town council, prolong their somnolence into the late afternoon. The workers return to the shops at will; but by two o'clock full activity has been restored everywhere. A second session of children is in the school, the women are back at the river, the clerks and tax collectors back at their desks. Later on in Mud Alley two prostitutes can be seen squatting in the lengthening shadow of the wall of the municipal corral, discussing the rising cost of rice. The barkeeper's mother-in-law sits in the doorway of the bar making lace by twining threads along a pin-marked pattern resting on a cushion. Her grandchildren sit by her side watching, while inside the bar her daughter is cutting leather into strips that will go to make sandals. At the State Tax Collector's office, the collector and his clerk are busy making out a transit permit for a pack of mules taking coffee to a distant city. The president of the council has finally thrown off his slumbers and has dropped into the office only to change the scene. He has just amused himself by accusing the collector of being the richest man in town. Soon the mayor stops by also and the conversation shifts to ways and means of protecting the clerk from the political persecution which threatens his job. The president of the council wearies of this subject and withdraws, walking slowly toward Chico Silva's store where he will probably find one of the telegraph line riders, a postal agent, and perhaps the school directress's husband to speak with. As he crosses the garden he stops to give some directions to the man who is watering the flowers. A group of children are spinning tops on the stone apron of the jail. Inside the bar, the barkeeper's son is practicing billiards while a traveling photographer strums some tunes on an old guitar. The barkeeper himself, old Waldemar, Negro and well-respected member of the town council, is playing checkers with a pensioned soldier. While in a hundred different houses women and girls are sewing, knitting, crocheting, making lace, ironing, and cooking. At four o'clock the church is opened for afternoon prayer; few attend. Now a horn blowing in the distance signals the arrival of a truck. It comes lumbering up the Rua da Ponte. All work stops along the route. People come to the windows and doors to stare silently at the lordly owner, who wears sunglasses and an officer's shirt, while swarms of children race gleefully alongside, trying to beat the truck to the pension.

As the long shadows from the westerly rim of the

escarpment slant across the square, the church bell tolls the hour of Ave Maria. The bar begins to fill up; a group forms about Waldemar and the pensioned soldier, who are still playing checkers. A municipal clerk stops in at the bar to fill a small bottle with *cachaca* before going to the river for his regular evening bath. All along the square the storekeepers are pumping their kerosene pressure lamps. In the twilight by the river a girl removes the day's wash from the rocks. Several persons have waded into the water and are washing their hands, feet, and faces in the cold, swift-flowing current. A small herd of cows comes home from the pasture across the river, accompanied by a drove of barking dogs. Darkness descends on Minas Velhas and with it the cold. Shadowy figures in enormous woolen cloaks move across the squares. Ulisses, the town watchman lights the five gas lanterns which in their ancient colonial frames are all that remains intact of an older and more extensive public illumination system. The only other lights in the streets come from the few stores which keep their doors open despite the cold wind now blowing down from the *gerais*. All the houses are shut tight and no light escapes into the street from the kerosene lamps which illumine the interiors. After dinner, which is dispatched as quickly as lunch, small groups of men begin to form inside the stores. Each store has its regular nocturnal habitués who band together by political and class preference. Other men wander from store to store listening to the different conversations going on in each. In one, Heraclito expounds his theory of why Brazilians are poor; in another the priest leans against the counter and reminisces about Rio de Janeiro; at Chico Silva's the justice of the peace is describing the details of a stabbing which took place in an outlying district. At 8:25 there is a general convergence of drifters upon those stores which have radios (power furnished from storage batteries) in order to be present at the nightly news service of the Esso reporter on Radio Nacional—the most listened-to program in Minas Velhas.

The billiard table in the bar has meanwhile become the center of a group of young spectators who sit around the wall on wooden benches watching the older boys display their skill.   In the back room an informal gathering of members of the *Jaz,* a small section of the *filarmonica* (town band), is working on some popular *sambas.*   They, too, have their admiring spectators, some of whom furnish vocal accompaniment.   The group in the bar is paralleled by the group in the Social Club where there is another billiard table.   In the back room at the club a card game is in progress.   In front, women and girls are looking over the latest newspapers from Salvador.   Outside the club, the moonless night "footing" is taking place, slightly disanimated by the cold and darkness.   At nine o'clock, Rogaciano, the man who keeps the animals out of the garden, performs his second function for the public good.   He blows a whistle.   He does this because there is a municipal ordinance which requires that all commercial houses close their doors after nine o'clock.   Having done his duty, Rogaciano goes to bed.   Since the law is an old one and no one is quite sure any more why it was passed, the stores stay open for an hour or so afterward. By nine o'clock, however, the majority of the townspeople are asleep.   By ten, the club is empty.   By eleven, all the stores are definitely closed.   By eleven-thirty, the bar is likewise closed, and the last few stragglers can be seen hurrying home with an occasional flashlight to guide them.   The streets thereafter are left strictly to the dogs, the ghosts, the thieves, and the young man or dissatisfied husband who may be detected furtively entering Mud Alley.

ECONOMICS 2

IN TRANSPORT and in all types of extractive or productive activities, Minas Velhas displays a tremendous degree of technological lag. Power-driven machinery is nonexistent, tools are makeshift, and techniques laborious. Mule trains are still the chief means of local transport, and on the farm agriculture is practiced with nothing more complicated than the hoe. Such technological backwardness is ordinarily associated with a rural or folk society. That this is not necessarily the case is quite obvious, though frequently forgotten. There were great European cities before the industrial revolution. In West Africa the Nuba, Yoruba, and other Negro kingdoms managed large urban conglomerations distinct from the peasantry without the benefit of an alphabet or a knowledge of electronics. While the technological advances of the industrial revolution have usually acted to intensify urban trends, they alone are not the indispensable prerequisites for many characteristically urban phenomena.

OCCUPATIONAL SPECIALIZATION

One of the most significant differences between a folk and an urban culture is the amount of specialization required by the daily regimen of making a living. In a truly folk or rural community such specialization is kept to a minimum. Aside from a basic sexual division of labor and a few specialists such as a shaman, canoe-builder, or potter, all members of a typical rural community are capable of satisfying individual or collective needs by means of approximately the same types of activity. Urban societies characteristically present a multitude of economic pursuits each of which is known only to a small percentage of the population.

In Minas Velhas, the strength of the urban complex is nowhere more clearly shown than in the extensiveness of occupational specialization. An impressive variety of remunerative activities are engaged in. These are listed below in six groups:

GROUP I. MANUFACTURE

1. Brass-smith (*Latoeiro*)
2. Blacksmith (*Ferreiro*)
3. Saddle maker
4. Shoemaker
5. Harness-part maker
6. Lacemaker
7. Brickmaker
8. Tinsmith (*Funileiro*)
9. Fireworks maker
10. Goldsmith
11. Flower maker
12. Luggage maker
13. Dressmaker
14. Tailor
15. Carpenter

GROUP II. MENIAL

16. Prostitute
17. Gravedigger
18. Woodcutter
19. Water carrier
20. Washerwoman
21. Cook
22. Miner
23. Beggar
24. Laborer
25. Bricklayer

GROUP III. PROFESSIONS AND SERVICES

26. Butcher
27. Sacristan (*Sacerdote*)
28. Priest
29. Dentist
30. Musician
31. Folk Doctor (*Curandeiro*)
32. Pharmacist

GROUP IV. CIVIL SERVICE

33. Teacher
34. School Inspector
35. State Tax Collector
36. State Tax Clerk
37. Federal Tax Collector
38. Federal Tax Clerk
39. Postal Agent
40. Clerk of Civil Actions (*Escrivao de Feitos Civeis*)
41. Notary Public (*Tabeliao*)
42. Clerk of Civil Register (*Oficial do Registro Civil*)
43. Post Office Treasurer
44. Telegraph operator
45. Court Clerk (*Escrivao do Juri*)
46. Municipal Bookkeeper (*Contador da Prefeitura*)
47. Municipal Treasurer (*Tesoureiro da Prefeitura*)
48. Municipal Secretary (*Secretario da Prefeitura*)
49. Assistant Postal Agent
50. Municipal Tax Collector (*Agente Arrecadador*)
51. Telegraph line rider
52. Soldier
53. Sheriff (*Delegado*)
54. Jailer
55. Justice of the Peace
56. Statistics Agent
57. Street cleaner
58. Mayor
59. Animal catcher (*Fiscal*)
60. Pension holder
61. Doorman (*Porteiro*)

GROUP V (CONTINUED)

62. Rat and flea killer (*Servicio Nacional Contra a Peste*)
63. Police Clerk

GROUP V. AGRICULTURE

64. Landlords (*Fazendeiros*)
65. Farmers

GROUP VI. COMMERCE

66. Innkeeper
67. Peddler (*Negociante Ambulante*)
68. Storekeeper
69. Trader and buyer [1]

Every occupation which yields some income, regardless of its relative importance to the individual engaged in it, has been included. The list, however, is incomplete as far as some highly refined specializations go, particularly with respect to Group I, Manufacture, where among the brass-smiths, blacksmiths and leather-workers, product differentials and a highly developed division of labor occur.

As for the occupational permutations per individual, all the groups except II, Menial, are noncombining within themselves. If Joao Silva is a luggage maker, he is not also a flower maker; or if Fulano is a postal agent, he is not also a teacher. Group II is different from the others in this respect. All the occupations in it are readily combined—in fact, the classificatory basis for the group consists in the inability of the individuals who belong to it to state their professions; they are considered to have none and are popularly known as *macaqueiros* (monkeys) because they jump from one job to another. Although the total number of specializations is small by comparison with the occupational diversity to be found in a large metropolis, it must be weighed both against the size of the population with which we are dealing and against the relatively retarded level of technology. There are 904 persons (fourteen years of age and over) in the city of Minas Velhas who account for this diversity, and the entire complex of skills and services associated with power-driven machinery plays no part in it.

Table 2 shows the distribution of the occupational

[1] Classifications are based on a house-to-house survey.

groups according to principal source of income per domicile in the urban zone.[2] The table does not indicate the complete number of persons engaged in any given activity; for example, there are nine teachers who reside in the city, but only five of these furnish the major part of their households' income. Where the chief of the house has more than one source of income, only the major one is listed.

TABLE 2. DISTRIBUTION OF OCCUPATIONS

MANUFACTURE

Metalworkers (*Latoeiros* and *Ferreiros*)	39
Leatherworkers	28
Lacemakers	6
Brickmakers	2
Tinsmiths (*Funileiros*)	2
Goldsmiths	2
Fireworks maker	1
Luggage maker	1
Dressmakers	9
Carpenters	2
Tailors	2
Flower maker	1
	95

MENIAL

Women (Water carriers, cooks, prostitutes, woodcutters, washerwomen, beggars)	31
Men (Laborers, woodcutters, road gangs, miners, bricklayers, beggars)	29
	60

PROFESSIONS

Pharmacist	1
Priest	1
Dentist	1
	3

CIVIL SERVICE

Communication	8
Education	5
Law, taxation, and administration	9
Others	10
	32

AGRICULTURE

Farmers (including sharecroppers and hired hands)	36
Landlords (*Fazendeiros*)	7
	43

COMMERCE

Buyers and commercial travelers	16
Storekeepers	16
Hotel operators	2
	29

Total Number of Households: 262

[2] Unless otherwise stated, all succeeding tables are based on independent studies and questionnaires.

For the last fifty years manufacture has been Minas Velhas's most important remunerative activity. It is performed for the most part with the aid of simple tools and rudimentary hand-operated machinery in small home workshops. Recently, however, factory-like installations have developed. But the supply of raw materials is uncertain and makeshift and the distribution of the finished product is still precarious.

From time to time attempts have been made to organize production by entrepreneurs who contracted with groups of artisans for their total output and who furnished raw materials on a more regular basis. Most of these attempts have been ephemeral. The metal industry in particular has failed to exhibit signs of capital concentration. It consists today of thirty-five independent workshops, none with a capital value of more than 3,000 cruzeiros (about $100 U.S.); the average annual value of the total production of one of these workshops in terms of primary sales value is about 7,500 cruzeiros. Only an insignificant percentage of production is at present subject to any sort of entrepreneurial mediation; the owner of the workshop himself buys the raw materials, does the work, and tries to secure a primary buyer for the finished goods. On the other hand, the leather industry has shown signs of emergent capitalistic forms. Home workshops have been expanded, and in one case a bona fide factory constructed. In the leather industry there are less shops and more artisans per installation, and division of labor is highly developed.

METALCRAFT

Four types of metal artisans are found in Minas Velhas: blacksmith (*ferreiro*), brass-smith (*latoeiro*), tinsmith (*funileiro*), and goldsmith. The blacksmith works exclusively with iron, heating scrap and hammering it on an anvil. The brass-smith works with nickel alloys. He, unlike the blacksmith, smelts his materials in small graphite containers and pours the molten mass into earthen molds. A primitive sort of lathe is also an indispensable part of his workshop. The goldsmith works only in gold, while the tinsmith's medium is the kerosene can, which he cuts with a shears.

The latter two are presently of only minor significance. But eighty years ago there were more than twenty goldsmiths in Minas Velhas; today there are three, two of whom are old spinsters. Some exceptionally fine gold jewelry—rings and filigree brooches—were once produced by Minas Velhas's artisans, and many examples are still to be found locked away among the family heirlooms. Knowledge of the fine points of the art now rests with two old women, who are recluses. But encroaching feebleness has practically put a stop to their work, and it seems likely that in a few more years, except for simple wedding bands, tie pins, and chains, the gold handicraft will disappear altogether. At the opposite end of the scale of artistic pretension are the tinsmiths; these humble artisans are dedicated to the making of funnels, pots, and *fifos*—the lamps of the poor. The last consist of small glass bottles, cast-offs of different sizes, with a wick passing through the top. The bottles are set into the metal frames which the tinsmiths make from their indispensable kerosene cans.

There are twelve blacksmith workshops. Each with but minor variations is like the others. The heart of the shop is a rude furnace built of adobe (figure 1). The furnace is essentially a high thick table with a hole in one side connected to an excavation in the surface. Into the hole fits the tube of a horizontal leather bellows which is suspended between two upright wooden posts. The head of the bellows is connected by a thong or chain to a wooden pole that rests on a crosspiece between the posts. A second thong hangs from the other end of the pole; this is pulled downward by the operator, expanding the bellows. An iron counterweight hanging from the top of the bellows provides the reverse motion. The forge burns wood charcoal which is heaped into a small mound above the excavation. The heat generated is sufficient to soften but not to liquefy iron. A tree trunk embedded in the floor holds the anvil. Also to be found in the workshop are a vise, hammers, files, and a drill. The last is a curious mechanism, somewhat like a primitive fire drill. Leather

FIGURE 1. A BLACKSMITH'S FORGE

thongs twisted around an iron shaft are snapped taut by lowering a handle through which the shaft passes. A sewing-machine handwheel is used as a balance and flywheel.

The blacksmiths produce a variety of products associated with harnesses: bridles, bits, spurs, stirrup frames, and saddle frames. Some of them specialize in making knife blades. A few make knives complete with horn handles, but for the most part it is the brass-smith who buys the blades and adds the handles.

There are sixteen brass-smith workshops, most of which are equipped with the same sort of furnace as that which is found among the blacksmiths. In addition, all of the brass-smiths have a rudimentary lathe (figure 2). It consists of two moveable blocks of wood that are tenoned into a horizontal board. Metal points extend from the blocks. The object to be turned is sup-

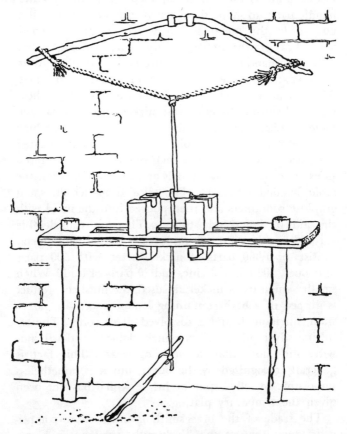

FIGURE 2.   A BRASS-SMITH'S LATHE

ported by the points, and the blocks are hammered together and locked in place by wedges below the board. Above the lathe is a horizontal wooden bow, usually fastened to the wall. A leather thong leads from the center of the bowstring to the end of a wooden pole.

The other end of the pole rests on the floor. The thong is given one full turn around the object in the lathe. By depressing the pole with his foot, the brass-smith succeeds in spinning the part he wishes to shape or polish. The tension of the bow reverses the motion.

The lathe is used to clean, shape, and polish knife-handle parts, to shape the wooden cores of whip handles, and to fit the metal sheath which covers the wood. Some brass-smiths produce only knife handles, others only whip handles; a few produce both. Another group concentrates on the production of bridles and spurs. Those who make bridles and spurs and some of those who make whip handles cast nickel alloys in earthen molds. These molds consist of two metal rims which are filled with a cohesive soil. The part to be duplicated is tapped into the soil and then removed. The impressions are connected by runnels and the two halves of the mold banded together. The alloy is melted in small graphite containers and then poured into the mold with the aid of homemade tongs. There is considerable variation in the mixture employed. A good white metal consists of 1,000 parts of nickel mixed with 500 parts of copper, 100 parts of zinc, and 20 parts of lead. When smaller amounts of nickel are used, the finished product is dipped in a bath containing lemon juice, salt, potassium, nitric acid, and a dissolved silver coin. The resulting silver plating is extremely delicate and will not withstand more than a week of wear. This fact is generally recognized by the buyer, but it is nonetheless impossible to sell a spur or bridle which has not been given the temporary plating.

The trade of the brass-smith is much more complicated than that of the blacksmith, though the blacksmith claims that his is the more difficult craft. "The blacksmith has only his eye to guide him," claims Joao Celestino, one of the town's best artisans. "The blacksmith works with a big hammer and makes little blades. He has to think as he works."

About a third of the brass-smiths and blacksmiths

work by themselves without any assistants. The rest have either apprentices, employees, or wives and children to help. Apprentices will serve up to six months or a year without remuneration, depending upon age and rate of learning. Usually they are cousins or nephews of the owner of the shop. There are only about eight employees in the entire metal industry. They all receive piece-goods wages of from one-quarter to one-third the selling price of the article they produce or help to produce. Where members of the same household are concerned, receipts are pooled and administered by the head of the family. Those workshops which have workers in addition to the owner usually exhibit a division of labor. One man will prepare the molds, a child will work the bellows, a wife and son will file and polish. One brass-smith workshop where all the men of the family have left to seek employment in Sao Paulo is run entirely by women. The head of the shop is Ligia, a middle-aged widow who learned the craft from her husband. She herself prepares the molds for making bridles and stirrups. A daughter and daughter-in-law attend to the smelting and pouring of the metal. Several grandchildren are always on hand when the time comes to work the bellows. All the other processes are performed interchangeably.

The learning of metalcraft as well as leathercraft is not especially dependent upon father-son transmission. The florescence of these industries has a time-depth of only three generations. Almost all of the large families are represented, and there is ample opportunity for any interested youth to learn with an uncle or cousin if his father is employed in something else. Most of the learning is done by informal observation and experimental imitative attempts.

LEATHERCRAFT

Another important industry in Minas Velhas is leatherwork. Except for the sewing machine, it too, like the metal industry, depends on primitive manual techniques. Leatherwork shops, however, range in size from one-room installations to an entire large building; and from one to twenty-five workers are associated with these shops. The industry produces saddles, stirrups, mud guards, stirrup straps, neck and tail harness assemblies, and shoes, boots, sandals, knife sheaths, and whips.

Three independent workers produce sandals; one independent worker concentrates on making knife sheaths. All the other workers—about forty in number—are connected with five larger installations. The smallest of these is run by Waldemar, the bar owner and town councilman. It is located in two different rooms adjoining the bar and has but two workers, one of whom is Waldemar's wife. The other is a piecework employee. Production is restricted exclusively to sandals. The woman cuts and stitches the top leather while the employee cuts the soles and assembles the finished product. Waldemar himself does not contribute to the work.

A larger shop, owned by Sr. Orlando, is dedicated to the production of shoes and sandals. Work goes on in two rooms of Orlando's house. In one, Orlando and five employees cut soles and assemble; in the other, his wife and daughters cut top leather and stitch with sewing machines.

The third installation, owned by Sr. Izidro, is likewise located in the domicile. Sr. Izidro, however, is the only worker who is normally to be found on the premises. The others work for the major part of the time in their own homes. Izidro furnishes the raw materials and pays piece-goods wages to six employees, including a son, daughter-in-law, two girls, a young man, and a woman. The only time these persons appear in the shop itself is when they are in need of more material or have finished goods to turn in. Production is centered upon the various kinds of harness straps.

The fourth installation belongs to Sr. Otacilio, who is also a barber. Again, it is located in the owner's domicile. Otacilio and his son make saddles; five other persons make sandals—Otacilio's wife, daughter, and son, an apprentice, and an employee. In addition there are three girls who stitch harness parts in their own homes.

The fifth, newest, and by far the largest installation is that of Sr. Braulio. All of the aforementioned leather products are produced. An entire building, constructed especially for the purpose, houses twenty employees. One room is dedicated to shoes and boots, another to sandals, one to stirrups, and two to saddles. There are storerooms, an office, and a salesroom. Three or four additional workers continue to work in their own homes —Braulio's brother, who makes saddles, and some girls who do hand-stitching. The factory has five large sewing machines, one of which is capable of piercing soles. Braulio himself, though a highly skilled craftsman, no longer makes anything. He now takes care of sales, planning, and supervision and a manager assists him in these tasks.

In the larger leather shops, division of labor is more highly refined than in the metal industry. This amounts to an additional type of occupational specialization. It is determined not so much by differentiation of skills as by the exigencies of the productive schedule.

Some idea of the extent to which division of labor has progressed in the larger workshops may be gained by a description of shoemaking in Sr. Otacilio's shop. Two women and three men are engaged in this activity. The two sexes usually work in separate rooms and the fundamental division is between the operations performed by the women on the top leather and the operations performed by the men on the soles. The top leather is a shiny industrial product imported from Salvador and Sao Paulo. The sole is a regional product processed on farms in the valley of Gruta.

The top part of a woman's shoe consist of two pairs of overlapping toe straps, a heel strap, and a connecting ankle strap. Let us call the two female workers A and B and the three male workers C, D, and E. (1) A cuts the top leather into narrow strips the size and shape of the various straps. She takes them into the next room where (2) C, D, or E glues a group of them into a thin piece of sole. A takes the sole with the strips glued on the back to B who (3) stitches the strips to the sole with a sewing machine. Then (4) A and B recut the strips which now have glued and sewn reinforcements. The two women (5) rivet the toe straps together, rivet a buckle to one side of the heel strap, and rivet the ankle strap to the other side. They also (6) punch holes in the ankle strap. Meanwhile, (7) C and D have been cutting out the soles. When the top assembly arrives, they (8) place it on a wooden form and nail it to the upper sole. (9) A short thick piece of leather follows next to form the arch support. (10) The bottom sole is nailed over this. (11) B trims the sole with a knife. E has, meanwhile, (12) been making the heel which consists of three layers of sole glued together. (13) Either C, D, or E finishes the shoe by nailing on the heel.

It will be noted that although the process is plainly conceived as consting of a number of discrete operations which ought to be performed simultaneously and continuously by workers assigned specific roles, a great deal of flexibility still remains. B may finish stitching and go to help A cut strips, or A may work along on the second strip-cutting operation until B finishes stitching and joins her. Either C, D, or E may drop his sole cutting to take up the assembly of the upper and lower units, depending on how many such units are ready, or how far he may have progressed with the task of cutting. Occasionally, if one of the women falls behind in certain of the operations, one of the men may help her out. Hence, over a period of days or weeks all but five of the thirteen operations may have been performed by every worker: only C, D, and E do the heels, or do the assembly; only C does the trimming; only B stitches the strips with the sewing machine. In any given day, however, the observer is most likely to find that all or most of the operations described above are performed on a discrete basis.

The variations in size, type of organization, and the

product differentials of the various leather shops are not as hopelessly confusing as they may seem to be at first glance. Both the metal and leather industries offer a rather unique opportunity for observing the early stages of a process which on a world-wide scale has culminated in one of the fundamental features of modern societies —the emergence of the capitalistic factory out of the home workshop. In Minas Velhas, the leather industry stands on the threshold of the era of power-driven machinery. The complete record of the transition to this crucial stage of industrial development remains visible: the one-man home workshop, the expanded home workshop, the expanded home workshop acting through an entrepreneurial function to incorporate a series of outside workers, and the shifting of the workshop from the home to a special structure which consolidates all the workers under a single roof.

ENTREPRENEURS

In Minas Velhas, expansion of the home workshop and the limited application of the entrepreneurial function has occurred against the background of a larger society whose capitalistic forms have considerable time-depth. Knowledge of these forms has always been part of the world view of many of the urban residents. The role of capital in all realms of economic enterprise is well understood. If anything, it is overemphasized. One of the most recurrent themes for businessmen, miners, farmers, and artisans alike is the plaintive search for the "boss" (*patrao*)—the fatherlike figure who gives people work, provides them with raw materials, lends them money, and buys their products before they are produced.

During the twenties two bosses appeared for the brass-smiths and blacksmiths. These capitalists provided raw materials and bought finished goods on a regular contractual basis for almost every workshop in the city. They never got to the point of building a factory because both of them, as soon as they had amassed some wealth, moved out of the city and became merchants in

Salvador. Ten years later another boss of the metal industries arose. He too, however, followed the footsteps of his predecessors and departed for the big city. At the moment the scores of independent metalworkers await the rise of the next big entrepreneur as one awaits the coming of a messiah.

In many respects Sr. Braulio, owner of Minas Velhas's largest industrial establishment and known throughout the community as "O Senhor," played this role for the leatherworkers. "He has helped so many people . . . he has given work to so many of us . . . he is the man who civilized the industry of Minas Velhas," are examples of the praise which his fellow townsmen heap upon him.

Though Braulio has succeeded in extending the entrepreneurial function further than anyone else, his factory has not brought any fundamental social or economic changes to the community. For a while the workers who made shoes were paid regular salaries—an important innovation had it endured. But Braulio found it impossible to maintain a rigid production schedule and had to revert to the prevailing piecework system under which the worker participates in the losses owing to his own delinquency. The harness-partmakers and the saddle makers in Braulio's employ never deviated from this system.

Division of labor in the shoe and boot room of the factory is the same as the flexible organization which has already been described as characteristic of a large home workshop. Moreover, the work in the harness-part and saddle rooms is not substantially different from that which a single artisan and a helper would perform. In these respects the factory betrays its recent emergence from the home workshop. The two rooms devoted to saddle making, which each contain an artisan and his assistant, give the impression of two home workshops which have simply been displaced and put into adjoining rooms under the same roof. The only distinctive features of the factory are that it is larger than the shops and that it turns out a greater quantity of goods.

Braulio has made no attempt to introduce a more rigid or more extensive division of labor. He is quite aware of the advantages which would thereby theoretically accrue, and there would be little resistance on the part of the workers to increased specialization. But in order further to refine the work organization of the factory, more workers would be needed, and production would have to be expanded in order to provide them with wages. The difficulties inherent in the present distributive system, however, make overproduction a constant danger. The fact is that despite the crudeness of their organization and technology, the industries of Minas Velhas can easily produce more than they can sell. Overproduction is as much a threat to these handcraft artisans as it is to a maker of television sets.

DISTRIBUTION

The principal means of distributing the industrial product of Minas Velhas is the peddler. The peddler undertakes protracted sales trips throughout the interior on foot and by mule. He carries the merchandise with him—from one to fifty thousand cruzeiros worth of mixed leather and metal products. Each trip may last anywhere from two weeks to several months. Twenty-five years ago places as distant as Matto Grosso, Goyaz, and Sao Paulo were covered. Today trips frequently include points as distant as Belo Horizonte, Itabuna, Bom Jesus de Lapa, and Xique-Xique. Setting out from Minas Velhas, the peddler goes from city to city, stopping wherever there is a public fair. All the goods which he carries with him are bought from the manufacturer conditional to sale, i.e., the manufacturer agrees to accept payment upon the traveler's return and also to take back whatever merchandise the peddler has been unable to sell. The peddler transports the goods and makes the sale to the consumer, but he assumes none of the risk. This fact is an index of the enormous cost of transportation and the scarcity of risk capital. At the time the traveler takes the goods from the manufacturer, a price is agreed on. Any receipts about this price are kept by the traveler. The markup for fair prices is 50 to 100 percent above the manufacturer's price. Under these conditions expanded production for the manufacturer is next to impossible. He must wait until the sale of his product to the consumer before realizing a cash return. Risk-sharing retail outlets are absolutely unavailable. In addition to peddlers, Sr. Braulio uses four retail stores in various cities in which he places shoes and boots. But the cash return here is also indefinitely conditional to sale. The storekeeper never assumes even a long-term obligation to pay for the merchandise which he accepts. He pays for what he sells and then only when he sells it, which may be a year or more beyond the date of manufacture, or never. Meanwhile, Braulio is forced to go on buying raw materials, producing more goods, and paying wages without ever knowing the real size of his inventory. Small wonder that the entrepreneur in Minas Velhas is cast as an heroic and messianic figure.

Table 3 shows the value of industrial products leaving Minas Velhas per month over a period of four years.[3] The figures should probably almost be doubled in order to arrive at the true values since the peddlers are notorious for undervaluing their wares when it comes to paying taxes; whether they can be trusted or not as absolute totals, the figures are still interesting from the point of view of monthly fluctuations.

There is a tendency for export activity to occur in spurts which more or less reflect the irregular rate of production. The period of greatest industrial activity occurs during the months of March through June, roughly equivalent to the harvest season; the period of least production can be correlated with the planting and growing season—October through February. The export figures do not reveal this fact since the high totals for November and January represent high production rates in the preceding months and not in these months themselves. The November and January peaks in ex-

[3] Collated from the local State Tax Office.

TABLE 3. MONTHLY INDUSTRIAL EXPORTS FROM MINAS VELHAS

(In Cruzeiros)

	1947	1948	1949	1950
January	..........a	22,200	16,000	22,000
February	..........a	7,200	15,500	5,000
March	9,400	3,300	13,800	12,000
April	18,600	15,700	16,000	17,500
May	2,200	21,000	12,100	21,600
June	12,100	3,000	2,700	5,000
July	29,400	28,500	33,500	36,300
August	11,700	12,900	6,000	12,500
September	13,000	9,500	9,400	3,900
October	5,000	15,000	13,000	10,400
November	0	10,200	20,200	26,000
December	0	1,000	6,300	0

a .... = Data absent.

port are due exclusively to Sr. Braulio's habit of ship-
ping to his retail outlets large quantities of shoes and
boots which have been returned by travelers or which
have accumulated in the factory during the preceding
year. Production during these months is actually at a
low point in all the industries.

The regularity of the export peak in July, which follows the period of greatest industrial activity, needs to
be explained. These shipments go to Bom Jesus da
Lapa—the "holy" city some 250 miles away on the banks
of the Sao Francisco River—and are coincident with the
great pilgrimages which occur during July and the early
part of August. Many of the brass-smiths and blacksmiths look forward to this event as the one time of
certain sales during the entire year. The regular low
point in export activity which occurs in December is to
be correlated with the prevailing notion that December
is the month of thunderstorms. Whether the storms
occur or not, none of the peddlers will risk an extensive
journey in December.

The metal crafts depend almost exclusively on the
peddlers not only for distribution but for supply of raw
materials as well. A peddler who has made an extensive

trip rarely returns with empty packs. Wherever he goes he is on the lookout for scrap iron, zinc, copper, lead, and nickel alloys. Though natural ferrous ores occur near Minas Velhas, no attempt has ever been made to utilize them. None of the other metals are native to the region. Adequate supplies of all the metals except the nickel alloys are maintained—iron from old hoes, brake drums, and rails; zinc from automobile radiators; copper from old sugar-cane cauldrons. Nickel, however, is a constant source of anxiety. The chief supply of this metal at the moment is made up of Brazilian 400-reis coins, officially recalled by the government, and old slipper-style stirrups. The present Brazilian coinage does not use nickel. Large quantities of the old coins are melted down each year.

The manner in which the majority of these coins are located is quite unexpected but typical of the many makeshift and precarious arrangements that characterize Minas Velhas's economy ever since the end of the gold-mining era. The coins are brought back from Bom Jesus de Lapa by the peddlers. Thousands of these nickel relics are brought to Bom Jesus by the pilgrims who probably have been hoarding them for years in order to make the pilgrimage. Some are sorted out by merchants at the fair which is in progress for almost a month. The largest part, however, comes from the alms boxes at the shrines. Church officials sort them out and sell them by weight to the peddlers from Minas Velhas. The latter in turn resell them to the brass-smiths.

Other raw materials are obtained at the local fair. Bulk leather, upholstery for saddle cushions, and the various woods needed for whip stocks are regional products. Top-grain leathers, plated rings, buckles, rivets, nails, and screws are bought in the big cities: Sao Paulo, Belo Horizonte, or Salvador.

CRAFT INTERDEPENDENCE

Despite their dependence on distant and sometimes irregular sources of raw materials, the industries display in combination a rather remarkable degree of self-sufficiency.   The manner in which the various industrial specializations complement one another accounts for this condition.   The blacksmiths produce knife blades to which the brass-smiths add handles; they make iron bits which fit into the brass-smiths' nickel bridles; and they make iron stirrup and saddle frames which are indispensable to the stirrup and saddle makers.   The leatherworkers in turn make straps for spurs produced by the brass-smiths and blacksmiths, and they also make sheaths for the brass-smiths' knives and whips for their whip handles.   Some of the simple tools are made by the blacksmiths for use in the other industries—thongs, pliers, and punches.   When the rasps and files of the brass-smiths are no longer sharp enough for working the nickel alloys, they are sold to the blacksmiths who are still able to use them.

Hence, from the point of view of industry as a whole, many of the independent shops should really be considered as units in a larger informal organization which consolidates discrete crafts.   Moreover, this is true not only for the main industrial categories but also within these categories themselves for crafts which in some cases remain nameless.   Knife sheaths, for example, are made from scrap leather left over from the process of making shoes and sandals.   One leather shop concentrates on making saddles, another on complementary straps and hitches.

In the making of whip handles, there are sometimes as many as three different brass-smith shops involved, each dedicated to producing a specific part of the handle. One shop fashions the wood stock and does the assembly; another casts and polishes the ring which goes on the end of the stock and forms the hand grip; and the third works at the task of beating down old nickel coins into sheets which will be used by the first shop to cover the wood.   It is the owner of the first shop who owns the finished product; he buys the rings from the second and pays the third to beat down the coins.

All three men consider themselves to be independent workers, and they all call themselves brass-smiths. They all work in their own workshops. The owner of the finished product acts as a contractor who utilizes the skill and equipment of the others. This arrangement is similar to that of the leather entrepreneur who gives out work to be done in the workers' homes. There are important differences, however. The principal criterion of the contracted as distinguished from the employed is that the former supplies his own raw materials. Thus the blacksmith knife-blade maker buys his own scrap; the brass-smith whip-ring maker buys his own nickel. The man who beats down the nickel coins is an exception; he is given the coins to work on. An important difference still remains, however, between him and the employed girls who stitch harness straps, for example. The latter work exclusively for one individual at a time and perform only one sort of operation. The coin beater, on the other hand, is the master of other skills, has the same tools and equipment in his shop as the man who pays him, and does other things besides beat down coins—such as making silver-handled whips and silver bracelets and chains for which he himself supplies the raw materials.

Offhand, it would seem that the contract artisan must inevitably tend to become more rigidly integrated in the industrial structure, that the coin beater must eventually give up his other skills and concentrate on being a coin beater. But the man who supplies the contract has only limited capital. As long as he cannot guarantee the coin beater that there will be work over an extended period, coin beating remains an expedient and the artisan must have something else to fall back on when the capital runs out.

ECONOMIC INDIVIDUALISM

Though an attempt has been made to emphasize the symbiotic aspects of the crafts, we ought not to lose sight of the dominant pattern, which is one of a large number of independent, duplicative, and competitive installations. This pattern is typical not only of the particular crafts which have been discussed, but generally of all the economic enterprises and work habits of the entire population under study—urban and rural groups included.   Reductions in duplication are almost completely dependent on the organizing force of individual owners of investment capital.   Such individuals are infrequent and inclined to abandon their efforts upon receiving a return sufficient to permit migration to larger cities.   Coordination of the production of individual artisans has never progressed to the point of eliminating several other rival installations.   On the level of the individual artisan, voluntary merger or systems of formal cooperation involving the pooling of equipment and joint efforts at distribution and the procurement of raw materials are unknown.   The individual artisan recognizes the ability of the boss—the strong fatherlike entrepreneur—to effect more advanced modes of industrial organization.   But the pattern of non-cooperation and the resistance to merger persists on the level of the entrepreneur who, like the individual artisan, resists the formation of cooperative associations with the rest of the local capitalists.

It would seem that the eagerness of the worker to accept a boss is paradoxical in view of his alleged desire for independence.   In Minas Velhas, however, working for a boss does not carry the imputation of reduced independence.   Even while working in Sr. Braulio's factory, the individual easily maintains the feeling that he is working more for himself than for someone else. The prevalence of the piece-goods wage is both symptom and result of the workers' attitude.   No time clocks are punched, production schedules are loose, and daily fluctuations are benignly tolerated by Sr. Braulio, who explains that all the workers are either friends or relatives.   The workers simply feel that they sell each article or part of an article they produce just as if they were working for themselves.   The selling price is less, but then they have not had to buy the raw materials. And even more important, they are assured of being able to sell all that they produce. *From the point of view of the workers, the boss is not someone who buys one's labor but someone who buys the products of one's labor.* Hence, the two work patterns—the desire to work independently and the desire to work for a boss—are actually complementary rather than opposing.

The pattern which would oppose both of these is that of working together—the formation of voluntary systems of cooperation larger than the systems produced by intra-family cooperation within the domicile. If this pattern existed there could not be, as there are, thirty home forges all of the same size and capacity, not more than five of which are in continual operation throughout any given working day, and none of which operates continuously throughout the year. Nor would there be five different shops in which sandals are made without a thought of merger by the owners. The fact is that neither in industry, commerce, nor argriculture can there be discerned well-developed patterns of cooperation as distinguished from the mere expediency of certain specializations. The average citizen of Minas Velhas has little or no experience in large-scale cooperative enterprises; the task of gaining a living is never considered communally. The economic destiny of each man is thought to be each man's private concern. The community as a whole is unaware of any collective responsibility for its general economic condition. No one feels that collective action ought to be the means of general prosperity, much less that collective action is feasible.

We asked Miguel, who is about to give up his shop and go to look for work in Sao Paulo, why a group of brass-smiths did not pool their resources and send someone to Salvador to buy sheet nickel—a source of the metal which is preferable from the point of view of regularity and economy to the present one. Miguel answered, "We are all weak. There is no one to make the effort. There is no lion in our midst." Another characteristic response to this and similar questions involving group initiative is a shake of the head while brushing the thumb with the index finger: "Nao ha dinheiro" (No money). The only known way of organizing the work efforts of the group is by the use of the coercive effects of capital. The concept that the organization of work through voluntary cooperation can create capital or that capital may be collectively rather than privately owned is rarely expressed in this or any other form. Capital is a quality of the boss, the foreigner, and the government, with the last being regarded as a sort of derelict "super-boss."

Conspicuously absent in both the town and the villages are the *batalhoes,* the cooperative labor groups which are popular ways of building or repairing a house in the Reconcavo of Bahia,[4] and the *mutirao* (sometimes *butirao*), the important agricultural labor battalions noted for other areas of Brazil.[5] Several informants testify that such institutionalized forms of cooperation were occasionally used in the days of their childhood. But there have been none for the last fifty years, and according to the same sources, they never were important.

The way in which care of the town garden was planned provides an illuminating insight into how the labor of one individual is conceived in relation to the labor of another. The garden is circled and crossed by a series of walks that divide it into a number of sections. A prominent family was solicited to take care of each of the sections. Each family was to plant and weed its section independently of the others. When the plants began to show their heads above the ground, the authors of the plan were dismayed to find that the variety of treatment given each section had resulted in an extremely displeasing mélange. One section had tall plants, another short; one had bright flowers, another none; one had a circular arrangement, another no arrangement at all; one had several different kinds of plants, another had only one kind. The characteristic

[4] Harry W. Hutchinson, "Vila Reconcavo."
[5] Emilio Willems, *Cunha.*

propensity toward specialization had done its work. The families worked side by side but not together. None of them consulted the others as to what they were going to plant, or stopped to consider their responsibility toward the over-all effect. This example is especially significant since it concerns a task which was explicitly recognized as requiring a communal effort.

Another such example has to do with the attempt to level one of the squares (Praca do Capim) into a field suitable for playing football. Sr. Luis, a storekeeper and resident on the square, decided that it would be a good thing if the unsightly holes and ridges were eliminated. He talked it over with one of his neighbors and decided to appeal to the mayor for aid. The mayor told them that he also thought that it was a good idea. Although the municipal government could not give them any financial assistance, it was willing to lend them tools and wheelbarrows if they undertook the task. Luis then wrote up an appeal for money and passed it around town. About 700 cruzeiros were collected and work began at once. "Volunteers" were paid at the rate of 15 cruzeiros per day—as much as many of them would make at their normal activity. Moreover, much of the work was performed at night, by moonlight, so that the "volunteers" did not suffer the loss of their regular daily remuneration. The effort was sustained only until the money was exhausted—about a week—and then it ended as suddenly as it had begun, with perceptible but futile modifications of the square's topography. Sr. Luis was accused of fraudulent bookkeeping and indignantly refused to undertake a second appeal. We questioned several of the homeowners on the square as to why, since they thought that the holes and ridges were objectionable, they did not get together and work at it in their spare time. One answer was that the county ought to pay for such work; another, that only a few would contribute labor while the rest would stand around and watch.

PAST AND FUTURE OF THE CRAFTS

The question of the emergence of a fully developed factory system for the industries of Minas Velhas requires a frame of reference considerably greater than that of the community alone. Events on a state-wide, nation-wide, and perhaps world-wide scale must be considered. When they are, the question of the sheer survival of these industries supersedes that of their eventual organization. More than half of the total industrial product is related to the horse and mule complex. These animals are at present by no means threatened with extinction, but there can be little doubt that the role they are destined to play is a rapidly diminishing one. Long-haul bulk transport by trucks throughout the state of Bahia has already cut their importance in half. The threat of motorized transport has another side to it, however, which is more imminent and more devastating than the first. The unfurling network of motor roads has rendered the simple, powerless industries of Minas Velhas vulnerable to the competition of metropolitan-based factories in advanced stages of mechanization. Despite the low cost of labor in Minas Velhas, a pair of shoes which costs 200 cruzeiros at Sr. Braulio's factory is not the match of a pair of shoes of the same price from the shops of Salvador or Sao Paulo. The cost of transportation has until recently acted as a barrier against the intrusion of machine-made products in the region covered by the peddlers of Minas Velhas, but this barrier is now crumbling fast. Peddlers have recently begun to appear in Vila Nova with shoes produced in the neighboring state of Pernambuco. These shoes are only slightly more expensive than those produced by Sr. Braulio.

Electrically plated products are a great threat to the metal industries of Minas Velhas at their present technological level. In order to achieve a polished white metal surface for his bridles, the brass-smith must use a core high in nickel content through and through; those craftsmen in distant places who have at their command electric nickel-plating machines save enormously on expenses for raw materials. All the knife blades produced in Minas Velhas are subject to rust after brief exposure and the preferred nickel- and chrome-plated blades are appearing in ever increasing numbers throughout the interior.

In yet another more subtle but equally important way, the invasion of machine products constitutes a threat to Minas Velhas's artisans. At present there are only two artisans who give their products an identifying mark; e.g., Joao Celestino punches three small holes on the upper portion of his knife blades. In the past this practice was more widespread. The artisans explain its passing as due to the steadily increasing emphasis on "junk" (*obras de carregacao*)—products which are slapped together hastily with little or no attention devoted to detail and excellence of finish. Today, quantity and not quality is the aim of most of the metal artisans. A "clean job" (*obra limpa*) is produced nowadays only on commission. There are still many individuals left who have the skill necessary to produce a work of art; but few opportunities occur for this skill to be fully expressed. Contrary to what might be expected of an industry which is still essentially in the homecraft stage, the artisans of Minas Velhas are more often than not ashamed of the articles they produce, rather than proud of them. The struggle to produce in quantity with only "one's fingernails to work with" has meant a working day filled with as much routine and automatism as that which plagues the modern factory worker. While division of labor remains relatively uncomplex and there is an intimate contact between each worker and the finished product, the contact itself is becoming less and less rewarding. The quality of the average spur, knife, bridle, or stirrup produced in Minas Velhas has been consciously degraded in a way which can only induce a feeling of frustration in most individuals who, like the majority of craftworkers in Minas Velhas, consider themselves to be artists. "We have to keep working as fast as possible all the time," complains Joao Celestino. "These days life doesn't give us a chance to make a decent piece of work."

This degradation results from the inability of the artisan profitably to match the perfection of machine-made products. The process of polishing and designing with the available equipment is laborious and time-consuming. A straighter edge, a smoother curve, a less visible seam are luxuries in which the average artisan can no longer indulge. The enormous amount of extra labor required to achieve a machinelike perfection in shape and finish requires a selling price far beyond that of comparable machine-made products. The alternative is to undersell by reducing standards of perfection.

STORES

The proliferation of commercial establishments in Minas Velhas is a phenomenon directly related to the prevailing concept of an individualized economic destiny in the urban ethos. There are twenty-two such establishments divided into three generally recognized categories: four *lojas*, sixteen *vendas*, and two *botequins*.

The *lojas* are large-scale, firmly rooted businesses with credit in Salvador and stock on hand worth from 15,000 to 30,000 cruzeiros. All four carry cloth clothing, pots, pans, dishes, other household items, kerosene, and cigarettes. Two of them sell bread and biscuits made in their own bakeries. They are distinguished from the other stores by their size, their lack of emphasis on food, and their handling of cloth and clothing.

The *vendas* are small with little or no commercial credit and stock on hand ranging from 1,000 to 10,000 cruzeiros. Most of them are located in the owner's domicile. Their chief emphasis is on foodstuffs—dried meat (*carne de sol*), crude lard (*toicinho*), cord tobacco, sugar, onions, coffee, *rapadura* (brown sugar in blocks), corn, cheese, bananas, and *cachaca*. Many of them also carry some pots and pans, kerosene, and a few flashlights; one *venda* owner runs the town's third bakery.

The *botequins* are smaller still and sell only food products, especially fruits and vegetables—bananas, oranges, lemons, tomatoes, and other fruits when they are in season.

There are eighteen stores, then, in this city of fifteen hundred persons which depend upon the sale of food-stuffs (including *cachaca*) for their mainstay. All of them carry the same type of food. Their combined annual sales do not exceed 200,000 cruzeiros (approximately $10,000 U.S.). The principal source of food-stuffs for these stores is the regular Saturday open fair. The number of food stores is quite remarkable, not only from the standpoint of their small scale, but also when it is considered that the merchants pay the same price as everyone else at the fair, and that the fair is open to everybody. Many families buy enough food each Satur-day to last them through the week. Clearly if this were the case for all the families there could not possibly be so many stores all handling the same wares. The fact is that the proliferation of the *vendas* is feasible owing to the inability of about one third of the population to maintain such buying habits. These families are con-tinuously in debt; their income is irregular and depends upon the intermittent sale of some goods or service. Many must buy their food from day to day. The food stores perform the service of buying food and keeping it on hand so that the poor families may buy on the same basis as they gain their income. The *vendas* which sell to them at prices 15 to 20 percent higher than those of the fair also function as sources of short-term loans. Each *venda* has its regular customers to whom the owner of the *venda* will grant credit over a period of weeks and sometimes months.

This explains how the proliferation of food stores is feasible, but it does not explain why there should be so many individuals with a capital of three or four thou-sand cruzeiros who can think of nothing better to do with their money than to open a *venda* when it is obvious that the relatively enormous number of stores and the small number of customers precludes the possibility of anything more than a marginal return. Nor does it explain why there is no tendency whatsoever for several of the stores to merge into larger and more efficient units.

Owning a *venda* does not bring wealth, but it is one of the most desirable occupations known to the community. Reference has already been made to the conspicuous role which the chair plays in the life of the storekeeper. The *venda* owner has lots of time to sit; he has endless opportunities for ruminative chats with the people who happen by. One storekeeper explained his choice of trade with the remark that he likes to "do things with money." This should not be taken merely at its face value, i.e., that he would rather have money work for him than have to work for money. Beyond the obvious desirability of escaping from physical labor and a life of lolling semi-security, there is another implication: not only does being a storekeeper involve less work, but it is also, in terms of the locale, more romantic and more stimulating. This concept stems from the very heart of the urban tradition. For over two centuries in Minas Velhas there has never been any doubt that prestige and manual labor are incompatible. Owning a store is like owning and knowing how to operate a machine that makes money; aside from the intrinsic fascination of the machine, the value placed upon the mental agility necessary to keeping the machine in order is far above the value placed on sheer physical effort.

The failure of these small establishments to effect mergers forms part of the same syndrome which has already been described for industry. There is no one to take the initiative. The supremacy of the pattern of the individual owner in his home-based installation has never been threatened. None of the storekeepers feels that expansion is the requisite of success. The idea of growing bigger and putting half a dozen of one's competitors out of business is scarcely given a thought. Each man wants a place for his store in his home, wants his regular customers and his leisure; becoming the owner of a store is conceived as the end of a struggle and not as the beginning of it.

GOLD MINING

All the occupational specializations and their associated technologies cannot be treated here in detail. One activity—gold mining—deserves more attention than the rest by virtue not of its actual importance in the economy but because of the extent to which it continues to figure in the aspirations of the townspeople.

For the most part, the technique of gold mining has remained unchanged for centuries. Both alluvial deposits and veins occur in the region. Many unsuccessful attempts have been made to divert river beds and exhaust the water from the deep river pools. Syphons, small gasoline-driven pumps, and, occasionally, diving suits, have been pressed into service, but the main effort usually depends on kerosene tins and back breaking effort. Veins are looked for near streams and rivers since water is always needed to wash the gold.

The key instrument for any miner is a circular wooden dish with a slightly conical bottom, called a *batea*. The ore, which has either been shoveled up from the river bottom or broken off from the rocks suspected of containing veins, is placed in the *batea*, which performs the function of a rude centrifuge. Water is added and the *batea* is floated on the stream. By whirling, tipping, and dipping the *batea*, the miner manages to thin out the ore until only the finer and denser particles remain. More water is added, and by more whirling and tilting the remaining particles are spread out along the sides. Unwanted substances are scooped out. The final traces are spread out and water is trickled over them, washing away all but what flakes and particles of gold may be present.

At the moment there are only five or six persons in

Minas Velhas seriously engaged in gold mining. About an equal number are engaged in crystal and slate mining. But as recently as 1932 and again in 1939, there were sudden bursts of activity in gold mining which involved upwards of a hundred townsmen working in or near the city. These were years of drought and depression when the industrial products became worthless and only gold and currency had value in terms of food. Many of the local artisans claim that they owe their lives to the ability to find gold during these lean years. The number of person—men, women, and children—who at one time or another have tried their hand as miners must come to well over 20 percent of the urban population.

Few people in Minas Velhas doubt that there are immense riches awaiting any large-scale attempt at exploitation. Here too the search for a boss goes on perpetually. Many of the town's most prominent citizens as well as the poor and uneducated regard the mineral resources of Minas Velhas to be its most important asset and its only hope for the future. One of the most consistent and bitterest complaints leveled against the government is its failure to perform mineralogical surveys in the area. The traces of platinum and bauxite, the considerable quantities of iron and crystal, together with the negligible amounts of gold and semiprecious stones which are constantly being turned up, maintain the feeling that boundless riches lie buried in the mountains which surround the city. Folk belief is saturated with occult phenomena revolving around the presence or effect of gold. A common explanation of the wealth of rich families is that gold or buried treasure was found by them. When our field team arrived in Minas Velhas, its members were immediately identified as mineralogists, geologists, or engineers. Early in our field work a week rarely passed without some townsmen appearing in the doorway to ask the ethnologist to identify some strange-looking rocks. One man, formerly the town's sheriff, tried for an entire year to interest the ethnologist in opening up a mine on some property he owned near Serra do Ouro. He never was convinced that our questions about the townspeople were not simply designed to mask our real purpose, which was to find gold. When this was denied, he would wink knowingly and offer to tell us all that we wanted to find out.

This concern with mineral wealth inevitably brings to mind the hopes and motivations of the founders of Minas Velhas. The heritage of the early adventurers— the tendency to regard the environment with rapine eyes and the belief that the creation of wealth can and ought to be instantaneous—is clearly visible among their heirs. While the average citizen of Minas Velhas is filled with pessimism about the possibilities of creating wealth above ground, he is eternally optimistic about the wealth that already lies created below it. The subsoil is a *deus ex machina* of the community's economic tragedy. This is what moved Sr. A. G., the local historian, to say that Minas Velhas is a beggar with jewels in her pocket.[6]

AGRICULTURE

For the townspeople, agriculture is a secondary but not negligible economic pusuit. There are forty-one town families whose cash income and/or food supply depends on farming. Of these, seven are relatively large-scale landlords (*fazendeiros*) who do not actually participate in the work, and the remainder are about equally divided between small-scale farmers (*roceiros*), sharecroppers (*meieiros*), and hired hands. In addition, there are about twenty more heads of families who own property in the rural area worked by sharecroppers and hired hands. For these landlords, the income derived from agriculture is strictly secondary. The State Tax Clerk, for example, owns a small farm about two miles from the city. After dividing the crop with the share-

---

[6] Lucrecio Bomfim, the State Tax Collector, on hearing this remark glumly reviewed the tale of poverty which his books told him and retorted: "Then she must be a thief."

cropper who lives on the land, the Tax Clerk receives only enough corn and mandioca to supply his family's needs for about six months.

The seven large-scale landlords are called *fazendeiros* (plantation owners). This term is applied to any individual who owns a large amount of land, receives the major share of his income from it, and does no agricultural labor. In the vicinity of Minas Velhas, landlords of this type are mainly town dwellers. They either inherited the land and moved away from it or bought the land and never moved onto it. Outside of Minas Velhas, particularly in the valleys of Gruta and Vila Nova, there are many landlords who spend most of their time on their plantations and who keep town houses which they visit but occasionally.

A second group of landowners are the *roceiros* or farmers. The farmer himself and members of his family work his land. He may be assisted by a few sharecroppers and hired hands but never to the extent that he is freed from labor. The farmer's domicile is often situated off the land which he works; this is the case for about half of the farmers who live in the villages and for all of those who live within the town.

The most common type of agricultural worker is the sharecropper. Many of these own small parcels of land; others are completely landless. They provide the main labor force for work on the plantations. Some sharecroppers live on the plantations all year round; others live in the city or on their own small parcels of land in the villages and travel back and forth to the land they work. Some work land on more than one plantation. The sharecropper pays for the use of the land with a portion of the crop.

Hired hands receive salaries. There are few persons, however, in Minas Velhas or in the villages who work for agricultural wages the year round. They are most in demand during critical harvest and planting seasons and for milling sugar cane. The hired hands usually come from the ranks of the urban and rural small-scale farmers, sharecroppers, and also the *macaqueiros* who live in the city. Thus it is not unusual in both town and villages for a single individual to cultivate his own small piece of land, cultivate someone else's on a share-crop basis, and work at certain times of the year in still another place for wages.

The plantations owned by the town's landlords are relatively small, ranging in size from 12,000 to 36,000 square meters and in value from 100 to 500 contos ($3,300 to $11,500 U.S.). It should be emphasized that due to variations in soil and water conditions, size constitutes an unreliable index to value. Four to eight families of sharecroppers (about twenty to sixty persons) are to be found living on the premises. Two families may share the same quarters, but more commonly each has its separate house. The houses are owned by the landlord who occasionally, but not necessarily, assumes the burden of maintaining them in a good state of repair. The landlord allots a specific portion of land to each sharecropper and indicates with what crop he wishes it to be planted. Each sharecropper plants a number of different crops but usually corn, beans, rice, and mandioca are planted by all the sharecroppers on the plantation; other crops may be planted only by some of them. The specific soil and water requirements of such crops as rice and sugar cane may conspire to produce a portion of the plantation dedicated exclusively to these crops. Otherwise all the corn is not planted in the same place, nor all the mandioca in the same place, etc. Each crop is scattered about the plantation. Hence, the average plantation looks like a series of separate small adjoining farms, each one duplicating to some extent the crops to be found in every other. This sort of apportionment is but another expression of the by now familiar work pattern. Each sharecropper works his own section independently of the other share-croppers, just as the three saddle makers who work for Sr. Braulio pursue the same craft in different rooms, and just as the care of the town garden was apportioned, each family with its own section.

At the harvest of any particular crop, the sharecropper surrenders one quarter or one half of the total production to the owner. According to popular account, the share is determined by whether or not the landlord has supplied the seed. If the sharecropper himself supplies the seed, he need surrender only one quarter of the crop; if the owner has supplied the seed, his share is one half. In practice the determination of the share may be traced to the quality of the land. A landlord whose land contains rich soil and abundant water rarely will permit his tenants to plant their own seed. He will insist that the sharecropper accept the seed offered to him and thus bind himself to surrendering one half of the harvest. Actually the giving of seed in many cases is more a contractual mechanism signifying agreement on a particular rent price, rather than a mechanism of credit. Thus, in a crude way the owner is able to proportion the cost of the use of his land to that of its value.

The sharecropper is never specifically bound to dispose of his share of the crop by selling it to the owner. But the owner is the fatherlike boss of his workers. In case of emergency he can be counted on to provide money for medicine, a funeral, or a marriage. During the lean months between harvests he also functions as a source of short-term loans and credit. By the time the crop is ready, the average sharecropper has already pledged the major part of it to the landlord. Rather than go to the trouble of selling it at the fair, the sharecropper simply turns it over to the landlord in return for the liquidation of his debts.

Most sharecroppers are permitted to raise a small number of chickens and pigs and an occasional cow as their own. Certain secondary crops such as potatoes, gourds, bananas, *andu* (white bean), and yams also do not normally fall into the category of crops from which the landlord expects a share. The owner seems to tolerate these sidelines as long as they do not occupy space which might be utilized for other purposes and as long as they do not interfere with the sharecroppers' main concern. Such crops are principally destined for the sharecroppers' own domestic needs.

LARGE FARMS

Uricuri, the *fazenda* of Sr. Jose da Silva, who is the present mayor of Minas Velhas, is typical of the plantations owned by prominent townsmen, and also to a large extent of those within the county. It is situated in a small, well-watered valley, five miles distant from the city. Sr. Silva, who besides being mayor is one of the town's two typographers, visits his property about once a week—sometimes with members of his family, who all normally reside in Minas Velhas. Uricuri has five houses set about three hundred yards apart and hidden from each other. Four of these are inhabited by the sharecroppers and their families; the fifth is reserved for Mayor Silva. Altogether, there are about 24,000 square meters of arable land which Sr. Silva estimates to be worth about $6,600 U.S. The cash crops are sugar cane, mandioca, rice, corn, beans, bananas, and pineapples; secondary crops for Mayor Silva's and the sharecroppers' own consumption are *andu,* watermelon, gourds, potatoes, papaya, and coffee. The wild *uricuri* palms from which the *fazenda* takes its name are not exploited for their wax; the nuts alone are eaten. A small number of orange, lemon, and mango trees are also cultivated. In addition, Mayor Silva owns fifteen head of cattle which are kept tethered in sections devoted to pasture. There are also six oxen used by the sharecroppers to transport supplies and for milling mandioca and sugar.

Uricuri, like most of the other *fazendas* in the area, has its own mandioca and sugar mills. The technological level of this equipment is similar to that found in the town's industrial installations. Mayor Silva's mandioca mill is located in a shed adjoining his country house. The mill itself consists of a large horizontal wheel whose axle is embedded in the ground. A long beam fits into the axle above the wheel and extends out over the rim of the wheel. A yoke is fixed to the beam against which one or two oxen may be made to push. Leather thongs circle the wheel and twist out over an arrangement of pulleys to the milling unit which is a small horizontal wooden cylinder studded with iron teeth (*boneca*). The cylinder whirls at high speeds and the mandioca roots are fed against it and pulverized. The pulp is then gathered up and put into a press in order to extract the poison. The press itself consists of a wooden trough with a heavy lid. A long beam is fixed to the top of the lid, and its weight forces the lid down upon the pulp. The poisonous liquid runs out of the bottom of the trough and is used as an insecticide. About four hours are required to extract the poison. The purified mash is then rubbed through a strainer (*peneira*) to eliminate husks and lumps. (The residue [*crueira*] is an excellent animal feed.) The flour is then ready to be toasted. A large open-hearth oven resembling an oval skillet is used for this purpose. The floor of the oven is made of slate; its walls are of adobe. Care must be taken to prevent the flour from scorching. Hence a long wooden hoe is used to toss and mix it about.

The sugar mill (*engenhoca*) is a slightly more elaborate installation. The milling unit consists of three large vertically mounted rollers. The center roller, which is geared to the other two, is turned by oxen. Two men feed the rollers, inserting the cane through one side and feeding it back through the other. The sap falls into a funnel which empties into a trough situated in a pit-house below the level of the mill. It is then placed in a large copper cauldron (*tacha*) set on top of a wood-burning oven and boiled. Wood ash is thrown in to help coagulate the impurities, which are skimmed off the top by means of ladles. The purified syrup (*mel*) may then be made into bricks of *rapadura* (crude brown sugar) or filtered to make sugar. Sr. Silva has facilities for making both products. *Rapadura* is made by simply pouring the syrup into wooden forms and letting it crystallize. Sugar is made by filtering the syrup in a V-shaped wooden trough known as a *bangue*. The trough is filled with several layers of syrup sandwiched between layers of earth mixed with cow dung. The syrup drips down through the earth and dung and out the bottom of the trough, leaving the purer crystals trapped between the layers. The sugar is then boiled again, skimmed of impurities, and left to recrystallize.

Uricuri produces about forty-five oxcart loads of sugar cane per year. Twenty cartloads go to make 2,000 kilograms of *rapadura,* which have a value of about 6,000 cruzeiros. The remaining twenty-five cartloads go to make 1,800 kilograms of sugar with a value of 7,200 cruzeiros. Half of the total belongs to Sr. Silva; the other half is split among the four sharecroppers. The share for sugar cane is always one half since the mill and the firewood are donated by the landlord. A little over a cartload of wood is required for each cartload of cane. The crushed cane (*bagaco*) is occasionally burned in the furnace as an auxiliary to the wood, but it is rarely used alone. Mayor Silva's monthly income from the sale of all of his products is about 3,500 cruzeiros. Sales take place in Minas Velhas and in the other nearby fair towns. Data is lacking as to what proportion of the produce is consumed locally and what proportion through resale finds its ways to more distant markets.

All agriculture in the area around Minas Velhas is done with the hoe. There are only three plows in the entire county of Minas Velhas, and even these are not used. Mayor Silva owns one of them, but has been unable to persuade his sharecroppers to use it. "They can't get used to it," he says. "When I'm there watching them they'll use the plow. When I'm not there they take up their hoes again." The sharecroppers claim that the land is too stony and too hilly for using the

plow. The real reason for their resistance to the innovation is probably a combination of these two factors—
motor habits and adverse topographical features—plus a
third and equally important one—the small, patchwork
layout of the plantations. The plow can be used to best
advantage on long continuous stretches. Owing to the
practice of allotting each sharecropper a parcel of land
and of staggering the areas devoted to a particular crop,
such conditions rarely exist.

AGRICULTURE IN THE VILLAGES

In contrast to the town, all the people of the villages are
agriculturalists. While there are landowning farmers,
sharecroppers, and hired hands in the rural areas, there
are no plantation owners and no landlords for whom
agricultural income is of only secondary importance.
Unlike the townspeople, almost every man, woman, and
child in the villages, at one time or another, picks up a
hoe and tills the soil.

The small, semi-subsistence farm is the most typical
form of land organization in the villages. Generally
speaking, each agricultural family grows enough staple
foods to supply its own minimum annual needs. The
villagers' involvement in the cash economy of the area is
perforce of a less vital nature than that of the town
dweller who must depend on a cash income for the purchase of his basic food supply. This dependence can
only be phrased in relative terms, since the villager does
need cash for the purchase of hardware and of agricultural products for the cultivation of which his land is
unsuitable or too small. Hoes, knives, cloth, sewing
machines, lamps, matches, drugs, and kerosene must be
paid for with cash, and such products as sugar cane, rice,
tobacco, *cachaca,* and cheese would be completely absent from many rural households if they could not be
purchased from other farmers at the fair.

There are three recognized planting seasons in the
gerais: October-November (*das aguas*), January-Febru-
ary (*da quaresma*), and June-July (*de seca*). The last is

feasible only with irrigation. Heavy rains may occur anywhere from October to March. (This period is popularly referred to as the winter, though in the Southern Hemisphere it is, of course, the summer.) Beans are the only crop which is sometimes planted more than two times per year. Due to the irregularity of the rains, it is rare that all three crops should come in, however. Corn, rice, and potatoes are planted one or two times. Yields vary tremendously from year to year, from soil to soil, and from season to season.[7]

Agricultural technology is very primitive. In none of the villages is the plow used, even to the limited extent to which it is used on Sr. Silva's *fazenda*. The hoe is the universal instrument of work. The advantages of using fertilizer are known but rarely practiced because of the scarcity of animals. Seed selection is largely unknown, with disastrous results. In Baixa do Gamba an unconscious sort of selection was observed to be responsible not for improving the stock but for deteriorating it. Due to the important role corn plays in the subsistence diet, the farmer normally consumes the best cobs as soon as they appear. The half-filled, stunted, irregular, and otherwise defective cobs are left over to provide the seed.

The land is planted as many years in succession at it will yield a minimal crop. When practically nothing has shown its head above ground, the land is left fallow for one to three years, depending on how hard pressed the owner is. The feeble secondary growth is burned off before planting again. The ruinous toll of this regime is recognized by the farmers, but they have no alternative owing to the smallness of their property. The same land is planted again and again. Migratory "slash-and-burn" agriculture, typical of many regions of Brazil, has long ceased to be feasible in the mountain region of Bahia.

In Serra do Ouro farming is performed on a series of

[7] Some actual rates reported by different farmers for one year are as follows: Corn: 1/16, 1/80, 1/160; Beans: 1/2, 1/4, 1/8, 1/160; Rice: 1/12, 1/160.

high fertile ridges surrounded on all sides by unworkable soils. The high elevation makes the planting of some temperate crops feasible. Wheat has been tried for many years but with inconclusive results. It is claimed that the toll taken by a small bird called the *chupa-chupa* makes a good harvest impossible. An additional obstacle is the lack of milling facilities. No mill capable of making wheat flour exists in Serra do Ouro itself. The nearest is located in Vila Nova. The processing here, however, is rustic; the local bakers in Minas Velhas and Vila Nova refuse to use the flour, claiming that it is too dark and that the bread made from it crumbles apart. They prefer, instead, bleached American and Argentinian wheat which sells for more than twice the price of the local product. Hence, little advantage is taken of the exceptional climatic conditions, and the same basic products—mandioca, rice, corn, and beans—are emphasized. Only one atypical crop is produced in quantity—quince—which is sold to several small factories in the county of Minas Velhas and made into preserves (*doce*).

Few of the agricultural products of both *fazendas* and farms find markets outside of the immediate area. When they do, primary sales usually take place in the local fair towns, and an intermediary then assumes the task of transport to more distant markets. Minas Velhas rarely has out-of-town buyers present at its fair despite the fact that the prices of food staples in Salvador are two- and threefold those current in Minas Velhas. The high cost of transport, lack of capital, and lack of initiative on the part of the local merchants, together with the timidity of the farmers over the prospect of an indisposable surplus, all act to restrict production principally to the needs of the local consumers.

Rural work patterns contain the same emphasis upon individualized effort as do the urban work patterns. In the local setting, the concept of an individualized economic destiny is as applicable to the villager as to the townsman.

For example, among the landowning farmers of the

satellite villages, partition of inherited land is rarely carried out by legal or formal methods. The cost of legal papers and assistance is prohibitive to the perpetually short-on-cash farmers. Most frequently the land is held in "common" (*comun*). But this condition merely means that each heir is permitted to work the amount of land to which his share in the inheritance entitles him without the specific plot of ground having been demarcated. In the event that an heir is not present his share of .the land is not held vacant but is worked by the others. If he should return after a period of absence the others must make room for him. In practice, however, the particular segment which an heir works corresponds to the segment which he worked during the lifetime of the deceased. A child, for instance, who goes to work on his father's property is usually assigned a specific area in which he may plant what he chooses. As he grows older this segment is enlarged and he spends more and more of his time on it. If he marries and maintains good relations with his father, he and his wife may tend exclusively to the segment and not work at all on the rest of the property. Upon the death of the parent the children continue to use the same plot plus a portion of the land which the deceased formerly worked. By the laws of the state, however, they have no particular claim upon any specific segment of the total inheritance. Upon this difference between the legal and use-defined ownership, and the resistance to genuine communal property, rests an endless number of quarrels and legal actions. A typical case is the following one:

Candido owned about fifty hectares of land. He married and had five children. His wife died and the children inherited five hectares apiece. No partition was made, and each one continued to work the segment he was accustomed to. One of the children married a man by the name of Marcelino. A second and a third then moved to Sao Paulo. Before they left, Marcelino bought the ten hectares which they had inherited from their mother. The segment which these two children had always cultivated included a strip of bottom land excellently suited for growing rice. Marcelino assumed that in the purchase of the shares he became entitled to this land because it was here that the sellers had always planted. He forthwith proceeded to plant it with rice and continued to do so over the mounting objections of Altino, his wife's brother. When Candido died, the situation became worse. Altino maintained that all the land was in *comun* and that Marcelino had no right greater than the others to use the choice bottom. To discourage Marcelino he let his horse and mule wander into the rice field. Marcelino then built a fence to protect the rice from the animals. When he was absent, Altino opened the fence and let the animals in. The dispute continues, and there is no resolution in sight.

There was also a house on Candido's land. After his death, the children could not decide who ought to live in it. The problem was solved in accordance with the generalized rural and urban resistance to communal property by tearing down the house. Each heir carried off a part of it; doors, windows, furniture and roof tiles were removed, leaving only the adobe walls standing.

Another example of the lack of cooperative patterns may be drawn from irrigation practices.

Irrigation is an important feature of agriculture in Baixa do Gamba. A second crop of rice, beans, and corn is often produced in this manner. A large ditch comes off a waterfall above the settlement and runs for several miles along the left bank of the Rio das Pedras. This ditch was built about one hundred and fifty years ago by persons vaguely referred to as *os antigos*. It was probably originally used for gold mining. Twenty separate farms are serviced by this source. Each owner accepts the responsibility of maintaining only the section which passes through his property and considerable malfunctioning is produced by the failure to organize responsibility in terms of larger units. In May and June, the height of the dry season, when the full capacity of the ditch is most needed, ineffectual attempts are made to form cooperative parties in order to clean and deepen the channel, but the burden usually falls to those who have property on the lower end of the ditch since they suffer most from impediments farther up. The use of the water is regulated by unwritten agreement giving each property owner the right to tap the ditch during an average of two hours per day. No provision has been made for a definite timetable with the result that between the hours of seven and eight in the morning, which are preferred "because of the help of the dew," farmers in the middle of the course are likely to be without water (the lower end gets the water which left the waterfall during the previous night). If a man at the upper end wants to use the water for more than two hours a day, he makes informal inquiries about the intentions of the farmers below him, and vice versa. If the ditch breaks near the waterfall—as is common enough owing to the failure to institute any major repairs for several decades—though all suffer the consequences, it is only those near the front end who attempt the repair.

The most conspicuous features of agriculture in the village satellites are the shortage of arable land and the extreme dissection and scattering owing to the inheritance system. Despite the vast expanse of the *gerais,* only the area confined to the margins and bottoms of constant rivers is workable under existing techniques. For farmers like those of Baixa do Gamba, confinement to the river bottom has made landlessness for some a mathematical certainty. With each generation the land is divided into smaller and smaller segments until the plots are so small and their soil so exhausted that they will not sustain those who attempt to live off of them. The farmer then has the recourse of seeking additional land elsewhere. One common solution is to go to work as a sharecropper or hired hand on one of the *fazendas* in the valleys below. Another common solution is to work as a hired hand in the state of Sao Paulo.

At least half of the population of Baixa do Gamba

does not own enough land to maintain a subsistence
diet. Jose is a typical example. He himself owns no
land. His father sold all that he might have inherited
in order to pay off a debt brought on by the marriage of
one of his daughters. Jose, his wife, four children, and
his mother-in-law live on the mother-in-law's land. The
mother-in-law is too old to work and is dependent on
Jose for support. In return Jose and his wife have the
use of her land. All that this land has on it are a house,
some fruit trees, and pasture. The fruit trees yield a
small cash income:

TYPE OF TREE	ANNUAL VALUE
Goiaba	Cr $150.00
Lima	30.00
Orange	70.00
Coffee	224.00
	Cr. $474.00

It is clear that the family must look for additional
land. Jose and his wife, therefore, also plant as sharecroppers in three different places. Two of these are different but adjoining plantations in Gruta, and the third
is on a neighbor's property in Baixa do Gamba. Their
annual share at each of these places is as follows:

	A: GRUTA	B: GRUTA	C: BAIXA DO GAMBA	TOTALS
Corn	480 liters	220 liters	15 liters	715 liters
Beans	60 liters	160 liters		220 liters
Mandioca			360 liters	360 liters
Rice			240 liters	240 liters
Turnips	50 lbs.	50 lbs.		100 lbs.
Andu (white bean)	20 liters	20 liters		40 liters
Potato	68 lbs.	68 lbs.	34 lbs.	170 lbs.
Yam			34 lbs.	34 lbs.

On *A*'s and *C*'s land the figures represent three
fourths of the total yield. On *B*'s land Jose's share is
only one half. Jose is not permitted to furnish his own
seed on the latter's land because it has above average
soil. The figures for potatoes, yams, and *andu* repre-

sent the total yield; no share is commonly taken by the *fazendeiro* for these subsidiary products.

Gruta is ten miles away from Jose's home in Baixa do Gamba. Hence the number of places in which Jose and his family work, and their distance from each other, puts the family almost within the category of migratory workers. During all the months of the year except June through August, Jose and his family spend almost as much time away from home as in it. In Gruta they sleep in the mandioca shed together with two other families who are sharecroppers on *A*'s property. The three families, in the typical individualized fashion of the sharecroppers, cook and work separately.

EMIGRATION

For at least the past fifty years, but with increasing intensity since 1920, the diminishing ratio of land per individual has forced more and more of the young men of each succeeding generation to leave the villages and look for work elsewhere. The saturation and mismanagement of lands in the mountain region of Bahia has coincided with the era of great agricultural expansion in the state of Sao Paulo and, more recently, in the state of Parana. At least 30 percent of the adult male population of Serra do Ouro and Baixa do Gamba are presently working or have worked at some time in the past in these distant states. A hired hand is paid between ten and fifteen cruzeiros a day in Minas Velhas. In Sao Paulo and Parana he may receive between twenty-five and thirty-five cruzeiros a day, usually including medical care and other benefits. This enormous disparity in wages accounts for the exodus to other regions. Owners of *fazendas* in Vila Nova and Gruta complain bitterly about the shortage of hired hands, while women and children are becoming more and more important in local agriculture. Actually the shortage of manpower is merely a reflection of the inability of the landowner to pay wages comparable to those which exist in places ten days' travel away from home, plus the ability of the local workers to get to those places. It is also a reflection of the inability of the local distributive system to tap distant markets so that a rise in prices and an increase in quantity might permit wages high enough to keep labor at home.

A high proportion of the émigrés from the villages were found, however, to be only temporary migrants. In Serra de Ouro, only 20 percent of the émigrés were permanently lost to the community. The rest could be expected to return after a period abroad ranging from three months to a few years. The bulk of the movement involves young unmarried men. Many get married upon their return with the money they saved while working abroad and often the trip is undertaken with this objective in mind. It is the men in the age group between sixteen and twenty-five who most feel the pinch of the shortage of land; if they want to marry they must somehow find additional land or another source of income. Frequently the former involves waiting for the death of their parents.

After working for a year or two abroad, the young villager returns somewhat as a hero. Few actually manage to save much money, but the experience and the foreign mannerisms are considered to be great assets. They bring home presents like gramophones, cigarette lighters, and silk cloth. For themselves, a large wristwatch, a silk bandana, and a mouth full of gold-capped teeth are considered just compensation for the adventure.

With the improvement in transportation of recent years the tendency has arisen for the work to become not only migratory but seasonal as well. The trip to Parana now takes nine or ten days. Formerly this trip would have taken three weeks to a month. Hence it has now become common for the men of Serra do Ouro to leave in blocks of ten or twelve, go to Sao Paulo or Parana, take part in the harvest, and return to Serra do Ouro in time to plant their own crops. One old woman, dismayed at the constant mobility of her grandchildren commented: "Two came home today. Two are leaving next week. Always going and coming. Like ants."

Among the townspeople the movement is just as intense, but there is considerably less likelihood of return. Out of a sample of 127 individuals born in Minas Velhas who are at present in Sao Paulo or Parana or who have worked there in the past only 16 can be considered permanent residents of the town. The place of

TABLE 4. OCCUPATIONS OF URBAN ÉMIGRÉS

OCCUPATION IN MINAS VELHAS		OCCUPATION ABROAD	
Agriculture	33	Agriculture	52
Blacksmith	14	Machine operators	3
Brass-smith	13	Sugar mill worker (*usina*)	4
Shoemaker	5	Mechanic	1
Dressmaker	9	Laborer	3
Goldsmith	3	Cowboy	1
Carpenter	2	*Empreteiro* (Labor boss)	1
Miner	8	Tailor	2
Housewife	7	Bricklayer	2
Storekeeper	5	Baker	2
Peddler	3	Doorman	4
Bricklayer	6	Bookkeeper	2
Tailor	1	Bank employee	1
Washerwoman	1	Storekeeper	3
Servant	2	Student	1
No occupation	12	Carpenter	1
Unknown	3	Shoemaker	2
	127	Hatter	1
		Peddler	1
		Teacher	1
		Miner	1
		Blacksmith	1
		Servant	1
		Saddle maker	1
		House builder	8
		Dressmaker	8
		No occupation	3
		Unknown	16
			127

residence and marital status of many of the individuals abroad are unknown or forgotten, and only an insignificant number of those away are expected to return for anything more than a visit. Unlike the emigrants from Serra do Ouro who are all farmers, a great many different occupations are practiced by the emigrants from Minas Velhas.

The fact that the majoity of the town émigrés were unconnected with agriculture (see Table 4) may help to explain the difference between the rural and urban movements. Even among those townsmen who were engaged in agriculture before they left there is a larger percentage of absolutely landless hired hands than among the villagers. The city dweller is evidently more successful in cutting off home ties than the villager who has a piece of land, however small, which belongs to him, and which may be augmented someday when he inherits from his father.

In Minas Velhas emigration has had a serious effect upon the balance of the sexes, reducing the number of

TABLE 5. POPULATION OF MINAS VELHAS PER SEX AND AGE GROUP

AGE	MALE	FEMALE	TOTAL
0-11 months	19	30	49
1-6 years	121	120	241
7-14	122	143	265
15-19	74	79	153
20-29	68	137	205
30-39	64	90	154
40-49	30	92	122
50-59	32	65	97
60-69	24	54	78
70-79	15	35	50
80-89	3	4	7
90-99	3	3	6
Total	575	852	1,427

Source: These figures were extracted from the questionnaires of the 1950 census by special permission of the Instituto Brasileiro de Geografia e Estastistica.

male workers and increasing the number of self-supporting females (table 5). In the age group between twenty
and fifty years, the group upon which the bulk of economic activity depends, there are only 162 males while
there are 319 females—just twice as many women as
men. This fact explains why, as we shall see in the next
chapter, there are so many women in the third or
menial class who are heads of families.

In summary, it may be said that there are two main
differences between the urban and rural ways of making
a living, both of which stem directly from the importance of agriculture in the villages and its relative un-
importance in the town. The emphasis upon agriculture means first a lesser degree of occupational specialization, and second, less dependence on cash income for
basic subsistence. On the other hand, the emphasis
upon agriculture *does not* involve any fundamental difference in work patterns or in the way the individual's
economic role is considered in relation to his neighbors.
Farming then, in this specific Brazilian setting, is associated both negatively and positively with additional
rural criteria.

The importance of farming in the local rural-urban
differentiation is, however, much more considerable
than this partial correlation would seem to indicate.
Agriculture is not just another occupational specialty;
it is a wholly different category of labor. From the
viewpoint of the townsman, the man who is willing to
spend all day under a hot sun hoeing up the soil is *de
facto* deficient in civilized qualities. Occupations, like
skin color and financial capacity, are graded aspects of
the urban culture; they can be good and bad or high
and low. Agriculture is both bad and low from the
urban standpoint. While the townsman looks upon all
manual labor as degrading, farming involves the greatest
loss of status—much more than the manual labor of a
blacksmith, for example. The artisans of Minas Velhas
habitually think of their work as involving more skill
and brains than the sheer brawn and animal muscle

thought to be sufficient for work in the fields. As a matter of fact, the handicraft workers of Minas Velhas call the town's industries arts (*artes*) and literally refer to themselves as artists (*artistas*).

"Forty acres and independence" would be a meaningless slogan to the poorest of blacksmiths if it did not also include the phrase "with five sharecroppers." Out of fifty city school children who were asked what they wanted to be when they grew up, not a single one answered "farmer," though two of the boys said "plantation owner." To an educated or wealthy townsman, the idea of using farm tools is so alien as to be ludicrous. For example, when a state engineer was sent to survey the possibility of installing a hydroelectric plant in Minas Velhas, Mayor Silva and the president of the town council, among others, accompanied him to the prospective site. While the engineer was setting up his instruments some municipal workers proceeded to cut down the underbrush in order to facilitate triangulation. The councilman, Sr. Morales, himself a wealthy plantation owner, borrowed one of the workmen's bushknives and began to hack at the vegetation. Everyone stopped to laugh at this gesture. "More strength!" shouted the workmen. "Watch out for your eye!" said Mayor Silva. After a few more hacks, Sr. Morales gave the knife back and sat down on a rock to enjoy the rest of the work, satisfied with his little joke.

Though agriculture is to some extent part of the urban scene, it is not part of the urban ethos. The town is oriented away from the fields while the villages are oriented toward them. The ideal relationship of the townsman to the land is one in which a sharecropper intervenes between him and the soil. The ideal of the villager is to get hold of enough land and water to feed his family. The townsman dreams of getting rich from the soil; the villager dreams of planting seed.

CLASS AND RACE[1]   3

MINAS VELHAS is a highly rank-conscious community. At a brisk pace it requires no more than five minutes to walk from one end of the city to the other, but measured in terms of social distance the ends of the city are very far apart. Sub-cultural varieties of behavior based on class differences supply perhaps the strongest expression of the urban complex. Class and not the community is the next largest unit of social structure beyond the family. Class barriers, as we shall see, divide the community into two separate, and to a certain extent, hostile camps.

Two classes are recognized by the townspeople themselves. They are called interchangeably: (A) "the whites" or "the rich" (*brancos-ricos*) and (B) "the negroes" or "the poor" (*pretos-pobres*). The members of these two groups are easily identified; they belong to different social clubs, attend separate dances, and hold competitive festivals. The stratification of the community is much more complex, however. Each class may be further divided into two social strata, yielding a structure whose four parts will be referred to as groups A^1, A^2, B^1, and B^2. The distinction between these groups is based on a combination of criteria involving economic, occupational, educational, and racial ranking "gradients."[2]

CRITERIA OF RANK

Let us first consider the cultural values upon which each of the various ranking gradients is based. In doing so, it will be helpful to bear in mind that such an analysis must be couched in terms of ideal rather than actual

---

[1] Sections of this chapter have previously appeared in *Race and Class in Rural Brazil,* Charles Wagley (ed.), UNESCO Publications, Paris, 1952.

[2] That is, a scale of values ranging from good to bad or high to low.

behavior. While each gradient has its own proper range of values, it is never applied in real-life situations as a discrete or autonomous system. An individual's rank is determined always by a combination of all four major criteria and never by one in isolation.

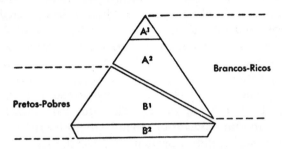

FIGURE 3. CLASS STRUCTURE OF MINAS VELHAS

The values on the economic gradient are self-evident. All that the culture defines as worth owning or doing is more readily accessible to the rich than to the poor. There are some families that own as much as five thousand times more property than others. Annual cash incomes frequently differ by a factor of ten or more. Wide differences in housing are common. Some houses have no furniture to speak of; others are filled with chairs, benches, tables, and a bed for each member of the family. Some women own but one or two dresses, a single undergarment, and no shoes; others have a dozen or more dresses, a score of modern European undergarments, silk stockings, and several pairs of shoes and slippers. Men's wardrobes likewise differ enormously in size and quality. These differences in wealth also account for substantial differences in everyday behavior. Some men do no work; some women do not cook, wash clothes or dishes, iron, sew, or carry water, since they can afford servants to do all the normal household drudgery. Wealthy families set their tables with different foods—fresh meat, bread, milk, potatoes, and canned goods—which poor families cannot afford. Wealthy men have leisure to enter politics, money to wage campaigns and hold political office, and time and clothes to go to church more often. The wealthy woman's wardrobe permits her to take part in the evening promenade in the town garden, to attend all the ordinary and special masses in church, and to become a leader in the religious sisterhoods. Wealthy men travel, know the life of the big cities, and send their children to be educated in colleges and universities. No one in Minas Velhas has ever entertained the slightest notion that there are some things that money cannot buy. "Money is everything."

The values on the educational gradient are also quite clear. The more years an individual attends school, the better he is thought to be. The educated speaker attempts to approximate the complexities of written Portuguese, which differs profoundly from the language of the ordinary people. Long strings of synonyms, full use of the subjunctive and compound tenses, and attention to euphony are powerful honorific symbols. The familiarity with uncommon words and erudite grammatical forms automatically bestows an air of distinction upon the speaker and assures him of silence and respect from the uneducated, rich as well as poor. Sheer literacy lifts a man above his fellows; the individual who can read and write is not only sought after to decipher letters from distant friends and relatives, but in the rural zone he usually supplies counsel on community and personal problems. So much of the prestige of the most important figure in Baixa do Gamba was bound up in the circumstance of his being one of the few literate adults in the settlement that when the creation of a municipal school was proposed, he was among those who fought against the project. Additional prestige derived from education stems from the fact that literacy is a requirement for voting. Elections and politics are taken seriously in Minas Velhas, and the man who cannot vote is distinctly inferior to the man who can.

The occupational ranking gradient is determined by considerations of more or less menial labor, more or less intellectual effort, and more or less control over others.

Those who are completely dependent upon the strength and endurance of their own physical powers—like farmers, the water carriers, the woodcutters, etc.—are at the bottom of the list. The artisans whose crafts demand a special skill in addition to sheer physical effort rank slightly higher. Higher still are the storekeepers and commercial travelers. Still higher are those who command the labors of others—the landlord farmers, who do no work in the fields, and the owners of large workshops who merely supervise production. Those who own large machines like trucks or a flour mill share this level. Owners of special professional monopolies, lawyers or dentists who control the destinies and welfare of others, rank still higher. The top of the order belongs to those who command both the labor and destinies of a large part of the community—the politicians, mayor, councilmen, and political party leaders. For women, the bottom of the order belongs to those who work exclusively with their bodies—field hands, water carriers, washerwomen, wood gatherers, prostitutes, etc. Women with skills like sewing and lacemaking come next. Higher are the housewives, arranged according to how much of the drudgery they have to do themselves. The top of the order belongs to the schoolteachers and others who have freed themselves completely from menial tasks.

The disapproval accorded menial labor ought not to be too rigidly correlated with the actual amount of work effort involved. Such correlations are usually at fault when entire populations have been branded as lazy or indigent. Menial labor is avoided in Minas Velhas at least as much because the culture labels it degrading as because it involves sweat and aching muscles. Women, for example, try to avoid washing clothes or fetching water from the river not simply because it is hard work but because it is shameful to be seen doing these things. Not a few women wash clothes inside their back yards rather than be seen at the river. A house may be situated only a few feet from the river, but if funds are available, a professional water carrier will be paid to bring the water into the house. Many women prefer to borrow water from their neighbors rather than go to the river themselves. The women of one household go so far as to wrap the water jar in a shawl when they steal out of their house to fill it. The gathering of firewood is also looked upon as a degrading activity. Many women consider it to be worse than washing clothes. "Me go into the bush?" exclaimed a housewife whose husband did not have enough money one week to buy wood from their regular source, "that's not for me. I'd rather let everyone stay hungry than go out and look for wood. Even when I was single and there was wood a couple of steps away from the house, I never went for it."

The racial ranking gradient contains less obvious values than the other three ranking gradients. The fact that wealth is considered to be better than poverty needs little explanation in the context of Western civilization. Values attached to racial types on the other hand are more complex and need to be described at greater length. For the moment, it will suffice to know that ideally the white is considered better than the negro, and that the mulatto occupies an intermediate position between the two.

HIGHEST AND LOWEST STRATA

Group A¹ is sometimes consciously identified by the people of Minas Velhas in the expression *gente que tem destaque* (people of distinction). This term is reserved for a limited number of men and women who are the community's most important figures. All of the heads of families said to have *destaque* have either incomes higher than 1,500 cruzeiros a month or property in excess of 50,000 cruzeiros. In addition they all hold some important bureaucratic post. "The people of distinction" control all the political and economic power. They give most of the orders, do least of the work, make the most money, and have the most leisure. They own an abundance of clothing including luxury articles like raincoats, sweaters, silk underclothing, and umbrellas; they live in big houses, sleep in their own beds, have servants to cook, wash, carry water, and take care of their horses; they have well-nourished bodies, own radios, and most of them have traveled and know the life of the big cities.

The people who belong to this group are also often referred to as the "elite" of Minas Velhas, and in many ways they constitute the remnants of a regional aristocracy. Three "traditional" families account for most of its members. These families, however, do not trace themselves back to the period of intensive mining. The names which appear in the subscription books for the erection of the town's early churches and which are associated with the donation of the most slave labor and the largest gifts of gold are the names of the ordinary present-day citizens of the town. The earliest aristocratic lineages were probably obscured and declassed soon after the exhaustion of the mines. As everywhere in the interior of Brazil, the richest and wealthiest among them quickly moved back to the coastal capitals. Those who remained behind became impoverished and contributed to the rank and file of artisans and small businessmen.

New leaders of the community appeared during the second quarter of the nineteenth century. As the basic wealth of the mountains slowly shifted from the barren rocky heights where gold was found to the at first neglected plains and valleys, new fortunes in cattle and agriculture developed, controlled by men who lived outside of the town of Minas Velhas, in far-flung parts of the region. Among them were the barons and *Coronels* of the Empire who with the help of small personal armies came to exercise the despotic political power characteristic of so much of the interior throughout the nineteenth and the early part of the twentieth centuries. During that period the political affairs of Minas Velhas were largely controlled by two landed families who had their estates in the nearby town of Vila Nova.

The various local barons and political chiefs founded families which were endogamous in their class. They married from one town to another, seeking always to adhere to families of comparable wealth and power. Part of this regional aristocracy was continually drifting away to the coastal cities to become doctors, lawyers, and politicians, many of whom figured prominently on the national scene.

Hence, the family lines of the present-day "elite" of Minas Velhas interlace and crisscross with the most prominent families in more than a dozen disparate communities scattered throughout the region. The three families which make up the framework of the highest stratum of the upper class have been part of the local political oligarchy for three or more generations. All of them have been connected and reconnected by marriage. The highest proportion of spinsters and the highest incidence of cousin marriage occur in this group. From these families, have come a long series of men who have attained regional, state-wide, and national renown.

The Bomfim family, for example, which stems partly from the union between the granddaughter of a local baron and a Portuguese merchant banker, numbers among its living relations: two judges; a mayor's wife; two tax collectors, one of whom is the state collector in Minas Velhas; the director of the local post office; an ex-mayor of Minas Velhas; the wife of the "millionaire" of a neighboring community; the wife of a district attorney (*promotor*); and a recently elected deputy in the state legislature. The Bomfims are connected by several marriages with the Limas, who boast among their ranks: an ex-mayor of Minas Velhas; several tax collectors; two physicians and one dentist (one of the doctors has been the mayor of a neighboring community for twenty years); the husband of the sister of the same "millionaire" who was married by a Bomfim; and the wife of one of the local political chieftains who is now a merchant and a political power-seeker in the state capital. Scores of people from these families have emigrated to the coastal metropolises. In the big cities they are apt to lead rather anonymous lives and appear as undistinguished members of the middle class. Wherever they live in the interior, however, they are, or are married to, the local bigwigs—the rich landowners, political chiefs, and the doctors and lawyers who dominate their respective communities.

Members of elite families will occasionally marry with recent upstarts who do not belong to the specific oligarchic tradition if the wealth of these new arrivals is great enough. *Nouveau riche* is, however, such a relatively rare phenomenon in Minas Velhas due to the virtual stagnation of the economy that the "traditional" families have managed to preserve their identity. If the economy were an expanding one, with abundant opportunities for rapid capital formation, the number of newly prosperous citizens would be sufficient to inundate the "traditional" families, destroy their monopoly on political power, and render them insignificant as vehicles of prestige. As it stands now, however, marriage into one of these families is still looked upon as the final badge of success in a career of political and economic opportunism. The rare individual who has risen in his lifetime from artisan or storekeeper to a position of financial and political authority usually seeks a marriage with one of the abundant white-skinned, well-dressed, well-groomed, well-mannered daughters of the elite. Moreover, the elite still seem to prefer celibacy or cousin marriage rather than marry a candidate who does not meet their high standards. Thus the two Portuguese merchant-bankers who founded the Bomfim family had nineteen children between them—seven males and twelve females. Two of the males and five of the females never married (they all lived to be adults). Of the remaining twelve, six married each other, i.e., their cousins.

"There wasn't a man in town who wouldn't have jumped at the opportunity to marry the Bomfim daughters; the sons could have chosen at will. They wanted *gran-finos* (elegant people)," explained one old disappointed suitor.

Hence, what we are here calling a stratum of a class has at its core the remnant of what was once a class by itself. From a static viewpoint it would still be correct to isolate the three major families and treat them as a separate aristocratic group. The situation is obviously transitional, however. Sr. Braulio, the owner of the leather factory, for example, comes from a poor and undistinguished family. Yet he is accepted as a complete equal by members of the traditional best families and no house in town is barred to him. Up until a few years ago, the girls of the Bomfim family are said to have refused to participate in the evening promenade. "They used to consider it a *diminicao* (loss of face) to be seen on the street with their arms linked with girls of other families, even the richest. Today they aren't like that any more." The informant went on to explain that the change occurred when one of the older girls, Gerolina Bomfim, took a job as secretary in the town hall. Due to her inexperience, Gerolina found herself in an inferior position with respect to another young woman who had been at the job for a longer time. "She had to get rid of some of her airs and started to go with other girls who weren't her relatives. Ever since then, all the Bomfim girls walk in the street and dance in the *Clube* like anybody else."

In sharp contrast to the elite live the *macaqueiros* (stratum B²). Included are the more than fifty urban families that subsist on a marginal or submarginal level. They own no property and their income is 400 cruzeiros or less per month. Almost all of this money is spent on food. Bread, cheese, milk, meat, and refined sugar rarely or never form part of their diet. Their houses have one or two rooms in an advanced state of disrepair, with few windows, leaky roofs, and earthen floors. Illumination is provided by smoky, open-wick lamps, and chairs and tables are rarities. If there is a bed, it is likely to be used by four or five adults and children. Most sleeping is done on a mat on the floor. There is no kitchen and meals are eaten in a squatting position.

These people are almost all illiterate. They work as water carriers, washerwomen, road workers, prostitutes, field hands, etc.; some are beggars. Their jobs are menial, seasonal, and intermittent; they go from one thing to another—hence the term *macaqueiro* (like a monkey). Their clothes are so torn and few in number that they are even ashamed to go to church. Partly for the same reason their children do not attend school. At the religious and secular *festas* the *macaqueiros* appear on the fringes, unable to bid at the auctions, dance at the dances, or walk in the processions.

In many respects this is an outcast group. It manages barely to meet the basic requirements of metabolism by abstaining from a series of social refinements deemed by the rest of society to be as necessary as food itself.

MIDDLE STRATA

The largest part of the community belongs to the two middle strata. While groups A^2 and B^1 pertain to two different social classes, no very great economic, educational, or occupational differences exist between them. Both groups are dominated by artisans, storekeepers, and minor civil service employees. Members of both groups characteristically own their own homes, have regular jobs, send their children to school, dress up for special occasions, and eat the same quantity and type of foods.

The two middle strata are thus easily distinguished from the extreme upper or elite group and the extreme lower or submarginal group on the basis of economic, educational, and occupational criteria. But these criteria are insufficient when it comes to distinguishing between the two middle groups themselves. The decisive factor here is likely to be race. This does not mean, of course, that the racial ranking gradient is not operative on the other levels. There happen to be so few wealthy

Negroes in Minas Velhas that the effect of racial rank need hardly be considered in analyzing the constituency of the elite. Similarly there are few whites who rank low enough on the other gradients to qualify for the sub-marginal group, so that here too the effect of racial rank is not a particularly live issue. But the two middle strata taken together are filled with individuals of every racial type in approximately the same proportions as these types occur in the total population. The darker individuals, however, belong to the lower middle stratum and, hence, are part of the lower class. The lighter individuals belong to the upper middle stratum and, hence, are part of the upper class.

If there were no racial ranking gradient, there would be only one middle stratum. The meaning of this fundamental social cleavage and the ways in which it makes itself felt in everyday behavior will be made clear further on. It will be more convenient for the moment, however, to continue our analysis of the actual economic, occupational, and educational differences as though there were, in fact, but a single middle stratum. This procedure will yield a simplified view of the community's standard of living and of the economic and social inequalities which are so integral a part of the urban complex.

DIFFERENCES IN RANK AND THE STANDARD OF LIVING

In this section various indices of the actual economic, occupational, and educational gradients are shown in tabular form. A sample of 100 households was used involving a total of 571 persons. Representativeness was gained by selecting the households on the basis of the occupation of the chief wage earner for each household. Occupations from every category shown in Table 2 (p. 47) were included in a ratio of approximately one to two and one-half.

The households classified as belonging to Groups A[1] and B[2] were identified first, on the basis of income, property, and type of occupation. A few upward and

TABLE 6. URBAN SAMPLE

GROUP	NUMBER OF HOUSEHOLDS	PERCENT	NUMBER OF INDIVIDUALS	PERCENT
A¹	10	10	65	11
A²–B¹	64	64	383	67
B²	26	26	123	22
Total	100	100	571	100

downward adjustments were then made on the basis of the field team's personal familiarity with the rank of the people involved. Naturally, there are some border-line cases where the classification is doubtful, especially when racial and educational rank deviate from the level of the other criteria. But in general neither race nor education are deviant enough or crucial enough to move an individual into or out of Group A¹ or B². As we have already indicated, the racial ranking gradient has a critical value in only a negligible number of borderline cases except when distinguishing between the two middle strata. The latter are here regarded for the time being as a single aggregate residue. In addition, the educational gradient plays an especially minor role in determining actual social strata because the full range of the gradient does not occur; i.e., no one in the sample has completed more than twelve years of school, and only 2 percent have gone beyond the primary level. A high degree of linkage between the major gradients comes out clearly in the tabular treatment and is itself perhaps the best proof of the validity of the way in which the sample was classified. The sample was divided as shown in Table 6.

TABLE 7. AVERAGE VALUE OF PROPERTY

GROUP	HOUSEHOLDS	TOTAL VALUE OF PROPERTY	AVERAGE VALUE
A¹	10	Cr $1,783,990	Cr $178,399.00
A²–B¹	64	775,325	11,973.80
B²	26	20,705	796.40
Total	100	Cr $2,580,020	

TABLE 8. RANGE AND DISTRIBUTION OF PROPERTY

CRUZEIROS	GROUP A[1]		GROUPS A[2]–B[1]		GROUP B[2]		TOTAL	
	No.	Percent	No.	Percent	No.	Percent	No.	Percent
0–100			4	6.2	13	50	17	17
100–200					1	3.8	1	1
200–500			2	3.1	5	19.2	7	7
500–1,000			2	3.1			2	2
1,000–2,000			2	3.1	2	7.7	4	4
2,000–5,000	1	10	13	20.3	4	15.4	18	18
5,000–10,000			11	17.2	1	3.8	12	12
10,000–20,000	1	10	12	18.7			13	13
20,000–30,000	1	10	13	20.3			14	14
30,000–40,000			3	4.7			3	3
40,000–50,000			1	1.6			1	1
50,000–100,000	3	30	1	1.6			4	4
100,000–200,000								
200,000–300,000	1	10					1	1
300,000–500,000	2	20					2	2
500,000–	1	10					1	1
Total	10	100	64	100	26	100	100	100

Property and cash income may be taken as the basic indices of the economic gradient. In Tables 7 and 8, land, buildings, animals, tools, machines, and inventories are figured as property.

Differences in the amount of property owned range from a literal zero to large landed fortunes—relatively speaking, from beggars to millionaires. It is true that

TABLE 9. MONTHLY CASH INCOME PER HEAD OF FAMILY

INCOME (IN CRUZEIROS)	GROUP A[1]		GROUPS A[2]–B[1]		GROUP B[2]		TOTAL	
	No.	Percent	No.	Percent	No.	Percent	No.	Percent
0–100					6	23.1	6	6
100–200			6	9.4	6	23.1	12	12
200–300			9	14.1	5	19.2	14	14
300–400			8	12.5	7	26.9	15	15
400–500			8	12.5	2	7.7	10	10
500–700			7	10.9			7	7
700–1,000			15	23.4			15	15
1,000–1,500	4	40	5	7.8			9	9
1,500–2,000	2	20	5	7.8			7	7
2,000–2,500	1	10	1	1.6			2	2
2,500–3,000	3	30					3	3
3,000–								
Total	10	100	64	100	26	100	100	100

TABLE 10. PERCENTAGE OF INCOME USED FOR FOOD

GROUP	INCOME	OUTLAY FOR FOOD	PERCENTAGE
A1	Cr $30,485	Cr $12,099	40
A2–B1	64,489	44,895	70
B2	11,203	9,805	88

the rich people of Minas Velhas are simply middle class when it comes to comparing them with the rich men of the nation, but in terms of the local economy their wealth is almost as considerable as that of a millionaire in Rio de Janeiro.

The range of cash income, as shown in Table 9, is not as great as that of property, though still considerable for such a small town.

A more revealing index perhaps is the percentage of the family's income which goes for the purchase of food. Table 10 shows the total cash income of all the wage earners in each group as compared with their total outlay for food.

These basic economic differences ramify into a large number of additional features producing equally pro-

TABLE 11. TYPES OF DWELLINGS

GROUP	NUMBER OF HOUSES	TYPE I[a]		TYPE II		TYPE III	
		No.	Percent	No.	Percent	No.	Percent
A1	10	10	100				
A2–B1	64	2	3.2	49	76.5	13	20.3
B2	26					26	100
Total	100	12		49		39	

[a] By a Type I house is meant a house with all or most of the following features: fifteen or more rooms in good condition, separate kitchen, wooden floors, seven or more glass windows, wooden or cloth ceilings, plastered and whitewashed or painted walls, friezes inside and out.

By a Type II house is meant a house with any of the criteria for a Type I house in poor condition and/or the following features in good condition: five or more rooms, separate kitchen, tile floors, four or more windows with wooden shutters, decorative bands.

By a Type III house is meant a house with any of the diagnostics for a Type II house in bad condition and/or the following characteristics: less than five rooms, no kitchen, earth floors, less than four windows, no decorative bands, no plaster on walls.

TABLE 12. HOUSING

	GROUP A[1]	GROUPS A[2]–B[1]	GROUP B[2]
Average rooms per house	13	8	4
Average beds per house .	8.1	4.0	1.8
Average beds per person	1.2	0.7	0.4
Kitchen	100%	80%	15%
Toilet	40%	3%	0%
Shower	60%	3%	0%

TABLE 13. DISTRIBUTION OF OCCUPATIONS

	GROUP A[1]		GROUPS A[2]–B[1]		GROUP B[2]	
	No.	Per-cent	No.	Per-cent	No.	Per-cent
I. Professional, Administrative, Executive, and Managerial						
Factory owner	1					
Tax collector	2					
Teacher	1					
Postal director	1					
Landlord farmer	3					
	8	80	0	0	0	0
II. Rank-and-file civil service						
Pensioned			2			
Telephone and Post Office			4			
Clerk			1			
Police			1			
	0	0	8	12.4	0	0
III. Commercial						
Storekeeper	2		3			
Peddler			3			
Others			4			
	2	20	10	15.6	0	0
IV. Artisan						
Brass-smith, Blacksmith ..			18		1	
Leatherworker			10			
Others			8		2	
	0	0	36	56.4	3	11.6
V. Menial						
Sharecropper			4		5	
Farmer			3		1	
Miner					2	
Municipal worker					4	
Prostitute					3	
Gravedigger					1	
Woodcutter					2	
Others			3		5	
	0	0	10	15.6	23	88.4

TABLE 14. YEARS OF SCHOOL

YEARS	GROUP A¹		GROUPS A²–B¹		GROUP B²	
	No.	Percent	No.	Percent	No.	Percent
0			57	28	47	77
1	1	3	16	7	2	3
2	4	10	33	16	1	2
3	4	10	25	12	2	3
4	6	17	23	11	4	7
5	14	38	33	16	3	5
6			9	4		
7	1	3	5	2		
8–12	7	19	6	4	2	3
Total	37	100	207	100	61	100

found contrasts between each level. House types, for example, show a high correlation with the main indices of the economic gradient.

More specific information about the differences in housing are summarized in Table 12 showing the number of rooms per house, the number of beds per house and per person, and the number of houses which have kitchens, toilets, and showers.

It is clear that no matter which index is used to express the economic gradient, Group A¹ and Group B² will occupy the high and low extremes respectively, and Groups A² and B¹ will occupy an intermediate position.

The occupational gradient has but one basic index. In Table 13 five grades of occupation are shown. Only the principal remunerative occupation of the principal wage earner of each household has been included.

The educational gradient may be shown in three ways:

TABLE 15. HIGHEST GRADE COMPLETED

GRADE	GROUP A¹		GROUPS A²–B¹		GROUP B²	
	No.	Percent	No.	Percent	No.	Percent
0	6	17	106	51	51	84
1			10	4		
2	1	3	20	10	5	8
3	2	5	23	12	3	5
4	9	24	30	15	2	3
5	11	30	10	4		
6			4	2		
7	1	3				
8–12	7	18	4	2		
Total	37	100	207	100	61	100

by the number of years of school attendance, by the number of grades completed, and by the incidence of literacy. Table 14 shows the number of years of school attendance for adults of eighteen years and over.

Sixty percent of the adults in Group A[1] have gone to school for five or more years, but only 26 percent of the adults in Groups A[2]–B[1] have gone to school for the same number of years, while 77 percent of those in Group B[2] have never gone to school at all. The same differential can be expressed in terms of the number of completed grades.

Fifty-one percent of the adults in Group A[1] and 8 percent of the adults in Groups A[2]–B[1] have finished primary school, while 84 percent of those in Group B[2] have never finished the first grade and none went further than the fourth grade.

Table 16 shows the percentage of persons who can read and write simple words and sentences.

TABLE 16. LITERACY

GROUP A[1]	GROUPS A[2]–B[1]	GROUP B[2]	TOTAL
92.97	78.87	25.87	69.17

There is no need to extend these lists further. The heterogeneity revealed by the basic indices of the town's standard of living ramifies into every facet of town life, reducing community cohesion, obscuring common goals and objectives, and preventing the formation of an effective *esprit de corps*.

Minas Velhas is a markedly heterogeneous community from still another point of view—that of race. In order to understand the division of the town's social strata into two classes, we must turn at this point to a discussion of the racial ranking gradient.

IDEAL RACIAL RANKING GRADIENT

The population of Minas Velhas consists mainly of two races—Negro and white—and the results of their intermixture. Occasional Amerindian characteristics may also be detected, but individuals of apparently pure American Indian descent do not exist. The two main stocks have combined to produce a continuous gradation in all the associated physical characteristics. In any rigid genetic classification few, if any, of the people of Minas Velhas would be either purely Negroid or Caucasoid; it is obvious that most of them are the result of Negro-Caucasoid mixtures. A highly refined classification is unneccesary since the socially derived "racial" classification, which alone has dynamic import, is related to physical characteristics in a markedly flexible and subjective fashion. A simple fourfold classification—namely, white or Caucasoid, Negro, mulatto, and *caboclo* (mixture of Caucasoid and Indian)—will serve to give us an adequate picture of the population. Based on the same sample of 571 individuals (100 households), the distribution of these types is as follows: white, 42.5 percent; Negro, 28.2 percent; mulatto, 26 percent; and *caboclo*, 3.3 percent. This distribution may be considered as more or less representative of the town, but the populations of two of the rural satellites differ strikingly from the town's in racial composition. In Serra do Ouro there are few Negroes, and in Baixa do Gamba there are few whites.

Throughout the area there are very few remnants of African culture patterns. The social behavior of the Negro and the mulatto is part and parcel of a regional culture in which all racial elements of the population participate. Not only are unmodified African traits rare, but also, when they do occur, they are not restricted to Negroes. The Negroes of Baixa do Gamba, like the whites of Serra do Ouro, have never even heard the terms *macumba* or *candomble*—the elaborate religious cults which are so deeply rooted in the Bahian *Reconcavo* and other areas of Brazil. They are all Catholics, sharing in common with other isolated rural communities of more typical racial composition the same underlying folk commentary on the official dogma and ritual, particularly with respect to *festas* and the magical interpretation of prayer. Elements of folk belief which are extraneous to the Catholic system, such as a belief in the enchanted state of gold, the emphasis on the curative powers of herbs, the large body of dietary taboos, and the various modes of witchcraft, are mainly of European origin and are shared by the people of Baixa do Gamba and Serra do Ouro. The crafts and agricultural techniques used in both villages are indistinguishable from the prevailing pattern of subsistence agriculture of the rest of the region. *Vatapá*, oil of *dende*, and other elements of African cuisine are not used. Perhaps the clearest example of African influence is the *samba*, which figures in religious festivals and at marriage celebrations as well as at almost any party. But the *samba* and other rhythmic forms are pan-Brazilian traits and persist independently of the presence or absence of Negroes. No evidence was found for any substantial difference in family structure between Baixa do Gamba and Serra do Ouro. Hence, in Minas Velhas as well as in the nearby satellite villages, there is no sub-culture which sets the Negroes off from the other members of the community.

Among the townspeople, the superiority of the white man over the Negro is generally considered to be a scientific fact. One of the school textbooks used in Minas Velhas declares:

Of all races the white race is the most intelligent, persevering, and the most enterprising . . . . The Negro race is much more retarded than the others.

The six urban teachers (who are all, incidentally, white females) agreed with this viewpoint. In their experience, they said, the intelligent Negro student was a great rarity. "It is a characteristic of the Negro race."

The townspeople tell a story which explains the origin of the Negro's inferiority in the following manner:

In the beginning of the world God created two kinds of man —the white and the Negro. One day He decided to find out what their respective attributes were, so He threw them into the bottom of a well and commanded them to get out as they might. The white and the Negro tried to climb up the walls, but without success. Finally the white, after thinking for a while, stood on top of the Negro's shoulders and pulled himself over the top. The Negro, left alone on the bottom, made no further effort nor cried out, and was left to die. It was on this day that God decided to make the Negro an inferior being and the slave of the white.

In most of his evaluation of the Negro as an *abstract type*, the white is inclined to deride and to slander. The mayor's son, addressing a group of friends, declared, "Everybody knows what kind of thing a Negro is. What I want to know is how did this curse ever come into the world in the first place when Adam and Eve were both white."

"They must be sons of the devil," someone else immediately replied.

Many informants maintained that "the Negro is more like a buzzard than a man."

All such statements, however, vary in the associated emotional tone. They are rarely said with hatred. The mood is generally lighthearted and tempered with earthy appreciation. There is no monotonous, heavy-handed undercurrent of bitterness or of revulsion. To the white and, to a certain extent, to the Negro himself, the Negro is primarily a curious, laughable anomaly. He is looked upon as a sport of nature, as a being with certain substandard and grotesque characteristics which make him rather amusing. A white man will say, "Negro desgracado. Que bicho feio!" (Miserable negro. What an ugly creature!), and smile broadly as though he were speaking of some rare, mirthful freak.

The predisposition to laugh at the Negro rather than to hate him and the prevailing mildness of the emotional tone accompanying the comparison between the white and black lead to occasional inconsistencies and seeming ambivalences. The Negro is sometimes presented as a rather likeable creature despite his faults, as in the following folk story:

Once a lawyer, a priest, and a Negro were traveling together. At the end of the day they made camp under a tree. They were very hungry, but all they had to eat was a single egg. The priest took the egg and blessed it. "Edite cuisinatorio," he said, and dropped the egg in a pot of water. The lawyer, not to be outdone, took the egg out of the water. "Edite decascatorio," he said, and stripped off the shell. The Negro grabbed the egg, and said, "Ti bebitorio," and ate it up.

The Negro in such tales plays the role of a somewhat lovable trickster. He is as much of a scoundrel as the two white men, but he is shown beating them at their own game.

This more kindly view of the Negro's simplicity should be viewed as a mere mood or nuance of the stereotype and in no way contradicts the underlying devaluatory theme. The stereotypes regarding the Negro in Minas Velhas are flexible enough to permit him occasionally to reap advantages from his faults. It would be a mistake, however, to view the faults put to best use as something other than faults, or to view mitigated derision as admiration. The same person may at one moment claim that the Negro is lazy and that "he sleeps during the day," and at another time admit that "the black race knows how to work harder than the white race." The last, however, is not really a point in the Negro's favor, since the capacity to do the type of work implied, namely, heavy physical labor, is scarcely something to be admired in Minas Velhas. The concept that the Negro is admirably suited for heavy physical exertion on the one hand, and that he is lazy on the other, seems to be a flat contradiction. But this contradiction does not signify any real ambivalence in the minds of the people of Minas Velhas. The *modus operandi* is disapproval of the Negro on both counts.

There are other contradictions in the many stereotypes which are expressed in Minas Velhas regarding the Negro. But, like the one mentioned above, these contradictions are eventually resolved by showing disapproval. One white informant, for example, who insisted that the white is better than the Negro in every conceivable way, quickly contradicted himself when it came to his opinion of intermarriage. "The mixture worsened the quality of the white," he said, "but in this respect the Negro was shrewder than the white. He caught the white women and married with them. He made himself better in the exchange. He whitened himself. The white was more stupid. She dirtied her family while cleaning his."

The people of Minas Velhas are familiar with two unusually well-organized statements containing stereotypes regarding the Negro. They are both in the form of rhymes with a verse for each letter of the alphabet. Some excerpts follow:

In former times there wasn't so much disorder when there was an emperor and the *negros* [3] had masters.

Everything about a *negro* is no good including his house which hasn't even got a ceiling. The only things he has are his teeth which God gave him so that he could tear *rapadura* [4] apart.

They are very foul-smelling, but there's no incense in the world that can make them smell better. No matter how little time I spend with them, I can't stand it.

The *negro* isn't human. God has nothing to do with him, and the *negro* has nothing to do with the saints.

The *negro* has an ugly face. He spends the day sleeping and the night robbing farms. The tail of the snake doesn't rattle the night he's about.

A good girl would commit mortal sin if she went with a *negro*. No saint would excuse her if she yielded to a *negro* without being shot first.

The *negro* is always unsafe. What he doesn't steal he takes when no one's looking. To help a *negro* is a great mistake.

---

[3] *Preto* is the polite term for Negro. The word *negro* is almost as offensive as the American *nigger*.
[4] Crude brick sugar.

When they see your foot they want your hand. I'm not going to help this animal because this animal is a thief.

If all the *negros* were to die, I would be happy. The *negro* in Brazil is like a plague on the wind.

The *negro* is the mainstay of the *negro* is the sickle, the axe, and the hoe, and a whip in the small of his back.

The *negro* spends a lot of his time washing himself, but the more he washes, the dirtier he gets.

They say they are as good as us, but I don't agree. Unfortunately here in Brazil *negros* become doctors and lawyers.

If you've seen a buzzard, you've seen a *negro*.

The *negro* hasn't got a face—he has a tin can.
He hasn't got eyes—they're lighthouses.
He hasn't got a mouth—it's a cave.
He hasn't got a nose—it's a tunnel.
He hasn't got ears—they're holes.
He hasn't got feet—they're slabs.
He hasn't got lips—they're rubber tires.
His beard is the beard of a goat.
His whole face is satanic.

Some specific features of the Negro stereotype are subject to the apparent ambivalences and contradictions to which we have already alluded; others, however, emerge as fixed and immutable principles which form the core of the urban white's attitude. These may be stated as follows:

1. The Negro race is subhuman and inferior to the white race.
2. The Negro does and ought to play a subservient role to the white.
3. The Negro's physical features, including physique, physiognomy, skin color, and body odor, are irredeemably displeasing.

The people of Minas Velhas recognize a great many physical types resultant from race mixture. These types are determined almost exclusively by the diagnostics of hair form, hair texture, and hair color, and skin color and skin texture. Physiognomy (wide lips, flaring nostrils, prognathism, etc.) is a tertiary consideration.[5] The value of each diagnostic may be safely thought of as being high if it corresponds with the features of a white man, and low if it corresponds with the features of a Negro. Actually the correspondence is with something more general, namely the ideal of beauty, to which the white man generally approaches more closely than the others. This ideal demands fine, straight, or wavy hair and smooth light skin. The set of physical characteristics by which the individual is judged to be more or less beautiful, however, comes to mean to a large extent more or less white or more or less negroid, not only from a physical point of view, but in a total behavioral sense as well. This may be stated as the following hypothesis: *The extremes of the racial ranking gradient are occupied by whites and Negroes, and the intermediate positions are occupied by racially mixed types.*

Some progress has been made toward substantiating this point of view by means of data which can be handled statistically. The data are drawn from the results of a pictorial test devised by our field group for use in Brazil. As used in Minas Velhas, the test consisted of three pairs of portrait photographs—a male and female Negro, a male and female mulatto, and a male and female white. The portraits were shown to ninety-six informants who were controlled according to color, class, sex, and age. The procedure was to lay down a set of portraits and ask the informants to select the subjects who showed more, less, and least, respectively, of a given attribute. Six attributes were inquired about: wealth, beauty, in-

---

[5] Among the most frequently distinguished types are: *moreno, chulo, mulato, creulo,* and *cabo verde*. The *moreno* has wavy hair with the skin coloring of a heavily sunburnt white. The *mulato* has crisp, curly hair and is darker than the *moreno*. The *chulo* has crisp, rolled hair and his skin is the "color of burnt sugar or tobacco." The *creulo* has fine wavy hair, is almost as dark as the *chulo*, but has smoother skin. The *cabo verde* has very straight hair and is the color of the Negro.

telligence, religiousness, honesty, and ability to work. The response is shown in Table 17 for all sexes, classes, and colors, and for both female and male photographs.

The highest score for the mulatto consistently falls in the intermediate position. For the white it falls on the high extreme and for the Negro on the low extreme, with

TABLE 17. RELATIVE RACIAL ATTRIBUTES [a]

ATTRIBUTE	PORTRAIT		
	White	Mulatto	Negro
Most intelligent	77	62	53
Less intelligent	68	93	31
Least intelligent	47	37	108
Most beautiful	107	75	10
Less beautiful	64	98	30
Least beautiful	21	19	152
Most wealthy	113	46	33
Less wealthy	44	96	52
Least wealthy	35	50	107
Most religious	82	62	48
Less religious	64	74	54
Least religious	46	56	90
Most honest	80	70	42
Less honest	64	74	54
Least honest	46	56	90
Best worker	12	63	117
Worse worker	49	96	47
Worst worker	131	33	28

[a] The figures in italics in Tables 17 and 18 indicate where the highest score falls for each respective type in relation to most, less, and least of each attribute.

the exception of the attribute "ability to work," where the situation is reversed. All six indices may be summarized by Table 18, which shows the totals of all six attributes combined as a progression in a three-valued ranking system. Because of the low esteem generally accorded manual labor, the highest score of "ability to work" has been taken as the lowest ranking value.

The nature of the racial ranking gradient is clearly shown by these tables.   It seems highly probable that an extension of the test to include a larger list of evaluatory diagnostics would not substantially alter the results.

The results of this test document another important aspect of the racial ranking system. The position assigned to each racial group in the scale of social value is similar, no matter which racial segment is consulted. Table 19 shows a breakdown of the three-valued ranking system as determined by each racial group in the sample.

There is a slight tendency for each racial group to rate itself higher than the others, but the difference is not great enough to alter the main outlines of the gradient.

The fact that the gradient was obtained from a sample consisting of all races, classes, and both sexes ought not

TABLE 18. RELATIVE RACIAL RANK

RANKING ORDER	WHITE	MULATTO	NEGRO
1st	590	348	214
2d	346	537	269
3d	216	267	669

to be interpreted as evidence that there is no disagreement about the racial stereotypes and that the Negro passively concurs with all the defamatory opinions of the white.   The failure of the Negroes' dissenting opinion to make itself evident in the test situation does not mean that the Negro feels he is irremissibly inferior to the whites, or that Negroes may not attain high social status. The results need to be explained in two ways.   First, the Negro concurs with the white in believing that he can achieve high rank not because he is a Negro but only in spite of it.   All racial segments see race as one of the diagnostics by which an individual's value can be measured.   Consistently, the Negro tends to minimize and narrow down the negative implications of being a Negro, and the white tends to exaggerate and broaden them. The white tends to strip the Negro of worth and dignity because he is a Negro, and the Negro tries to cling to his dignity and attain worthiness despite it. *But everybody believes it is better to be white.*

The second consideration is related to the complex phenomenon of subjective and objective racial identification as it pertains to the test situation. For the purpose of the racial apperception test, informants were assigned to the three catch-all racial categories we have been using on the basis of their approximate similarity to the standard anthropological exposition of racial

TABLE 19. RELATIVE RANK AS SEEN BY EACH RACIAL GROUP

RANKING ORDER AS SEEN BY WHITE INFORMANTS

	White	*Mulatto*	*Negro*
1st	209	104	71
2d	115	164	105
3d	60	116	208

RANKING ORDER AS SEEN BY MULATTO INFORMANTS

	White	*Mulatto*	*Negro*
1st	196	122	66
2d	108	194	82
3d	80	68	236

RANKING ORDER AS SEEN BY NEGRO INFORMANTS

	White	*Mulatto*	*Negro*
1st	186	122	76
2d	122	179	83
3d	76	83	225

types. This procedure is faulty by virtue of failing to take into account the frequent social and psychological transmutation which objective racial characteristics are likely to undergo. It is difficult to determine what portion of the thirty-two individuals classified by the observer as physically similar to the photographs of the Negro actually considered themselves to be similar to the extent of being able to make a psychological identification. Many of those classified as Negro laughed heartily when they examined the Negroes' portraits: "Is this a man or an animal?" one jested. "How disgraceful! Look at the size of his lips!" another exclaimed. Since the society recognizes a continuum of racial forms from most white to most Negro with a large array of intermediate types, the tendency is to flee from the crushing stigmata of the lowest type by taking advantage of slight physical deviation or by emphasizing social rank achieved on the basis of nonracial criteria.

The large number of intermediate types serves as a convenient mechanism for denying identification with the lowest. The Negro in Minas Velhas attempts to "pass" not by posing as white but by posing as anything but a Negro—as a dark *moreno*, or *chulo*, or *caboclo*, etc. And if these categories do not suffice he is liable to invent new ones. For example, a Negro storekeeper named Antonio who is well educated by the local standards, fairly prosperous, and active politically, never refers to himself as a *preto*, although physically he has every reason to do so. He prefers rather the euphemistic term *roxinho* (a little purple) and alludes to his son as "that slightly purple fellow over there." Each individual twists as well as he can away from the complete identification with the lowest echelon of the social order. The Negro has the opportunity of saying first, "My hair is not that kinky," or "My lips are not that big," or, "My color is not that black"; and second, "I may look like that picture, but I am not as poor, or as illiterate, as he probably is. Therefore, I am not like him."

Another important issue illustrated by the racial value gradient is that all positions are occupied to some extent by all racial types. The Negro scores at both extremes as does the white and the mulatto. While there is definite vertical arrangement, there is no absolute horizontal discontinuity. Unlike what occurs in other parts of the world (for example, the United States or the Union of South Africa), the Negro in Minas Velhas can be measured by the same yardstick as that which applies to the white. The Negro can be compared to the white even though on the average he may consistently emerge as inferior. The comparison proceeds not on an either-or basis—either white or negro, and if negro, noncomparable—but on a more-or-less basis—more or less like a Negro and more or less like a white.

This aspect of the gradient appears to contrast with the face value of the Negro stereotypes. In its extreme form such as displayed in the verses previously referred to, the defamatory intentions of the white would seem to preclude the possibility of comparison by stating that the Negro is a creature apart, like a buzzard or a chimpanzee, having nothing to do with God. But the fact that the Negro scores in the high extreme of the gradient does not alter the white's fundamental conception of the Negro as an inferior race. Actually there was not a single white informant who rated the portrait of the Negro higher than that of the white when it came to summing up the score for all the attributes combined, i.e., while the individual white occasionally rated the Negro higher than the white for a particular attribute, no individual white rated the Negro highest for the majority of them.

The ideal racial ranking gradient reflects both the wish or daydream of the white to be everywhere superior by showing himself to be consistently better in total than the Negro, and it also reflects the real situation wherein the white recognizes that the Negro is occasionally richer or more honest or more intelligent or more religious, etc., than he is.

ACTUAL INTERRACIAL BEHAVIOR

The actual behavior of the white toward the Negro differs from the white's ideal of what it ought to be.

A certain white man in Minas Velhas, named Carlos Silva, who in his youth had been a skilled metal artisan, has been going blind for the last twenty years. Ten years ago his eyesight became so bad that he had to abandon his profession. He now barely manages to keep alive by organizing *rifas*—lotteries in which a can of kerosene or a bolt of cloth is the prize. Carlos begs the storekeepers to sell him the kerosene at wholesale price, then he goes from house to house asking people to buy a chance. In his entire demeanor—clothes, walk, and talk—

Carlos displays to his superiors the abject deference of a beggar. Yet he was responsible for the following statement: "A *preto* may be a doctor (that is, any professional) and have *posicao* (status), but he always remains a *negro*. If you have a dispute with him over something you can always say 'You're a *negro*,' and he won't have anything to answer back with"; then he capped these sentiments by reciting a widely known quatrain:

> *Negro* even when a doctor
> Ought to be addressed as *tu*
> Because the worst race in the world
> Is the *negro*, the toad, and the buzzard.

But how does Carlos behave when he actually meets with a Negro who has *posicao*? When talking to Sr. Waldemar, the Negro councilman, far from using the deprecatory *tu* reserved for addressing inferiors, Carlos invariably used *o senhor*, one step higher than the normal *vôce*. A week after he had made the statement quoted above, Carlos was heard in Antonio's ("slightly purple") store using *o senhor* and trying desperately to talk Antonio into selling him a can of kerosene at the wholesale price. Neither of these Negroes remotely resembles a *doutor*, and there are none such in Minas Velhas at present. One day a full-fledged Negro *doutor* came to town. He was a state engineer sent to survey the possibilities for a hydroelectric installation at the request of the county. Everyone in town tried to sell him something, including Carlos who tried to sell him a *rifa*. Carlos told his tragic history and ended by asking "O Doutor, Vossa Excelencia," to please help him out.

Similar examples of contradictions between ideal and actual behavior could be cited in great numbers. The Negro is supposed to have a smell which nobody can stand for an instant, yet there was never an occasion in Minas Velhas when a white man left a room because there was a Negro in it. The Negro is supposed to be "offered a foot" and the white man is indignant "when he wants his hand," but no white man ever refused his hand to anybody because and only because he was a Negro. The stereotype speaks of the subhuman standards of the Negro as a father and husband and of the atrocious condition of his home. White girls are warned that self-respect and a Negro husband are incompatible but the population itself is one grand demonstration that this warning has never been completely heeded.

The principal reason for the difference between ideal and actual behavior is that the terms "Negro" and "white" denote clear-cut, readily identifiable physical groups for nobody but the physical anthropologist. It is true that in the ideal stereotype there is a group whose members are defined by physical criteria. In the actual dynamics of everyday life no group so constituted can be discerned. In every real situation the fact that an individual manifests a particular set of physical characteristics does not by itself determine a single status-role. There is no status-role for the Negro as a Negro, nor for the white as a white, except in the ideal culture. Race is but one of several criteria which determine an individual's rank and is thus but one of several criteria which will determine how the mass of other individuals will actually behave toward him. In other words, wealth, occupation, and education, the other three major ranking principles, have to a certain extent the power of defining race. It is due to this fact that there are no socially important groups in Minas Velhas which are determined by purely physical characteristics.

It is to be expected that when there are a number of diagnostics by which the social value of an individual in a rank-conscious society is determined, not all of the diagnostics need be applied with equal conclusiveness to each individual. In any society, an individual is most often thought to be higher or lower, better or worse, of more or less value, according to the extent to which he manifests a complex series of criteria. Most complex systems of rank are reciprocal in the sense that a high rating on one diagnostic index tends to obscure or raise the low rating on another. If most of the indices show high-ranking status, those which do not are benefited by an infectious upward shift. If the majority are low, the few which are high suffer the opposite effect.

The failure to state this fundamental principle of rank easily leads to a distorted picture of the race situation in Brazil. An important characteristic of race relations in Minas Velhas, as well as in most of Brazil, is the occasional ability of individuals of low-ranking physical types to rise to otherwise high-ranking statuses. Sr. Waldemar, the Negro councilman, for example, owns considerable land, a leather shop, and the town's only bar, and is sufficiently wealthy so that he himself need no longer work. Waldemar is treated with universal respect by both whites and Negroes. When one of his sons recently married a white girl, the wedding was attended by the town's elite, and congratulatory visits were paid to Waldemar's house by representatives of some of the town's best families. There is no doubt that Waldemar ranks higher in the class system than most whites. From time to time other Negroes in the community have enjoyed comparable prestige. Their numbers are few, however, and even if they were multiplied several times over, the basic evaluation of a Negro as a Negro, and not as a rich Negro or an educated Negro, would still be the same. That is, on the scale of physical types the position of the Negro, as we have seen, is unquestionably the least desirable. *High rank in other respects can only be achieved in spite of, never because, one is black.*

Much has been made of the expression which is heard in Minas Velhas as well as in other parts of Brazil that "money whitens." The unstated corollaries—"whiteness is worth money" and "blackness cheapens"—also need to be emphasized. No matter how many handsome suitors an ugly millionairess may have, the low social value of ugliness remains a cultural datum. Similarly, the occasional Negro who rises to high social levels does not diminish the importance of race as a ranking principle. In Minas Velhas race helps to produce the town's most important social cleavage.

THE SOCIAL CLUB

On the best street, known popularly as Rua do Clube (Club Street), the largest and best cared-for building is that of the Clube Social—the traditional recreational center of the city. The Clube has a charter granted by the state of Bahia which declares its *raison d'être* as "benevolent, educational, and recreational." In practice, the Clube's charitable efforts are confined largely to an elaborate paper-work scheme of distributing nonexistent funds; its educational efforts reside in a dust-shrouded library of about five hundred books and pamphlets, most of them in foreign languages which no one can read; but the Clube's recreational function is well exercised. One room is dedicated to a billiard table which is used nightly by the youthful members. Checkers and backgammon are played in another room that contains a radio and a file of Salvador newspapers. In a back room a card game can usually be found in progress. The largest room is reserved for the frequent dances which the Clube sponsors, and which are considered the town's most important social events. The Clube's president, Lucrecio Bomfim, who is also the State Tax Collector, is quick to assure visitors that all one needs to do to become a member is to pay a few cents a month.

The dues are in fact insignificant, but only about one-third of the town's families actually belong. Many families, especially those of the lowest stratum, are effectively excluded by the rule that a coat and tie must be worn by all who enter the building. In addition, it is one of the fundamental axioms of life in Minas Velhas that the girls at the Clube's dances will not dance with everyone who happens to have paid his dues. During the score of dances which were observed at the Clube only one Negro was ever seen on the dance floor. He was the son of Waldemar, the councilman. His partner, moreover, was always one of his white sisters-in-law. The rest of the dancers were white or mulatto.

The Clube's festivals provide an excellent opportunity to see who's who. At every dance those who cannot enter the Clube, as well as those who can, make their appearance. The out-group gathers around in the streets and presses close against the open window of the ball-room, peering in at the proceedings with vaguely wistful eyes. The crowd outside stays there as long as the dance goes on. Sometimes they are as numerous as the dancers. The light which streams out of the ball-room shows most of them to be Negroes. But many mulattoes not much darker than those who are dancing and a handful of whites also appear. If you ask the people inside the Clube who the people standing outside are, you will get two interchangeable answers— *os pobres* (the poor) and *os pretos* (the Negroes). If you ask the people outside who the dancers are, you will get three interchangeable answers—*os brancos* (the whites), *os ricos* (the rich), and *gente da alta* (high-class people).

By and large the people who belong to the Clube are white. Those who are not have an excess of money or some other prestige factor in a ratio inversely proportional to their racial "deficiency." By and large the group at the window is Negro; those who are not Negroes have a deficiency in money or some other prestige factor inversely proportional to their racial "excellence." Neglecting occupational and educational criteria for the moment, it can be said that the "whites" consist of people with the following characteristics: (1) white and wealthy, (2) white and of average wealth, (3) white and poor, (4) mulatto and wealthy, (5) mulatto and of average wealth, (6) Negro and wealthy.

The "Negroes" consist of people with these characteristics: (1) white and poverty stricken, (2) mulatto and poverty-stricken, (3) mulatto and poor, (4) Negro and poverty-stricken, (5) Negro and poor, (6) Negro and of average wealth. Approximately 90 percent of the town's Negroes, 50 percent of the mulattoes, and 10 percent of the whites cannot dance at the Clube. Schematically, the class structure of Minas Velhas may be represented by the figure on page 97. The oblique cleavage in the diagram between A^2 and B^1 is meant to illustrate the fact that some of the individuals in B^1 rank higher on the economic, occupational, and educational gradients than some of the individuals in A^2.

THE SOCIETY OF THE POOR

Carnival is the high point of the social calendar of Minas Velhas. The traditional center of fun-making is the Clube Social, where highly animated masquerade dances are held on three consecutive nights in an atmosphere saturated with intoxicating ether perfume. From time to time the celebrants organize *cordoes* (files) and march into the streets where they dance and show off their costumes. Though many whites from distant cities attend and take part in the Clube's *festa*, the *pretos-pobres* have been openly bitter about not being able to enjoy themselves as well as the *brancos-ricos* in this supposedly universal holiday. A small group of political adventurers, *brancos-ricos*, but opposed to the ruling clique, have taken advantage of this sentiment and have attempted to create a new political force by championing a separate carnival for the *pretos-pobres*. The proposal of these power seekers, many of them members of the Clube Social, was enthusiastically supported by a large number of *pretos-pobres*. Few of the latter were aware of the ambitions of their self-appointed standard-bearers, but even if they had been, the events which followed would have taken place anyway. As one of the organizers said, "They have been thinking about this for twenty years, but they [the *pretos-pobres*] were too stupid to do anything about it themselves." As the scheme gathered momentum, its scope became more ambitious. It was decided that a mere carnival for the *pretos-pobres* was insufficient, and that there should be more than one opportunity per year for the non-Clube members to dance, play games, and enjoy themselves.

In the spring of 1948 a mass meeting was held in which plans were made for the organization of a new club that would be a rival to the Clube Social. The new club proclaimed itself to be dedicated to "charitable, recreational, and alphabetizing" ends. It was officially named Sociedade dos Pobres (Society of the Poor), though it promptly became more popularly known as the Sociedade dos Pretos (Society of the Negroes). Plans were made for the approaching carnival and for the construction of a club building. Some vacant ground next door to the Clube Social was suggested as a fitting site for the new edifice. The land and some material were actually purchased, but after the first carnival the activities of the Sociedade as well as work on the building languished due to organizational inexperience and the mounting resistance of the *brancos-ricos*. Three consecutive *preto-pobre* carnivals have been held to date, however, and as far as the class structure is concerned, it is unimportant whether the new club ever gets built or not. Some excerpts from the minutes of the Sociedade's first meeting may help to show the profundity of the social schism to which the new club owes its origin:

> The floor was given to the *orador* [official speechmaker], and he said more or less the following:

My friends and countrymen! "Society of the Poor"—What a beautiful title! What an attractive name! "He that is humble," says the evangelist, "shall be exalted." This association is really organized by the poor for the poor. But it is necessary to fully understand that the poor in total with their honest and fertile labor constitute a richness and a strength which the rich egotist never will be able to destroy . . . . What a sublime idea inspired the founders of the Association of the Poor! Let us analyze it. "Alphabetizing," that which alphabetizes. This association is created in order to teach the A-B-C's to its members—at least so they can sign their names. "Recreational"—this association was established in order to provide its members with leisure hours when the cares of life shall be set aside by games, dances, and sambas which are so well loved by all. "Charitable"—this association will create a fund . . . in order to render aid to those of its members and others who are in need . . . . The public powers, after learning about our aims, will certainly have to give us their support . . . .

> And so, amid the enthusiastic acclamations of those who no longer are saddened by their humble places, for they now understand that the right to have a club is not the exclusive privilege of the rich, was founded the Association of the Poor.

The *preto-pobre* carnivals are more than merely a mechanism for permitting the underprivileged to enjoy themselves. The preparations for carnival are extensive and begin as much as two months before the holiday. Each year a new crop of songs must be learned and many practice sessions are held in order to make sure that everybody who will take part in the *cordao* will know the words. The *preto-pobre* practice sessions are performed with an undercurrent of more than casual determination. There is considerable talk of "beating" the *brancos-ricos*, i.e., of having the more brilliantly animated celebration. During the actual celebration the *preto-pobre* group leaves the scene of its dance, which is a large house rented for the occasion, and parades past the Clube Social. The members of the *cordao* show off their costumes, sing, leap about, and make as much noise and bustle as they can manage.

Such institutionalized expressions of the rift between the two classes were not absent before the advent of the *preto-pobre* carnival. Two other competitive institutions go back to the beginning of the century. The first has to do with the once religious, but now mainly secular, Festival of the Kings (*Festa dos Reis*). This holiday originally featured a representation of the journey of the Magi to the manger at Bethlehem. Now it is marked by a slow torchlight procession of young girls through the streets. The girls are dressed alike; they dance along slowly in two files singing to the accompaniment of castanets and a few musical instruments. They eventually make their way to a predetermined house where the rest of the evening is given over to the usual ballroom dancing. Each year the procession has a different theme which is expressed by the costumes and the songs. In Minas Velhas there are two such festivals, one for the *pretos-pobres* and one for the *brancos-ricos*. Some years the two different *festas* are held simultaneously; the rest of the time, depending on who takes the initiative, only one group or the other may perform the celebration. Strong emphasis is placed on perfecting the costumes and the procession so that the *Reis das Pretas* may be "better" than the *Reis das Brancas.*

Another focus of rivalry is the town band. From about 1910 to 1940, there were two *filarmonicas* in Minas Velhas, each with more than twenty musicians. One was associated with the Clube Social, and the other with the now defunct religious Brotherhood of Rosario (Irmandade do Rosario), which was also known as the "Brotherhood of the Negroes." When the Church of Rosario fell into ruin and had to be demolished, the Brotherhood disbanded, leaving the musicians on their own. For a while the Clube's band was dominant; then in 1922 the *preto-pobre* musicians reorganized and began the "Artisan's Lyre." A period of intense competition ensued, with each organization trying to outdo the other in the splendor of their uniforms and instruments. At festivals they marched up and down the streets playing different songs and trying to drown each other out. The Clube even went so far as to hire a professional musician to gain replacements; when the music master died, however, the Clube's band slowly deteriorated, and for the moment the "Lyre" reigns supreme.

The Brotherhood of Rosario itself was an interesting example of the class schism. It existed contemporaneously with a "white" brotherhood. Like the Sociedade dos Pobres, most of its leaders were white, but the rank and file were Negroes. A feud developed between the priest and the local political strong man over the administration of the Brotherhood. The squabble had political overtones mixed with racial and class differences in much the same manner as was later true of the Sociedade dos Pobres. While the bickering went on the church began to leak and finally the walls collapsed, ending the argument.

Another example is the *festa* of Sao Sebastiao. For seventy-five years the organization of this holiday has been confined to members of a single Negro family, for whom Sao Sebastiao is the chief saint in the household pantheon. It has become known as a *festa dos pretos*, though *brancos-ricos* attend the special mass and bid in the auction which is an important feature of all such religious celebrations. The presence of a large number of whites at last year's auction elicited the following comment from one of the Negro organizers: "They [the *brancos-ricos*] don't let us go to their *festas*, and when we have ours they butt in so much that they seem to be the owners."

It must be emphasized, however, that such examples of formal institutions which are duplicated because of the class differential are not very numerous. This does not detract from the enormous differences in the behavior of the various social strata. There are great differences between the classes in Minas Velhas, but inter-class tension is mostly restricted to the area close to the narrow margin between the *brancos* and *pretos*. To imagine that the competitive situation we have been describing is an instance of an economically based general "class struggle" would be a severe distortion of the facts. The fundamental justice and correctness of the principle of rank and of the major ranking gradient are believed in by all members of the community. Nothing in Minas Velhas is more stable and more tenacious a part of the urban ethos than the belief that some people are better than others, and that the best deserve and get the best. The number of institutions which seem to express interclass tension are limited precisely because the bone of contention is not the principle of rank itself but how that principle is to be interpreted on a particular level of the hierarchy, namely, between Groups A^2 and B^1. Here the economic differential is insignificant; indeed, from a purely economic point of view, Groups A^2–B^1 would be but a single class. The tension arises exactly because of this essential lack of difference between the two groups. Those in B^1 seek not to destroy or level the class above them; they seek to enter it. They are mostly prevented from doing this not because of an economic but because of a racial factor. What is at stake, in other words, is the relative importance of the racial ranking gradient.

SOCIAL TENSION

The white-rich, Negro-poor cleavage in Minas Velhas is associated with a degree of social tension unusual in Brazil. A possible explanation of the open competition between the upper and lower class lies in the lack of agreement between the ideal racial ranking gradient and the actual economic-occupational strata.

According to the ideal culture, the majority of whites ought to rank higher than the majority of Negroes. There is no widespread sentiment against some Negroes occupying status positions equal or higher than some whites (i.e., "whitening themselves"), but there is evidently a critical value for the number of such cases which can be tolerated. There is in other words implicit in the special configuration of the ideal racial ranking gradient a "quota" on the proportion of Negroes whom the whites are willing to rank equal to or higher than themselves. One result of the town's rather atypical emphasis on home industry and its large artisan class seems to be the violation of this quota.

From the point of view of race and class relations, the development of home crafts has meant that an unusually heavy concentration of dark-skinned people are to be found in the same economic-occupational strata as the whites. Table 20 shows the actual percentage of each

TABLE 20. ACTUAL DISTRIBUTION OF RACIAL TYPES
PER ECONOMIC GROUP

RACE	GROUP A[1]		GROUPS A[2]–B[1]		GROUP B[2]	
	No.	Percent	No.	Percent	No.	Percent
White	60	25.1	165	68.7	15	6.2
Mulatto	5	3.6	97	70.9	35	25.3
Negro	0	0	107	67.3	52	32.7

racial type in the three economically determined strata
of Minas Velhas. Note that approximately 70 percent
of each racial type is to be found in the middle group.

It is interesting to compare this figure with the results
of the racial apperception test on the question of relative
wealth. Using the three values, most, least, and less
wealthy, as roughly equivalent to the three actual strata,
some idea may be gained of the discrepancy between the
wished-for hierarchy and the actual one. While the
reader is urged not to take these numerical values too
literally, there is little doubt that the distribution curves
of the racial types in the actual strata are askew in relation to the ideal distribution.

Actually the whites, on the average, still enjoy by far
a higher standard of living than the Negroes, but more
Negroes than is perhaps normal for Brazil can match
them in this standard. The normal synchronism between the racial value gradient and the economic value
gradient is threatened to a considerable extent; the white
finds a large number of Negroes economically displaced,
higher than they should be, and he acts to restore the
balance which is called for by the ideal stereotypes.
While there is still no absolute prohibition against

TABLE 21. IDEAL DISTRIBUTION OF RACIAL TYPES
PER ECONOMIC GROUP

RACE	MOST WEALTHY OF EACH RACE (Percent)	LESS WEALTHY OF EACH RACE (Percent)	LEAST WEALTHY OF EACH RACE (Percent)
White	59	23	18
Mulatto	24	50	26
Negro	17	27	56

Negroes occupying positions equal to or higher than the whites, there is apparently a definite limit to the number whom the whites can safely permit to do so. This number is determined by the difficult-to-measure but certainly finite extent to which the gap between ideal and actual behavior may be stretched. The more Negroes that the white has to accept in the "white-rich" class, the more difficult it becomes for him to profess the low rank of the Negro as an ideal together with the principle that "money whitens." Hence, the more Negroes that money actually does "whiten," the more money is required for that whitening to take place. As the gap between the whites' wished-for social hierarchy and the real social hierarchy tends to increase, so too does the relative importance of race as a diagnostic of class tend to increase. An increasing number of Negroes find themselves denied participation on their level of the hierarchy simply because they are Negroes. The bitterness and ill-will generated by this exclusion are expressed by duplicative and competitive institutions such as the two clubs, the two bands, the two brotherhoods, and the two *Festas dos Reis*. Though the duplication is thus far restricted to a relatively minor list of institutions, there is a definite trend in that direction.

It is the Negro of "average wealth"—the literate, skilled, and self-supporting individual—who most resents the genuine racial barrier which excludes him from the white's domain. These persons are part of the large group of artisans who in their small-scale home workshops are all limited by an almost primitive machineless technology to the same meager level of production. Their tools are the same, their skills equal, they make the same products; yet some of them can dance in the Clube Social and others cannot. Sebastiana, for example, is a Negress and a highly skilled ironworker. She owns her own home forge and turns out stirrup frames which are in constant demand. Sebastiana has a reputation for being one of the more outspoken critics of the *brancos-ricos*, and often takes the initiative in organizing the *Reis dos Pretos*.

"People talk that I want to be better than the whites," she says. "But it isn't that. I am the mistress of my life. I know just what I do. I have my work just like they have, my craft just like they have, so why are they better than I am?"

Sebastiana's attitude contrasts strongly with the attitude of Negroes in Group B[2]. The latter are placed in few situations where race has crucial ranking value. Thus Jose, a poor Negro sharecropper, can find his way free to say: "The white people of Minas Velhas treat us nicely. They don't call us buzzards or *negros*. Dona Autelia (wife of the town's wealthiest landowner) gave my wife a dress once. She's a great lady."

There are many instances, however, where the negative effect of being Negro is felt outside of the middle group. Sr. Waldemar, the Negro councilman, for example, maintains but a dubious hold on the highest stratum, despite the excellence of his economic and occupational qualifications.

Waldemar's best friends are not members of the "elite." He maintains close relations with some persons in Group A[1], but the relationship is formal and Waldemar tends to belittle himself. At elite parties and dances he keeps in the background. When invited to be seated to have coffee and cake with the rest of the guests, he invariably declines and takes his refreshments standing. No one ever insists too much. The solicitude which is shown him as a councilman in such circumstances depends entirely on the certainty that he will not accept too much of it, that he knows his place in other words. He is invited to most formal functions of the elite, but he never visits their houses informally and they never visit his. When his son was married, Waldemar gave a dance. A handful of the elite came to congratulate him. They sat around stiffly for a few moments and then one by one took their leave before the party had really gotten under way. Though well liked and treated with respect, Waldemar just fails to make the highest grade. Because of his color he is not treated as an equal by the rest of the people in his economic bracket. This fact can be phrased differently: he is not treated as an equal because he is not rich enough or educated enough to overcome being a Negro. If he were the richest man in town (which he is not by far), or if he held a university degree, there is no doubt that he would be taken more seriously.

Waldemar is firmly established as a member of the white-rich class, but his position with regard to the elite is insecure enough to make him sensitive to situations in which the racial factor assumes critical importance. A situation of this sort arose in connection with the building of a school for one of the rural satellites. Since 1940, the county of Minas Velhas, with state and federal aid, has undertaken a program of expanding school facilities in the remote rural areas. Schools were created in almost all of the village satellites with the exception of Baixa do Gamba—the predominantly Negro group.

Whereas, before the beginning of the expansion, the villages considered schools to be a luxury which they could not afford and to which they had no right, it afterward became apparent that they were entitled to them. The people of Baixa do Gamba began to clamor for what had become the normal due of even poor farmers, and which apparently they were being denied simply because they were Negroes. Sr. Waldemar undertook to champion their cause. Some excerpts from a speech of his to the Municipal Council will help to illustrate the issues which were involved:

Mr. President, I asked for the floor in order to bring to the attention of this House the visit I made to the new Municipal School of Baixa do Gamba . . . . I still don't know . . . why this House did not receive with good favor my project to establish a school in Baixa do Gamba . . . even though after much debate and discussion it was approved . . . . But even after that crisis was passed and the project was approved, there appeared another and still greater one. The functioning of the school remained forgotten. This perhaps because a teacher wasn't found right away . . . but I believe that only one cause existed, namely: that the village of Baixa do Gamba is inhabited by Negroes. But as Negroes they also have the right to learn to read and write, since, Mr. President, the Negro is also one of God's children . . . .

[Now that the school has finally begun to function] we can see that the Negroes of Baixa do Gamba really do have the desire to read and write. The school will enable them later on to bring products more important than firewood and straw to our market, since the principal gate to progress for a people is education. From the [large] attendance at the school we see that the Negroes of Baixa do Gamba have a desire for good things despite the financial situation with which they are afflicted.

The tendency of the white to resist high Negro rank pertains to every level of society. Most of the time there is little opportunity for the effect of racial discrimination to become manifest, because the entire issue is obscured by the greater difference in behavior due to relative economic standing. Even in the lower class, however, as in the case of the school for Baixa do Gamba, a disturbing phantom sometimes swims into view.

TOWN AND VILLAGE SOCIAL CLEAVAGE

One additional aspect of the class structure and its relationship to the urban complex is the social cleavage between the town and the villages.

Each rural settlement, discounting absentee landlords who spend most of their time in the city, is a one-class community. The rural class has two strata, roughly on a par economically with Groups B^1 and B^2 of the city. In addition each village has at most one or two leaders who are treated as equals by the white-rich. Much of this equality, however, depends on the political climate and on whether or not the rural leaders are being curried for their vote-swinging influence in the rural zone.

The upper rural stratum consists of people who own and work their own farms, occasionally hire additional help, live in a four- or five-room house with a kitchen, and own a good suit, dress, and a pair of shoes which they wear when they come to town. Members of the lower stratum typically lack these features. Like Jose of Baixa do Gamba, they live on a day-to-day basis, eating the crops as soon as they are ready, and have little left to sell at the fair. If they own their own land, it is likely to be small and near exhaustion. Otherwise, they work as sharecroppers and field hands. They are characteristically clothed in rags, housed in leaky one-room shacks, and visibly undernourished.

In general the rank of the residents of the rural zone must be stepped down a grade in comparison with the townspeople. The rural B[1] group ranks between the urban B[1] and the *macaqueiros*, while the rural submarginal group ranks even lower than the urban B[2] group. This is because country people are regarded as inferior by almost every city dweller simply on the basis of their being country people. From the urban viewpoint, in other words, place of residence, whether in the town or country, is itself an additional principle of rank. The urbanite considers using a hoe to be a highly degrading way to make a living. A man who spends all of his time working in the fields is by definition a *tabareu* (a yokel). When the *tabareu* comes to town for the fair he is expected to wear ill-fitting clothing, use colloquial speech, and be proverbially slow and timid in his thought and behavior.

"These *gente da roca* (country people) are frightened by their own shadows," commented a lower-class bricklayer. "They've been dragged out of the bush (*pegado a dente de cachorro*) and are afraid of human beings."

Lucrecio Bomfim, the State Tax Collector, likes to tell about a visit he once made to Serra do Ouro: "I was walking my horse downhill not far from the village when I met a young girl carrying a can full of water. She turned around, took one look at me, and started to run. She ran so fast that all the water spilled out of the can. I never laughed so much in my life."

One of the men in the Bubonic Plague Control Service

who regularly visits the rural zone to spread DDT and set rat traps claims that he has great difficulty getting into the houses. "Those yokels lock the door when they see me coming. They say their children are being eaten alive because I go around feeding the rats. Imagine!"

Nothing could be worse in the eyes of the city dweller than the isolation and lack of *movimento* characteristic of life on the farm. Antonio, the storekeeper, talks about country people in pitying tones: "Poor, miserable unfortunates, way out there in the bush! Their lives are very dull. None of them know how to read and they have no amusements. The only thing they can do is drink *cachaca*, and that ruins them even more. For lack of any other *distracao* (amusement) they get married when they're eighteen and never get ahead in the world."

The townspeople's estimate of rural ways is based partly on stereotype and legend and partly on some very real and visible differences in behavior. Mistrust of strangers in Serra de Ouro, especially among women, can scarcely be exaggerated. The arrival of a total stranger is such a rare occurrence that women and children flee into the houses and close the doors and shutters.

As part of what seems to be an ancient custom, perhaps extending back to the period of Moorish influence in Portugal, all the women of Serra do Ouro wear a shawl over their heads and around their shoulders. In going to and from the fields, if a woman happens to pass a man who is not a member of her immediate family, be he a resident of the village or not, one of the loose ends of the shawl is brought up to the level of the eyes and held across the face until the man has passed. Since some of the shawls are quite long and reach down the back to below the waist, a townsman was able to report; "What a rude people! They take the shawl from their behinds and put it into their mouths."

The proverbial backwardness of the villagers may be correlated with a low literacy rate—only 39.3 percent of a rural sample over seven years of age, as opposed to

69.1 percent among the townspeople, could read and write simple sentences.[6]

The superiority which even the poorest townsman feels in relation to the villagers is manifested in many subtle but unmistakable ways. One of our best informants was a poor bricklayer by the name of Pericles, who made himself especially useful by accompanying the ethnologist to the various towns and villages in the vicinity of Minas Velhas. On excursions to Vila Nova, Pericles invariably dressed in a raggedy fashion, with a torn shirt, dirty trousers, no shoes, and badly in need of a shave. The manner in which he dressed for a journey to one of the villages, however, was altogether different. On the day before leaving for Baixa do Gamba, Pericles borrowed an old pair of boots and a can of shoe polish. The next morning he appeared freshly shaven, neatly combed, wearing his only suit, a borrowed tie, and an ill-fitting but highly polished pair of boots. "It's different in Vila Nova," Pericles explained. "There the people don't notice such things, but in Baixa do Gamba I can't look like those *tabareus*." Since Pericles was known in Vila Nova he felt that there was no sense in getting dressed up for a visit. In Vila Nova his status could not be improved by such a gesture, and it could not get much worse than it already was. On the other hand, as a townsman among villagers, there was a chance of losing face if he failed to dress in a superior manner. Dressing up in the town would be a pretension, but dressing up for the country was merely the fulfillment of a status position which might be weakened if he neglected to live up to it.

A similar phenomenon occurs at the annual festival of Baixa do Gamba's patron saint. Only three or four of the townspeople attend and these are all young men from the lower class. At the auction which is part of

[6] The complete rural sample consisted of 25 households in Serra do Ouro, 15 in Baixa do Gamba, and 10 from other villages and large farms making a total of 284 people.

most religious *festas*, the townsmen enter into the bidding with great enthusiasm and are inclined to swagger a little as they make off with the highest bids. The same young men at an auction in Minas Velhas, on the other hand, remain perfectly meek throughout and do not seek to compete in the bidding unless they are sure that no upper-class townsman has his eye on the same object.

The uninformed visitor to Minas Velhas can find no quicker way to alienate himself from the townspeople than to confuse life in the interior (*a vida do sertao*) with life in the country (*a vida do campo*). Native Brazilians from the coastal capitals are especially prone to this mistake. In the early stages of our field work, a young Brazilian member of the research team was invited to a dance at the Clube Social by a group of the "elite" girls. She accepted gladly and then to show her enthusiasm paraphrased a song then popular in Salvador with the exclamation: "Farmer's dance! How nice!" An embarrassed silence ensued. Finally one of the girls said angrily: "We don't have farmers' dances at the Clube Social. You have to go into the bush for that."

The majority of townspeople know almost as little about the people in the rural zone as the big city dwellers on the coast know about Minas Velhas. Hundreds of adults in Minas Velhas have never visited even the nearest rural settlements. The twelve miles between the city and Serra do Ouro might as well be a thousand as far as the townspeople are concerned. Mayor Silva has never made the trip. Sr. Waldemar, the councilman who fought on behalf of a school for the people of Baixa do Gamba, made his eloquent plea before the council without ever having visited that place. He made the pleasant hour and a half trip for the first time in his life when our field team rode out to take up residence there. Yet Waldemar, who spent his youth as a commercial traveler, knows Sao Paulo and Rio de Janeiro intimately as well as hundreds of small towns in ten different states. Of the officials of Minas Velhas, it may be said that they are more familiar with the streets of Salvador than with the trails leading out of their own town.   Except for a handful of gold miners, wood gatherers, occasional hunters, and those who own property in the rural zone, the average resident of Minas Velhas has only the vaguest notion of what lies off the main road and beyond the encircling hills.

For their part, the people of the villages are fully aware that they are looked down upon by the townspeople.   The villagers speak of the town as the *comercio*. This term refers to the fact that the town is the locus of business and particularly of cash transactions.   The fact that the townsman can and must pay cash for his basic food supply greatly impresses the rural farmer.   "The life of the *comercio* is only for people who have lots of money," says Jose of Baixa do Gamba.

The villagers wear their Sunday best when they go to fair.   It is a common sight to see people on the trails outside of Minas Velhas on a Sunday morning, walking along barefoot while holding a pair of shoes in their hands.   Only when they get to town do they put on their shoes.   The journey to town for the fair is regarded as a welcome relief from the monotony of working in the fields.   When they have sold their products and made their purchases in the stores, the villagers visit the bar and have a few drinks while enjoying the crowd and the conversation.   But by the afternoon they become impatient and are finally glad to quit the town and start back home.   "The *comercio* is all right for a few hours," says Jose's wife.   "I like the *movimento*, but after a while I get tired of it and I can't wait to start back again."

In summary, then, one of the principal facets of Minas Velhas's urban complex is the attention devoted to various forms of hierarchical grading.   Far from manifesting the socioeconomic homogeneity which the size and isolation of the town might seem to call for, Minas Velhas contains striking differences in those very aspects of the culture—wealth, education, occupation, and race

—which the community itself considers to be most important. These differences are of a sufficiently intense nature to have produced social strata separated from one another by deliberate social barriers in the form of competitive and duplicative institutions. In addition to this internal heterogeneity and stratification, there is a value placed upon the fact of sheer inclusion or exclusion of residence. This facet of the urban complex, namely, the conscious preference of the town to the country, is a particularly interesting one. Among the inhabitants of genuine metropolises, thousands of times larger than Minas Velhàs, such a preference may be much weaker or even expressed on behalf of the country. It permits us to speak with greater accuracy of the existence of an urban ethos distinct from the various urban phenomena which may be the mere functional accompaniments of urban agglomeration rather than its goal or purpose.

THE HOUSEHOLDS of Minas Velhas may be divided into three types: households occupied by husband, wife, and children; composite families; and households occupied by a solitary individual. In the urban sample of 100 households, 55 percent were of the first type, i.e., they contained only primary relatives and only two generations or less of them—one or both parents and children, parents alone, or siblings alone. In the same sample, 40 percent of the households were of the second type, i.e., they contained either three or more generations of primary relatives plus secondary relatives and relatives by marriage or a *compadre* (ritual kinship) tie. In addition, 5 percent of the households were occupied by only one person.

FAMILY COHESION

It is obvious that in terms of residence, the nuclear two-generation family is the predominant familial form in Minas Velhas. This is even more evident when the kinds of relatives included in the second or composite type of family are further analyzed. Only eleven of the forty-five composite households contained any vestige of the three-generation family in the form of a grandparent-child-grandchild combination. The meaning of this fact is clear: the overwhelming tendency for children upon marriage is to move out of the parental domicile and to establish a separate household. The remaining 89 percent of the composite households (34 percent of the total sample) consist mainly of a single married couple and their children plus one or two unmarried relatives of either the husband or wife—maiden aunts, widowed uncles, and younger brothers and sisters.

In keeping with this emphasis upon the nuclear family, each household consists of a relatively small number of individuals. Individuals per household are shown in Table 22.

The average number of persons per household for the sample is 5.7.[1] The average (excluding domestics) for Group A[1] is 6.0; for Group A[2]–B[1], 5.9; for Group B[2], 5.1.

TABLE 22. NUMBER OF INDIVIDUALS PER HOUSEHOLD
IN MINAS VELHAS

NUMBER OF PERSONS	NUMBER OF HOUSEHOLDS
15	1
14	1
13	3
12	2
11	3
10	1
9	5
8	8
7	7
6	12
5	14
4	9
3	20
2	7
1	5

The significance of the relative smallness of the residential unit in terms of the general importance of family bonds in Minas Velhas is not easy to estimate. Since the change of residence upon marriage usually, though not always, occurs within the town itself and not outside of it, the possibility of strong, affective, and functional familial bonds such as those said to be characteristic of folk and rural communities is not immediately eliminated. In addition, almost any townsman can name up to one hundred kin living in Minas Velhas or the vicin-

[1] It is worth pointing out that this figure provides the basis for a check on the representativeness of the 100-household sample used throughout the study. Since there are 262 occupied households, and the census population is given as 1,427, the average number of persons per household in the town as a whole is 5.4, agreeing closely with the 5.7 derived from the sample.

ity. This has to be the case since most spouses, except for those of Group A[1], are drawn from nearby towns and villages and Minas Velhas itself. The crisscrossing of family lines within this small area makes relatives abundant and keeps them close at hand. Nonetheless, even the limited change of residence which takes place upon marriage may be said to preclude the formation of the strong, extended patriarchical kind of family which is often considered to be the prototype of the Brazilian kin group.[2] While it is true that the average townsman can name many second- and third-degree relatives who live within the town or nearby, the range of close, psychologically affective, and socioeconomically important relationships is considerably narrower than this number might suggest. The separation of Minas Velhas's nuclear families into independent households has the important effect of proliferating the number of basic economic work units. Parents and siblings as the basis of the household unit cooperate, divide the labor, pool incomes, and practice a common budget with a degree of coordination and a measure of intimacy that is only possible for people living under the same roof.

Beyond the household circle, close kin treat each other with special deference, visit each other, borrow and lend freely, and count on each other for mutual assistance in crisis situations, but they do not normally participate in the same economic routine, and as far as making a living goes, each one pursues his separate course. Beyond the circle of primary relatives—parents, siblings, grandparents, aunts and uncles, and first cousins—these special patterns of behavior based on kinship decrease in importance and are subsumed by the underlying urban patterns which govern the behavior of unrelated persons. Thus the relationships between secondary kin are only slightly less subject to the various schismatic components of the urban complex—class differences, political strife, individualization, and lack of cooperation—than those between non-relatives.

It is frankly impossible to speak of characteristic fam-

[2] Gilberto Freyre, *Casa-Grande e Sanzala.*

ily relations in Minas Velhas without a great deal of oversimplification and the neglect of a multitude of exceptions. Often the relationship between an uncle and one nephew and the relationship between the same uncle and another nephew are liable to show considerable variation. Obviously, personality differences here are of extreme importance. The Federal Tax Collector, for example, lives in the same house with seven nephews and nieces, and is largely responsible for their economic support, but the State Tax Collector hardly sees his brother's children from one year to the next. With the understanding that the "norm" in these matters is an extremely elusive entity, we may proceed to some examples which seem to indicate that intrafamilial bonds in Minas Velhas are not of the intensity characteristically associated with folk cultures.

Occasionally between brothers and sisters and frequently between cousins, class differences intervene and dominate all interpersonal relations. Pericles, the bricklayer, for example, belongs to Group B². At carnival time his children took part in the *Carnaval dos Pretos* and neither he nor his wife can dress well enough to be active socially in the Clube Social. Pericles's half brother, Chico Silva, on the other hand, is a prosperous merchant, the town's Justice of the Peace, and quite solidly a member of the *brancos-ricos*. Pericles's children and Chico Silva's children never play together. Their wives never visit. (Pericles's wife is a laundress, Chico Silva's wife has two servants.) The two men maintain an amicable but distant relationship. Pericles can count on a certain amount of credit at Chico Silva's store, but if he runs too heavily into debt, Chico Silva becomes firm and refuses to give him any more. As far as daily life goes, the two men live in different worlds, and Chico has never attempted to elevate his half brother's status by offering him a partnership in his business.

The social distance between Sr. Braulio, the owner of the leather factory, and the several cousins, nephews,

and brothers-in-law who work for him is of the same
order. Braulio frequently claims that the only reason
he stays in business is that most of his workers are relatives and that they are depending upon him for work.
This is true to the extent that Braulio did give preference to his relatives in hiring employees. But when it
came to choosing a manager for the factory, Braulio
passed up a brother and a brother-in-law and selected
one of the few persons in his employ who was no relation at all. Braulio is constantly confronted with the
pleas of his less fortunate relatives, such as those of his
sister Pamela, for medicines, food, and clothing, and he
rarely refuses though the effort he will make on behalf
of a cousin is markedly less than for a sibling. Despite
this, Pamela's husband, Paulo, has remained at odds
with Braulio ever since the latter failed to make him
manager of the factory.

One of the most important components of the urban
complex in Minas Velhas is the emphasis upon politics.
It is uncommon for brothers to be allied with different
political parties, and local political leadership sometimes
is maintained by a family regime. Beyond the primary
group, however, political differences are frequently
damaging to intrafamilial relations. This is true of the
Bomfims, one of the town's best families. Two branches
of the Bomfim family, related through a common grandparent, have, for over a decade, supported opposite sides
in local political matters. Feelings are so embittered
that first cousins meeting on the street fail to acknowl-
edge each other. Lucrecio Bomfim has not set foot in
his cousin's house for over five years.

RITUAL KINSHIP

Like most Latin American communities, Minas Velhas
has a system of ritually extended kinship, known as
compadresco. The relative strength of this institution
has frequently been used as an index of urbanization.[3]

[3] Robert Redfield, *The Folk Culture of Yucatan*, p. 338.

In Minas Velhas, the *compadre* system, while still an important part of the culture, shows signs of weakness and disorganization.

In Minas Velhas children who are about to be baptized require two sponsors, a godfather (*padrinho*) and a godmother (*madrinha*). By virtue of the baptism, godfather and godmother become *compadres* of the child's parents. Christening, which is performed by the bishop on his periodic pastoral journeys, requires a male sponsor for a male child and a female sponsor for a female child. He or she also becomes a *compadre* of the child's parents. For marriage, the bride and groom require another godfather and godmother, respectively, though the godparents of marriage are often the same as those of baptism. An additional source of *compadres* used to be the *festa* of Sao Joao. Two friends holding each other's hands jumped over the embers of one of the bonfires characteristic of this *festa*. They recited together the phrase: "St. John slept, St. Peter awoke, let's be *compadres* as St. John commanded." Repeating this three times, they embraced and said, "*Adeus compadre.*" The *compadre* relationship created by this ceremony was never regarded with the solemnity which is often characteristic of the others. It is generally agreed, however, that all of the *compadre* relationships have waned in importance and that people no longer take them as seriously as they once did. It is said that formerly to be a *compadre* meant that a friend or relative was to be treated with the generosity, courtesy, and loyalty ideally associated with the relationship between siblings. Today, it is not unusual to hear the term *compadre* used indiscriminately between ordinary friends and acquaintances, especially when a favor or some consideration is being asked for.

It is when the *compadre* relation is used to reinforce a relationship based on ordinary kinship ties like those of grandparent, cousin, or in-law that it is most effective. It is then most likely to have the effect of uniting the parties concerned with bonds equivalent to those between the members of the nuclear family. The god-fathers and godmothers who take the greatest interest in their godchildren are those who are already related by ordinary kinship ties. In the villages the *compadre* system seems to be predominantly of this nature. Most of the godparents are chosen from among the child's grandparents and uncles. In this manner the father and mother of the child often become *compadres* of their in-laws. The child not only receives a sponsor who can truly be counted on to treat him like a son, but his father and mother may also be brought into friendlier relations with the family they have married into. Hence in the rural zone the function of the *compadre* system cannot be regarded as that of extending the family, which already includes several score of relatives living nearby, but of strengthening and intensifying the bonds between these relatives.

In Minas Velhas, however, more than half of an individual's *compadres* are likely to be unrelated to his family. Only in the upper class are godparents chosen more from among kin than from among outsiders. This is true because in the middle and lower classes the attempt to find effective sponsors for children entails the crossing of class lines.[4] Certain influential figures in the upper class are singled out by scores of parents with the result that it is not unusual for one man to have over a hundred godchildren and several hundred *compadres*. The fact that such godfathers are separated from their *compadres* and godchildren by class barriers is sufficient to rob the relationship of the kind of intensity which characterizes it in a homogeneous rural community. When, in addition, the manifest inability of one man to attend to the needs of a hundred godchildren is also considered, it becomes clear why in the urban context the institution is comparatively superficial and prone to

[4] Sidney Mintz and Eric Wolf, "An Analysis of Ritual Co-Parenthood," *Southwestern Journal of Anthropology*, VI, No. 4 (1950), have called this form of extension "vertical" in contrast to the "horizontal" extension in homogeneous groups.

becoming a mere formality. Table 23 shows by socio-economic strata the number of godchildren by baptism per head of household in Minas Velhas.

TABLE 23. GODCHILDREN PER HEAD OF HOUSEHOLD

GROUP	HEADS OF HOUSEHOLDS	TOTAL GODCHILDREN	AVERAGE PER HEAD OF HOUSEHOLD
A¹	10	336	33.6
A²–B¹	64	332	5.2
B²	26	19	0.7

Many parents choose an upper-class godparent in the hope that he will pay for the baby's clothes or give a gift of money. This is occasionally done, but the gifts are of insignificant value and do not alone justify the choice. If an important gift is given, it is usually between persons of equal social rank who can be expected to reciprocate. Thus Sr. Alvaro, the mayor's brother, gave the head schoolteacher's daughter a thousand cruzeiros for her baptism. Pericles, a poverty-stricken bricklayer, is also one of his *compadres* by virtue of the fact that Alvaro baptized his first son. When Pericles heard about the large gift which the schoolteacher's daughter had received he commented, "Water flows to the sea (i.e., the rich get richer). He didn't give my son a cent."

A godchild who is one of several score attached to a man of superior social standing rarely has occasion to come into contact with him; the bond between them is flimsy and artificial. Nonetheless, it is felt that it is better to have a powerful though disinterested godfather than an interested but weak one. The bond is felt to be a form of ultimate insurance; in the event of extreme emergency, the godfather is unlikely to ignore completely his obligation to render assistance. He will not, however, take his godchild into his house, rear him for a while, help him find a job and get married, as a godparent who is also a kinsman or at least of the same social stratum is likely to do.

From another point of view the godfather with a hundred or more godchildren is but an additional instance of the search for a "boss"—the strong man who will paternalistically resolve the material difficulties of his wards.

LIFE CYCLE

In the life cycle of the individual both similarities and differences between townsmen and villagers are to be found. New ideas are more prevalent in the town, especially among the upper socioeconomic strata, but they have not replaced many old patterns which are largely common to both town and country.

In both town and country, for seven days after the birth, the newborn child is kept in a darkened room in order to avoid the "seven-day sickness" (*mal do sete dias*). This disease (a tetanus infection) is identified by the darkened facial color of the infant and is said often to end in death. The seventh day is considered especially dangerous and the infant's daily bath is omitted. In the country, but rarely in the town, on the fourteenth day after birth, the child is returned to the darkened room for twenty-four hours. It is believed by the villagers that if a child does not contract the *mal* during these first two weeks he may still get it during his fourteenth year. Most townspeople are ignorant of this possibility.

Breast feeding everywhere usually begins on the second day. Boiled water and an herb tea are used until the flow is well established. Sugar and water, and boiled corn water (*cangica*), are taken by the mother to stimulate lactation. The infant is generally fed at his demand though many town mothers try to discourage feeding during the night. Three upper-class townswomen are reported to have bottle-fed their babies. Weaning usually begins at from six to eight months; it is often terminated quickly when a new pregnancy occurs, but there is considerable variation. Some women continue for one or two months, gradually reducing the number of feeding periods and substituting cow's milk and soups made from potatoes, rice, and meat. In town, children who resist weaning are sometimes sent away to live with their grandmothers. In other difficult cases, the leaf of a plant called *Babosa* is used to make a bitter paste which is put on the nipples.

In both town and country, toilet training begins early and is rigorous. At about eight to ten months children are taught to use the chamber pot; a little later they learn that elimination must be performed in private and that direct verbal references to natural functions must be avoided. The latter prohibition is especially observed by the townspeople.

Sex is an important ranking principle both in Minas Velhas and the villages. Just as everyone considers it better to be white than black, everyone considers it ✓ better to be a man than a woman. From the beginning the male child gets more of his father's attention than his sisters. The first words of a father upon being informed that delivery is over and that his wife is all right are usually, "Is it a boy?" Little girls quickly get the idea that even their younger brothers are stronger than they are. The boys are often permitted to flail out openly while the girls are constrained at the first sign of physical aggressiveness. A common sight is that of a girl of five cowering under the onslaught of her three-year-old brother, not daring to strike back. Women who fail to learn this lesson from their brothers are apt to learn it later in life from their husbands.

In town, girls are more rapidly and more thoroughly integrated into the household regimen—taking care of younger children, sewing, washing, etc.—with the result that except for school, their orbit of daily activity rarely takes them out of the house for the rest of their lives. Boys, on the other hand, gradually come to spend more and more time outside of the house. Serious remunerative employment is rarely begun by town boys until after thirteen years of age. In the rural zone where their labor in the fields begins to be useful from the time they are six, boys are important economically at an earlier age than in town. When the town boys are not in school they are usually out *vadiando*—playing marbles or tag, swimming in the river, catching birds—with a freedom of movement never equaled by their sisters or by their country cousins. A conscious effort is made to give preadolescent town children as carefree a life as possible. Their main business is to go to school and play games, though increasingly the girls are occupied within the house.

The town's artisans do not expect regular assistance from their sons until they are twelve or thirteen. In fact, when the time comes for a boy to learn a craft, his father is rarely the one to teach him. Some other person is preferred because the boy will "show more respect," i.e., the boy will work harder for someone else than for his father.

In Minas Velhas the boys play various forms of hide-and-seek, tug-of-war, cops and robbers, and follow-the-leader; they fly kites, spin tops, shoot marbles, play several types of tag including blindman's buff, set traps to catch birds, run foot races, roll hoops and push along spools in imitation of truck drivers, build swings, shoot at birds and small game with slingshots, ride around on top of sheep, swim in the river, steal fruit from gardens, and play soccer. The girls spin tops, play with dolls, play house, make believe they are in church, sew, and embroider. Boys continue to play their games until well into adolescence, but the beginning of menstruation effectively terminates this phase for girls.

In both town and country menstruating women have a great fear of taking a full bath and of getting their heads wet. Cucumbers, oranges, lemons, pork, lard, and deer meat are carefully avoided during this period.

A girl ate a salad with cucumbers for lunch. In the same hour she began to feel ill. The illness entered her lungs, and she spent five days in bed between life and death. It took six months more before she was all right again.

If you want to stop menstruating for a day for a *festa* or something like that, rub a piece of lemon on the sole of your foot. But this is very dangerous . . . a girl I know did this for *carnaval;* she caught tuberculosis and almost died.

A girl from around here ate some lard and she got herself pitifully sick. She had terrible pains and had to go to bed.

For relief of menstrual cramps, teas and hot coffee with butter are used in addition to several herbs and roots from the *gerais*. In town there is a greater reliance upon patent remedies purchased in the pharmacy, however.

All of the females' responses are colored by a puritanical sexual code, deviation from which is liable to have dire consequences. Female virginity is given great importance in both town and country; without it marriage is possible only in those cases in which the male can be coerced into assuming responsibility. Premarital coitus for women is extremely rare; methods for simulating hymenal rupture are known, but the women who need to resort to such devices are well known among the ranks of prospective husbands. The "lost girl" (*moca perdida*) who is unable to prove rape often finds prostitution as the only alternative for spinsterhood and the only way to have children. All of the prostitutes in Minas Velhas claimed that a seduction marked the beginning of their careers.

The sexual code for males is profoundly different. Men are given more or less carte blanche to do as they please and get away with as much as they can. Childhood masturbation, while never deliberately encouraged, is less likely to be methodically prohibited in males than in females, especially among the lower classes. The data, though frankly inadequate, seems to indicate a great deal of onanistic and some homosexual experimentation prior to marriage for both town and villages. The local idiom is rich in synonyms for onanism. One male informant asserted that he masturbated every day at least once: "Everybody here in town does it," he said. Many adolescent males claim that the girls are even more given to masturbation than they are. "They use everything—fingers, pieces of wood, bananas, their heels." A recurring story tells about a girl from a good family for whom a doctor had to be summoned in order to extract a variety of foreign objects from her vagina. Whether these claims have a basis in fact or were simply part of the male's opinion of women was not determined. Whatever the actual frequency of male onanism, it is certain that no great emotional stresses are engendered by it. The young male is expected to be sexually active; his experiments may be looked upon as ludicrous, but they are never considered sinful.

A good example of the tolerant attitude accorded the male libido is the one publicly recognized homosexual in Minas Velhas. This man, a hunchback, lives in Mud Alley. Like the prostitutes who are his neighbors, he is rarely seen in other parts of the town. It is generally known, however, that he solicits male children and gains their cooperation with bribes of fruit and money. The presence of the homosexual, like the presence of the prostitutes, is not a cause of concern to the rest of the community as long as his activities do not become too conspicuous.

The male is expected to have premarital heterosexual relations. The abundance of prostitutes in Minas Velhas makes this readily feasible for the townsmen. Village youths on the other hand have less opportunity. In town, a young man's indulgence is limited only by his fear of sickness and his supply of cash.

In both town and country the danger of premarital intercourse for girls prescribes a rigid pattern of separation of the sexes after puberty. The principal place of meeting for young townspeople is the Clube Social. Dances at the club and in private homes are the most prolonged form of young heterosexual association, though they are heavily chaperoned. Unchaperoned encounters occur during the nightly "footings"; flirtations by eye and word are carried on as the girls stroll back and forth on Rua do Clube and around the garden. A slight consistent attention by a young man, such as dancing several times in succession with the same girl, staring at her, or brushing against her as she passes, is enough to bring about the relationship of *namorando* (courting). The couple who are *namorando* are permitted to take walks together in the Praca do Jardim and along Rua do Clube; if they stray from these routes, however, there is much gossip, and the girl will be censured by her family. As the courtship progresses minor liberties are permitted; the young man becomes a frequent visitor at the girl's house and they often stand outside at night holding hands. When they go for walks now, the girl holds onto the man's sleeve. Kissing and other intimate bodily contacts seem to remain absent until after marriage.[5]

Social contact between young unmarried men and women in the villages is even less frequent and more cautious than in town. Dances in Serra do Ouro and Baixa do Gamba are held only once or twice a year, and of course there is no social club. Modern ballroom dancing is still frowned upon in many of the villages. One of the rural customs which the people of Minas Velhas find most amusing is that in Serra do Ouro boys often dance arm in arm with boys and girls with girls. Ballroom dancing in Minas Velhas itself seems to go back at least seventy-five years, but in all of the village satellites its introduction is of much more recent date.

There is a feeling, especially in the villages, that the bride's family ought to finance the marriage ceremony; in practice both families contribute according to their respective abilities. In the last few decades most of the town dwellers have been joined by both religious and

[5] The young men of Minas Velhas had great difficulty in understanding American "dating" habits. If the girl is foolish enough to go off alone with a man and "neck" with him, why doesn't he take full advantage of the opportunity?

civil ceremonies. The rural zone, however, continues to pay less attention to the civil bonds. In town, 9 percent of marriages were given only civil sanction, 28 percent had only church sanction, 54 percent had both church and civil sanction, and 9 percent had no formal sanction at all (*amigados*). In the villages, 52 percent of the marriages had only religious sanction, 44 percent had both civil and religious sanction, 4 percent had no sanction. In the rural sample, there were no cases of civil marriage alone. Thus in both town and country, though with much greater frequency in the villages, if one of the two services is to be omitted, it is usually the civil ceremony. In the rural zone the principal reason for this is the failure to accept governmental sanction as necessary to the marriage contract. The sanction of the priest is felt to be sufficient and the civil code is regarded as capricious and superfluous. In addition, if the Justice of the Peace and his clerk have to go to the villages, their fees, including cost of papers, stamps, and traveling expenses, amount to more than the average farmer or sharecropper earns in a month.

Some villagers interpret the fact that there are two forms of marriage ceremony to mean that they have a chance to marry twice. For example, a wealthy farmer's daughter was seduced by a neighbor. The latter, though denying his guilt, expressed his willingness to marry the girl. The farmer, however, disliked the fellow. He felt that his daughter had been seduced merely as part of a scheme that the young man had to share in her wealth. The farmer then gave permission for a church wedding. This cleansed his daughter of the sin she had committed and made her respectable once more. The groom's satisfaction was short-lived, however, for immediately afterward the girl was legally married to a more favored suitor with whom she went to live.

In addition to the greater number of civil marriages in the city, there is a big difference between urban and rural marriage ceremonies. For the church wedding in

Minas Velhas, the godfather goes to the groom's house and brings him to the house of the bride. Relatives and friends follow along behind. When they get to the bride's house they wait outside. The bride, accompanied by her godmother and friends and relatives, emerges and both parties proceed to the church. Bride and groom, godfather and godmother, walk up to the steps of the altar where the priest performs the service. The couple kneel and are blessed. The godfather puts the marriage ring on the groom's finger while the priest puts the ring on the bride's finger. For an extra fee the priest will take advantage of the opportunity to deliver some words of caution and advice. The couple then leaves the church arm in arm, surrounded and followed by the crowd of friends and relatives. They return to the bride's house where the civil ceremony follows immediately. At one end of a large table in the "visiting room" (*sala de visita*) sits the Justice of the Peace, and at the other end, his clerk. Bride and groom sit on the left and right of the Justice of the Peace accompanied by their respective parents and godparents. The clerk reads the acts of marriage, and they are signed. Drinks are offered, and then there is a dance. At midnight a special cake containing various miniature objects is cut. The person who gets the piece with a ring inside is destined to marry quickly, the one who gets a rosary never will. The dance continues until daybreak, but before it is over the newlyweds steal off quietly and retire to a separate room. Sometimes they reappear and sometimes they do not.

In the villages, national formalized institutions do not play so large a role as in the city. Folkways are the most important part of the celebration. There is usually no civil ceremony and no cake. When it is time for the bride and groom to retire, one or two of those present at the dance approach the godfather and ask, "Where is the newlyweds' house?" They repeat this question until the godfather decides, "It is time to put the newlyweds to bed." The godfather and godmother then lead the couple to a room in the same house which has been readied for the occasion. Bride and groom go inside while the rest of the company stands outside the door singing:

> Cry bride, cry groom
> Cry until you can no more
> Cry because he who marries
> Bachelorhood shall find no more.

The groom then hands out several bottles of *cachaca* which have been kept in the room, and the door is closed and locked. A *samba em roda* (dancers form a circle within which alternating partners perform) begins and lasts for about an hour. The marriage is not usually consummated at this time. When the *samba* is over, everyone shouts, "Viva os Santos Reis (*Long live the Saints*)!" The door is opened and the newlyweds rejoin the *festa*. Later when the guests are beginning to leave they return to their room.

If the girl is an only daughter or the last daughter to be wed, an added feature of the *samba em roda* in the rural zone is the part known as the *quebra panela* ("breaking of the pot"). A man dressed as a woman *sambas* with a ceramic tray filled with stuffed chicken, fruits, and scraps from the evening meal balanced on his head. The people who come into the center of the circle to dance with him push his belly with their own in order to make him drop the *panela*. At the end of the dance he lets it fall to the floor and break. The food is snapped up by the children and the dogs, all except the stuffed chicken, which is saved by virtue of being tied by a string to the man's fingers.

In the villages as well as in the town, the ideal for newlyweds is to rent, buy, or build their own house as quickly as possible. Until this can be done, they remain with the parents who can best accommodate them.

When a town or country woman becomes pregnant she usually continues her normal tasks until the last few days, but there are several prenatal taboos which she must observe. She must take care not to wear objects suspended from her neck such as a rosary or a key lest her child be born with disfiguring marks upon it. She seeks to avoid staring at ugly animals to prevent her baby from acquiring their characteristics. A sudden fright or shock is said to induce abortions. Wishing for a child of a particular sex is said to make it sickly, hence no thought can be given to naming until after parturition. The prospective mother must avoid walking under lemon trees or both she and her child will suffer illness. In the rural zone it is said that if a pregnant woman steps over her husband, she has the power of rendering him temporarily impotent. The same power is said to enable her to kill a snake by stepping over it or to tie it in knots by tying one of her garments in knots.

In Minas Velhas as well as in the rural zone, children are born without the benefit of a doctor. There are two practicing midwives in town, neither with any formal instruction, who collect fees (about 50 cruzeiros). The town midwife, upon arrival in the house of the woman in labor, changes to a white dress and takes antiseptic precautions. She washes her hands in alcohol, but is likely to dry them on a dirty cloth. From the moment she comes into the room she begins to pray in an inaudible whisper; around her neck she wears an amulet consisting of a prayer sewn between two pieces of cloth. The mother lies in a supine position with her knees raised. She wears a dress or nightgown and is kept covered. By external pressure on the womb the midwife attempts to stimulate contractions and steer the baby in the right direction. When major spasms have begun, she climbs on the bed and has the mother place the soles of her feet against her knees. She now tries to aid the descent of the child by inserting her hand in the genital tract. When the child emerges she cuts the umbilical cord with a scissors washed in alcohol and ties it with a thread treated in the same manner. The child is bathed in soap and water and wrapped in a cloth. When the afterbirth emerges it is collected in a basin and the father takes it to another room in the house or to the back yard, digs a hole, and buries it. He kicks the earth back in place with his back to the hole. When the umbilical cord falls off the child, it too is buried. No explanations for these rites are offered except that dogs and rats should be kept away from the buried parts. Abortions and stillbirths are treated in the same manner. The husband is usually the only man permitted to attend the delivery, though he frequently stays in an adjoining room until it is all over. Girls as well as young men are prohibited from watching the proceedings.

Rural births occur in much the same manner. The village midwife, however, lacks the rudimentary conceptions of antiseptic precautions which are performed conscientiously if not effectively by the urban midwives. No alcohol is used, no special dress worn, nor are clean hands considered a necessity.

Postnatal taboos are more numerous than prenatal ones. Village mothers stay in bed on the average between three and five days; townswomen stay in bed from five to nine days. Prohibited foods are squash, mangrove, lemons, oranges, deer meat, steer intestines, most fish, breadfruit, fresh meat of any kind, male pig, cock, and any breed of cattle or fowl *que tem raca,* i.e., a breed which, like zebu cattle, is pedigreed and not *da terra* (common). For at least a month, women should avoid walking up- or downhill. A full body bath ought not to be taken until after forty days. In Serra do Ouro there are many women who will not wash their hair until a year has passed. These taboos, like all other folkways, tend to be more closely adhered to in the villages than in the town. Townswomen generally agree that it is dangerous to wash one's hair soon after giving birth, but the time they wait is shorter than the period observed in the country. Moreover, there is a group of deliberately "progressive" women in the town, including most of the schoolteachers, some of whom boast that they have washed their hair five days after giving birth and their bodies two days later.

MARRIED LIFE

After marriage the urban husband is expected to continue visiting the prostitutes, but with lessened frequency and increasing circumspection. Most wives expect and tolerate occasional lapses in their husband's behavior as long as he makes a reasonable attempt to keep it secret from her and everybody else. If, however, a husband begins to devote too much time to a prostitute, serious domestic strife often ensues:

I never knew that my husband was so fond of the women. Right after we were married he started to go with the prostitutes. When I heard people talking about this, I became angry and got into violent arguments with him. In one of these he hit me, and I fell down. I was a fool, because I got up and tried to hit him back. . . . I took so much that day that I learned for good to take it without wanting to give it back. Despite all this he liked me very much. He used to go crazy when I left him and went to my mother's house and pleaded for me to come back with him.

If a woman is unable to make her husband desist from a relationship with a prostitute which has become regular enough to be known by her neighbors, she will often appeal directly to the other woman or try to intimidate her. For example, a storekeeper had quarrels with his wife about his frequent visits to Mud Alley. His wife, after having been molested physically, left Minas Velhas and went to live with her mother in a nearby town. When friends informed her that the situation had got worse, that Antonio now had the key to the prostitute's house and was paying her rent, she returned and in desperation paid a visit to the woman and begged her to leave her husband alone. The prostitute responded that she could not keep him out since he had the key to her house, whereupon Antonio's wife offered to pay for the installation of a new lock. The situation was resolved when the prostitute finally wearied of these constant pleas and threats and moved to another town.

There are about thirty women in Minas Velhas who

are known as *raparigas*. Only eight of these are real prostitutes in the sense that they will give themselves to any man who is willing to pay. Six of these live in Mud Alley. The remainder consist of women whose sexual behavior is known to deviate in one way or another. Some are widows who are concubines of married men; others live with a man to whom they were never formally married; others are former concubines or prostitutes who, because they are too old, can no longer earn any money or attract a new lover. The inflexible code for females lumps all of these offenders under the same term. Little distinction is made between an unmarried woman who has as many men as she can attract and an unmarried woman who has been living with the same man for a number of years. Only when a great deal of time has passed and the woman is quite old and has had several children will she come not to be thought of as a *rapariga*. The latter situation implies that before the beginning of the relationship the woman had not been a virgin or else the man with whom she is now living would have married her. Either she was a prostitute, a *moca perdida,* or a wife estranged from her real husband. All of these conditions are felt to be an aspect of but a single pattern of sin and are in fact closely linked together.

The ideal of the outright prostitute, for example, is to become a concubine to some man who will support her in return for exclusive sexual privileges, or better still, to live with a man who may not marry her but will at least support her children. Four of the prostitutes in Mud Alley have lovers (*amantes*) who pay their rent and provide them with *trem*—food and household items. As long as the lover continues to support her, the prostitute is not supposed to accept any other men. Occasionally a lover will permit a prostitute to accept all comers provided that she lets him share in the profits. But sooner or later the prostitute usually comes to have exclusive relations with one man over an extended period in which paternity may be recognized. Only time, however, can prove whether the relationship will be a stable one. Since there is no societal sanction that binds the man to her, the chance that the union will be a permanent one is actually slight. Hence, no matter what the form of nonmarital relations, there is a basis in fact for calling all the women who participate in them *raparigas*. One form of illicit relation leads to another and then back again without the woman ever being able to overcome her original violation of the code, whatever that may have been.

None of the prostitutes presently in Minas Velhas was born in the town. Some come from the rural zone and others from the neighboring cities. The younger ones stay on for a year or two and then move away to another place, looking for better business or a lover. In the main their stories are similar to that of Odete, an old ex-prostitute born in Gruta who now makes her living by cutting wood. When Odete was fifteen, one of her sisters married a widower who came to live in their house. Shortly afterward the new brother-in-law raped or seduced Odete and she became pregnant:

Finally my mother told me frankly that I couldn't stay in the house any longer among my sisters. I became very sad and told my mother that since they didn't consider me a human being any more, I was going to live like the beasts of the field eating grass like they do. [She accused her brother-in-law, but] he had the courage to deny everything right in front of me. So I told him some things with all the anger I had for him. I cursed him out and went away without saying good-bye to anyone. I went to the house of another sister of mine who was also "lost" and there I had a child who shortly afterward died. Since then I've been knocking around the world. I had five children who died, but God has left me one in my old age in order that I shouldn't end up like a tree without leaves.

The unusually large number of prostitutes and concubines in Minas Velhas is undoubtedly related to the surplus of women caused by male emigration.

Among the urban females from whom information

was collected about marital sex life there were several who considered intercourse a conjugal duty from which the woman derived scant pleasure. Explained a widow who professed not to have the slightest desire to sleep with another man again:

It is difficult for a woman to lift her skirt for another man who is not her husband because of the amount she has suffered with her own man. I prefer to live alone rather than submit again to a man.

But the sample was insufficient to determine with what frequency frigidity occurs in the total population. It is certain, however, that periodic odium and at least temporary frigidity are common features of almost every marriage in association with the hardships of excessive pregnancy and because of the male's failure to adjust his impulses to the various occasions such as menstruation, sickness, and pregnancy when the woman would prefer to abstain. There is no doubt that the majority of males fail to consider their wives' willingness to have sexual intercourse, whatever their excuse, and that they consider the woman's pleasure to be a mere by-product of their own. The wife of a bricklayer had this to say about her sex life:

When I married at sixteen years of age, there were many things that I didn't know yet. The first night is very difficult—only those who have gone through it know. The man is already accustomed to all that but the girl never tried it. It gives her such agony that she thinks she is going to die. But even so, the woman has the greatest pleasure on the wedding night because everything is a novelty to her. It's all so marvelous that she doesn't close her eyes the whole night long. . . . If afterward things stayed that way for the rest of life, it would be very good; but no, as soon as the husband accustoms himself to you, he thinks everything is automatic. He takes you like a machine. My husband has a real hunger for women. If he didn't why can't he wait for three days without having me until my period is over? When he started to go with the prostitutes, I decided to have relations with him even during menstruation.

A *ferreiro's* wife said her husband was "like a donkey . . . he doesn't respect sickness, much less menstruation (*como um jegue . . . nao respeita doenca quanto mais a regra*)." When she pleads with him to desist for a night, he answers, "Nonsense, it doesn't bother me; I'm accustomed to this (*Bobagem, nao fez mal, ja estou acostumado a isto*)." [6]

Another woman's husband agrees with his wife that they should abstain during menstruation because of the *porcaria* (filth), but against her wishes insists on having relations "until the moment of birth (*ate o menio estar nascendo*)" when she is pregnant. This is considered by many women one of the worst hardships of having children. Many of them profess to hate their husbands in the moments of sexual contact during the last months of pregnancy: "What pleasure can a woman have with her stomach that big and a child kicking around inside? She gets the impression that it is going to die suffocated with agony."

An interesting feeling called *antojo* permits the female to protest against the male's domineering, self-centered role. *Antojo* is the term for the sudden intense likes and dislikes which the women of Minas Velhas and the villages experience during pregnancy. It is believed that these violent cravings, usually for some food or article of comfort, can be ignored only at the risk of having the child abort or be born with some physical deformity. Women who have had miscarriages are likely to account for them in this fashion:

I had a desire to eat some fresh meat. My husband didn't have enough money so I spent the whole day without being able to stop thinking about it, with my mouth watering and a great deal of discomfort; the next day I had an abortion.

[6] In addition to registering disapproval, the comparison of the husband to " a donkey " also registers a certain amount of pride. The husband is thus shown to be very virile, which is as it should be. In her passive role, the woman expects a certain amount of rough treatment and would be disappointed if she did not get it. In a sense, she is " happy in her suffering."

Nowadays I've lost my shame about asking for something when I feel like that.

I wanted a beautiful red melon that I had seen in the street; when I got the money together to buy it, it had already been sold. I lost the child.

Other wishes are more bizarre; some are legendary, like that of the woman who wanted to eat part of her husband's leg and another who felt that she had to eat a certain dog. Since most of the desires are for foods, *antojo* may be looked upon as a means of assuring that husbands will make the extra effort which may be necessary to satisfy their wives' hunger during pregnancy. In addition, *antojos* are often negative, consisting of hatreds and repulsions. A woman may find it impossible to enter her kitchen or she may be filled with disgust by the smell of a rose or unable to stand the sound of a dog barking. One of the town schoolteachers took a violent dislike to her entire house and sat about morosely while her husband negotiated to move into another one until she had her child. Frequently the hatred is generalized and includes almost everything and everybody; most often, however, it is the male relative in particular who is felt to be especially noxious and among these it is the husband who is regarded with the greatest revulsion. Moreover, it is said that the most violent cravings and hatreds are associated with the birth of the first male child. The men of the town as well as the villages respect these *antojos* and indulge them to the best of their abilities. They probably serve the important function of relieving some of the woman's frustration which results from the male's dominant role.

In both town and villages, the husband contributes and maintains control over the largest share of a family's cash income. In the majority of households the wife has no independent source of income. There are many cases, however, especially in the lower urban socioeconomic strata, where the wife does earn money on her own, mainly by making soap, pastry, or lace. This money is usually administered by the woman herself and goes for the purchase of clothing and miscellaneous items for herself and her children. When the husband's income is particularly small or subject to seasonal fluctuations, the wife's income may be surrendered to him in order to buy food; this is always a male prerogative. On the other hand, if the wife has no separate remunerative activity, but merely assists her husband in his daily work, the man keeps all the money. For example, Almira helps her husband make bricks and tiles. Her husband digs up the clay, transports it to their back yard, and mixes it. Almira, with the help of her small children, molds the bricks in a wooden form. She and her husband work together baking them in the furnace. The man does the selling and receives all the money. When Almira or the children need to make a purchase she has to ask her husband for the money.

In Minas Velhas, it is the man of the house who does the shopping. This is true for purchases made in the stores as well as at the weekly fair. The townsmen often explain this by saying that their wives are too busy taking care of the children and cooking to leave the house. Others say frankly that women do not understand and ought not to be trusted with affairs of money. The use of money is felt to be the prerogative of the head of the house. "Me go to the fair?" said one townswoman. "God forbid. I never went to fair and I never go to the stores. Here in my house the master of the house is still living." At the auctions which form part of the religious *festas* women are present but they never bid. This is true of both town and villages. To bid here would mean to compete openly with males; hence, not even widows would think of participating.

Owing to the surplus of young adult females, an unusually active wage-earning role is taken by the women of Minas Velhas. Competition for husbands has increased the economic liability involved in the raising of daughters. As a compensation, many young women have acquired handicraft skills associated with metal- and leatherwork and embroidery, and contribute to the cash income of the household. For the most part, however, their wages are considerably lower than those of males and are insufficient to permit real economic independence. Most of the women who do maintain their own households without the benefit of a husband, whether by handicrafts or menial services, belong to the lower half of the social hierarchy. Despite the inevitability of a large number of households run by women, there is a great loss of prestige when a woman is forced to undertake a male occupation like that of blacksmith or brass-smith. Many married women continue to gain wages but only the schoolteachers frequently earn more than their husbands. The schoolteacher's husband is known as a *Filipe*—a term which implies that the man has traded some of his manliness for the luxury of being supported by his wife. Even the *Filipe*, however, does the shopping, and though his wife may strongly suggest when and how much he should bid at the auction, it is the *Filipe* himself who speaks up.

In both town and country, women are generally expected to stay in the background. In church the sexes are separated. The women outnumber the men by four to one, but the section nearest to the altar is reserved for males. Women who are employed by the craft shops work either in separate rooms from the men or in their own homes. At home the husband eats first. It is uncommon, except in the highest socioeconomic stratum, for an entire family to be seated at once at the dinner table. Father and one or two of the oldest male children are usually the only ones to eat at the table. The mother and females wait upon them and eat after they have finished. Many women and their children in the lower income groups crouch by the stove or by the water jar in the kitchen or sit upon the lintel in the doorway to the back yard, holding their plates in their hands. In those lower-class families where the woman has her own independent source of income, the husband frequently eats with her in the kitchen; father and favorite son sometimes sit on a box eating out of the same plate.

When there are visitors, the wife usually does not partake of the coffee which her husband orders her to make. Women in general tend to keep quiet and let the male do the talking in any public situation and in most private ones too. The laughable exception to this is the schoolteacher with whom the *Filipe* must wage a constant struggle to get a word in edgewise. In the villages, however, the secondary, retiring role for females is much more pronounced than in the town. The great timidity which the women of Serra do Ouro manifest toward strangers has already been discussed. In contrast to Minas Velhas, no women except widows have a source of income which they can spend as they see fit. In addition, while there are many households in town where both husband and wife will sit and have coffee with a visitor, this is never the case in a place like Serra do Ouro.

Some of the young townswomen have "liberated" themselves to the extent of learning to ride a bicycle. True, rather than risk public exposure of the upper part of their legs, these girls have had to confine their practice sessions to rather dark nights with the result that not many of them have mastered the art as yet. In the villages even such seemingly mild freedom is still very much impossible.

URBAN DISCONTENTS

When fifty urban school children were asked the question, "What do you want to be when you grow up?," their answers were as indicated in Table 24.

Here again the urban ethos, with its orientation away from agriculture and menial forms of labor, shows through clearly. The lure of change and modernity, and the aspiration after intellectual rather than manual ways of making a living, are evidence of a pervasive desire to lead an urban rather than a rural existence.

TABLE 24. OCCUPATIONAL PREFERENCES OF URBAN
SCHOOL CHILDREN

BOYS		GIRLS	
Truck driver	8	Teacher	20
Doctor	3	Doctor	2
Landlord farmer	2	Dressmaker	2
Storekeeper	2	Lacemaker	1
Teacher	2	Actress	1
Barber	1		26
Shoemaker	1		
Priest	1		
Lieutenant	1		
Ferreiro (Blacksmith)	1		
Airplane pilot	1		
	23		

Given a knowledge of the possibilities confronting the adults of Minas Velhas, one might correctly deduce from these answers the fact that adulthood is a great disappointment to many members of the urban community. The low esteem in which handicrafts and other forms of menial labor, including farming, are held is incompatible with the realities of the local economy. After marriage both husband and wife often assume the attitude that they have been trapped into a life of unrewarding drudgery. In the city the husband looks upon his ever expanding progeny as a dubious blessing. While his family grows steadily larger and there are new mouths to feed and new bodies to clothe, his income remains fixed. Young unmarried men are able to leave Minas Velhas and find jobs where cash is more plentiful and where they can amass enough capital to buy land or start a business, but the married man's brood is like a millstone about his neck. After a while he may begin to see his children as the means by which he may enjoy a life of greater ease, at least during his old age. Hence, in town, the child, far from being encouraged to follow his father's profession, is urged instead to avoid it. The wife, as we have seen, after the romantic hallucination of the first few months, discovers herself to be a machine designed to give her husband pleasure while he gives her babies. As the number of births mount up, she makes less and less of an effort to interest her husband sexually. Her own pleasure in the sexual act diminishes; the constant pregnancies sap her vitality and she ages rapidly. Her husband loses interest in a woman who is so worn out and begins to pay more attention to the prostitutes, which compounds the latent hostility between them. This sort of situation occurs quite frequently in the middle socioeconomic stratum; it does not happen in the upper group where financial security permits the nuclear family to expand without increasing tension, nor in the lowest where ambitions are kept to a minimum. Nor does it pertain to the villages where children plant and harvest most of their food from an early age and the women do not have to compete with prostitutes.

The plight of Sr. Paulo and his wife, Pamela, the sister of Sr. Braulio, illustrates the troubled destiny to which the aspiring urbanite in the environmentally misplaced little big city is frequently condemned. Paulo's father owned a store and was fairly well off. They could afford a cook and a washerwoman. Shortly after Paulo's father died, Carlos Prestes, the communist leader, and his army sacked Minas Velhas in their 1926 flight across Bahia. Paulo's father's store was destroyed and with it Paulo's share of the inheritance. In his youth, Paulo learned the trades of brass-smith and leatherworker. He started his own shop and did fairly well, but he spent all his money on prostitutes and new clothes. Later he contracted syphilis and used up all his savings on doctor bills. Then came the depression and drought of the early thirties. Paulo left Minas Velhas with a cargo of metal and leather goods and journeyed to the region of Conquista. Here he sold his merchandise and with the aid of a rich cousin opened up a small store. Word soon reached him that it had begun to rain in the interior, so he packed up and returned to Minas Velhas with two *contos* in cash, "which in those days was a great deal of money." He reopened his shop and divided his time between making and peddling spurs and bridles. Then he began to court Pamela, whom he had known all his life. "As soon as I got married, life started to get worse." His wife bore him eight children in twelve years. He soon found himself unable to replace the suits, ties, and hats to which he had become accustomed when he was single. "The money I was making wasn't enough to live on." Pamela had to do all the washing and cooking. In 1939 another drought struck the region and Paulo had to abandon his *arte*. Like most of the artisans in Minas Velhas at this time, he kept his family alive by working as a miner in the river. When the drought ended he was penniless and had to borrow from Pamela's brother to buy food. Sr. Braulio was just starting his factory then and gave Paulo a job. But Paulo, who had become irritable and restless, quarreled with his brother-in-law when he failed to make him manager. Today Paulo says that his life "has no future, unless a miracle happens." He is constantly in debt, his house is in a crumbling condition, and his clothing is so patched and old that he is afraid to be seen at *festas*. "If only I hadn't married," he keeps saying, "then when things got bad around here I could have gone to Conquista again or to Sao Paulo and gotten some money together." In a dream which he has had repeatedly, he sees himself marrying a beautiful young girl and moving into a big house on a plantation in a land far from Minas Velhas.

Pamela works ceaselessly taking care of the children and keeping the house in order. When Paulo fails to bring home enough money for the fair, she borrows from her brother. Occasionally Paulo gets drunk and beats her. As the years have gone by she has become more and more religious. Though she is unable to go to church as often as she would like, she prays constantly to the images in her room.

Antonio, the storekeeper, also tends to blame his troubles on an early marriage. As a young man he had served in the army, was pleased with the life, and wanted to pursue a military career. When his enlistment period terminated he came back to Minas Velhas intending to reenlist. He married instead and his wife talked him into staying; she refused to leave her family. He opened a small store which he has had ever since. It was Antonio's wife who had to plead with the prostitute in Mud Alley to keep her husband home at night.

THE PEOPLE of Minas Velhas are fully aware that they
are members of a large national state. Most townspeople know the national anthem or at least can recognize it when they hear it sung. Independence Day is
celebrated by the school children with parades and
speeches. Events of national concern regularly impinge
upon the urbanites' consciousness by radio, newspaper,
and word of mouth. The course of the Second World
War was followed with keen interest, and on V-E Day
the town erupted in a spontaneous victory celebration.
Many people still talk about the great quantity of drink
they consumed when the war ended. Brazil's failure to
win the 1950 world championship soccer matches played
in Rio de Janeiro was a source of great disappointment
to the town's young men who are themselves organized
into soccer teams that play in the Praca da Grama every
Sunday afternoon. The most important institutionalized links with the rest of the nation, however, are furnished by formal government and political parties.
Local government is a powerful urbanizing force, while
politics produce intense schisms to be considered along
with race and class in relation to the low level of community cohesion.

GOVERNMENT

The government of the county whose seat is in Minas
Velhas employs more people and owns more property
than any single private enterprise in the county. Each
year about 350,000 cruzeiros (about $11,600 U.S.) are
administered by the local officials. This sum is extremely small in the frame of reference of national economics, but in local terms it is far from insignificant.

In spending its limited funds, the local government
operates under the handicap of having to maintain and
expand a program of secondary urban improvements in

poverty-stricken and disease-ridden communities. <u>The local government is a self-conscious city-building corporation strongly determined not to let the county's poverty interfere with the prevailing notion of what a city ought to contain in the way of public works</u>.

The county's expenditures for the year 1949–50 were apportioned as shown in Table 25.

TABLE 25. EXPENDITURES OF THE COUNTY OF MINAS VELHAS
FOR 1949-50

	EXPENDITURE (IN CRUZEIROS)
I. Construction and Repair	
Stone pavements, Minas Velhas	6,612
Stone pavements, Districts	2,632
Paved street, Gruta	10,000
Bridge	57,379
Roads	59,999
Town garden (part)	29,954
Two police houses, Districts	32,879
Schoolhouse, Serra do Ouro	15,000
Schoolhouse, Formiga	20,000
Repair of church, Gruta	10,000
	244,455
II. Salaries and Pensions	
Secretary of Council	1,200
Mayor	6,000
Mayor's expense account	3,000
Secretary	3,600
Porter	1,800
Bookkeeper	3,600
Tax collectors (5)	8,226
Animal catcher	3,000
Treasurer	3,600
Jailer	1,200
Sheriff	2,400
Police Clerk	1,260
Schoolteachers (12)	14,800
Justice of the peace	2,000
Pensioned treasurer	2,250
Street cleaner	1,200

TABLE 25. EXPENDITURES OF THE COUNTY OF MINAS VELHAS
FOR 1949-50 (CONTINUED)

	EXPENDITURE (IN CRUZEIROS)
Courthouse attendant	3,100
Pension fund	1,260
	63,696

III. Administrative expenses and expenses for supplies

Furniture	400
Printing of budget	600
Material for police	1,041
Schools	2,516
Sanitation (sweeping streets and cleaning buildings)	9,391
Lighting, Minas Velhas	3,410
Lighting, Districts	6,685
Elections	17,543
Unspecified	2,880
	44,466

IV. Charity

Paupers' funerals	1,641
Clube Social's fund	500
Social work	1,071
Needy prisoners	590
Seminary, Caetite	2,000
	5,802

V. Miscellaneous

Agricultural exposition, Vila Nova	2,000
Aid to the production of cereals	300
Town band, Minas Velhas	5,600
Town band, Districts	2,000
Balance for market	664
Town library	305
Unspecified	13,076
	23,945
Total Expenditures	382,364

Outstanding in this budget is the emphasis placed
upon public works. New buildings, roads, bridges, and
paved streets are the highest expression of urban civic

standards. The success of each local administration and
the personal worth of the individual members of the
town council are judged by the amount of construction
performed under their auspices. The more new buildings, the better the record. Moreover, each councilman
strives to have some particular *obra* (public work) associated with his name that will serve as a permanent memorial to his efforts on behalf of progress. Since the
councilmen are not paid, such memorials are regarded
as just remuneration for services rendered. At the con-
clusion of the council's most recent term of office, one of
the members reviewed the record in this typical fashion:

It is with great satisfaction that this administration is drawing to its end, for in the space of four years it has left behind it a veritable carpet of finished *obras*. In every part of
this county, wherever you may go, an *obra* is rising. . . . Sr.
Heraclito Azevedo built a beautiful bridge in Gruta. Sr.
Teofilo organized gigantic works of progress in Formiga—a
public market and a police station. Markets and schools
arose throughout the county.

All such construction is accepted per se as "progress."
At the risk of doing violence to a set of values which
contain their own justification, it is worth pointing out
that little distinction is made between basic and superficial improvements. The local government feels
obliged to spend its limited funds in a way calculated to
meet certain aesthetic criteria of urban living as much if
not more than it feels obliged to deal with basic insuffi-
ciencies in health, education, and subsistence. Schools
and roads are, of course, basic in any program designed
to raise the standard of living. Paved streets, town gardens, and special houses for the justice of the peace are
perhaps not as fundamental. At any rate, school construction and operation account for only 13 percent of
the budget. There is no concern with public health at
all despite the complete absence of doctors in the
county. Large buildings for public markets are given
priority over measures designed to insure safe sources of
water, none of which exist. Assistance to local agricul-

ture and industry is also completely absent from the budget.

In the eyes of the townspeople the principal duty of all government is to produce "progress." But for basic improvements in the general welfare, the people look beyond the local authorities. The prevailing attitude is, "We are too weak to help ourselves. *O Governo tem que dar impulso* (The government has to give us a push)." *O Governo,* in this case, refers to something beyond the county, but to no specific bureau or agency. What the townspeople have in mind is the "boss" of super proportions embodied in the state and federal governments. Everyone, from mayor and councilmen to artisan and storekeeper, is firmly convinced that herein lies the solution to Minas Velhas's troubles. To the state and federal governments is attributed the semi-miraculous power of being able to bestow health and prosperity at one fell swoop in the time it takes to sign a piece of paper. As a matter of fact, the efforts of the county to live up to its concept of urban standards actually depends largely on a subsidy from the federal government. Table 26 shows the origin of local receipts for the year 1949–50. Almost two thirds of the county's income consists of the outright gift of federal funds which are made available to each county in the country under the present federal constitution.

TABLE 26. RECEIPTS OF THE COUNTY OF MINAS VELHAS

ORIGIN OF RECEIPTS	CRUZEIROS
Land and building taxes	4,288
Stores, industries, irrigation	83,383
Road tax	1,817
Official papers	380
Sanitation tax	1,159
Fair tax	6,938
Back taxes	28,959
Fines	1,337
Miscellaneous	5,597
Federal government	213,798
Total	347,655

There is a widely held belief that Minas Velhas's backwardness has resulted from the failure of the government to be properly concerned with the town's welfare. The lack of electricity, for example, is universally regarded as a tragic instance of the dereliction of this "super-boss." "Why doesn't the government make use of the Rio das Pedras waterfall?" everybody wants to know. The generally impoverished condition of industry and agriculture as well as the lack of electricity, roads, schools, and medical attention are all viewed as evidence that Minas Velhas has been abandoned and neglected by the most powerful of all worldly benefactors. "We live in this state of poverty and backwardness because we have been forgotten by the public powers," maintains Sr. Waldemar, the councilman. "Our hills are filled with precious metals, but the government takes no interest in them. They ought at least to send an engineer to find out what's there. They ought to send us tractors and plows and machines for our industries. And it's a shame that we have to live here without a doctor."

The urbanite thinks of the government as an immensely wealthy but unpredictable philanthropist. It is patently obvious to the townspeople that the government has more than enough money to build a hydroelectric station. That these sums must be used in other places for other purposes is small comfort to the people of Minas Velhas. In fact, this is precisely what they find most distressing—namely, that the government has "forgotten" them. With the proper approach, however, it is felt that the government can be made to "remember" and in few grand gestures relieve the town of all its problems.

The habit of regarding the government as a potential source of outright gifts was recently reinforced by a rather strange windfall that came directly from Rio de Janeiro. There was born in Minas Velhas in the last century the Baron ——, who became one of Brazil's most famous educators. The local historian, Sr. A. G., has been trying for twenty years to gain support for various projects designed to render homage to the Baron and his birthplace. Sr. A. G.'s first task was to prove that Minas Velhas was indeed the educator's birthplace, for others insisted that he was born in Vila Nova. When the facts had been established, Sr. A. G. had the Baron's house declared a monument and equipped it with a commemorative plaque. Then, by working through the Social Democracy Party (PSD), he tried to interest various state and federal deputies in a larger project. As a result, in 1949 a bill was presented in the Federal Congress providing for the creation in Minas Velhas of a "professional high school with courses in the humanities." A budget of two million cruzeiros was requested. In 1951, five hundred thousand cruzeiros of this sum was actually appropriated for the construction of a building to house a "professional school for minors." In order to sell this scheme, Sr. A. G. has named the Clube Social as the sponsor of the project, representing the officers of the Clube as ready with the detailed plans necessary for building and operating the school. The money has, therefore, been deposited in the Clube Social's account. But the Clube really had no such plans and no one, including Sr. A. G., has any clear realization of what a professional school for minors ought to consist. Undismayed, the PSD, which claimed credit for having attracted the super-boss's notice, put out a triumphant leaflet calling for the voters to express their appreciation of the gift at the ballot boxes:

Nothing can bring more benefit to this city than the establishment of a superior professional school for the development of the recognized calling of its children in the arts and letters. Furthermore, it will benefit the entire sertao, where not a single professional school exists.

Gratitude is the most noble sentiment of an esteemed people, and the population of this city, benefited in such a high manner, certainly will not belie its traditional past.

The townspeople were pleasantly surprised by this windfall. It was the gift they had least expected, but welcome nonetheless. "It would have been better if we could use the money to build a hydroelectric plant instead of this professional school," said Sr. Waldemar. "But at least we are no longer completely forgotten."

In the actual day-by-day administration of the county and in terms of local legislation, the local government which has its seat in Minas Velhas exhibits a degree of autonomy commensurate with the town's geographical isolation. Local edicts and ordinances concerning fiscal policy, the construction of roads, schools, and markets, while ultimately circumscribed by federal and state statutes, remain in detail dependent principally upon local conditions. In ordering the construction of a road, a tax on irrigation, a fine for unwhitewashed houses and stray pigs, a bonus for an employee, and hundreds of other similar items, the local executive and legislature wield their delegated powers apparently without interference from larger centers of government. This decentralization of power is more apparent than real, however. In addition to the state and federal statutes which, under the present constitution, include a uniform abstract fiscal code for all counties, local government is now and always has been deeply enmeshed in state-wide and nation-wide political events.

POLITICS

The political history of Minas Velhas is intimately linked with the political history of Bahia and Brazil. The rise and fall of leaders in the government of the county reflect the viscissitudes of the state-wide and national political drama. From 1890 to 1915, for example, the principal political leaders of Minas Velhas came from a single wealthy landowning family, the Soares of Vila Nova. Afonso Soares, the most influential of them, was appointed mayor of Minas Velhas by a decree of his friend, Marcelino, then governor of Bahia State. Afonso subsequently became a state senator and his sons and sons-in-law succeeded him as the local political bosses. Afonso, however, aspired to the governorship himself. When Marcelino failed to support this project in the 1916 elections, he was shot by arrangement of one of Afonso's relatives. Marcelino recovered from his wounds and, as part of his revenge, ordered that Carlos Bomfim, the Portuguese merchant, should replace Afonso's son as mayor of Minas Velhas. This edict was carried out. In the 1916 elections, the elder Soares was defeated by Marcelino's candidate, but his son was victorious in the local contest. Carlos Bomfim looked to the capital for help. Marcelino dispatched a squad of troops to Minas Velhas and Bomfim resumed his position as mayor.

Time and again in this manner, the results of national or state elections and revolutions have influenced the local political scene. The disposition of local political power—the utilization of it—is a local affair; but the power itself is linked to and ultimately dependent upon the power in the big cities. The local political *chefes* (bosses) cannot dispense with behind-the-scenes connections and intrigues, especially in Salvador.

The present-day *chefe* of Minas Velhas, Artur Morais, is well acquainted with this principle. Morais is a landlord from the district of Gruta. He was elected mayor for the first time in 1926 under the sponsorship of a state deputy who was a friend of his family. Up for reelection in 1930, Morais's regime came to a temporary halt when Getulio Vargas engineered his first *golpe* (*coup d'état*). Vargas swept the state governments clear of opposition and appointed *interventors* (administrators) to replace hostile governors. Ataliba Osorio, a stranger to Morais, was appointed *interventor* in Bahia. Morais decided to abandon his post as mayor until a friendlier figure should appear in the state government. He locked the town hall and for a year or so Minas Velhas was left without an effective local government. Meanwhile, the first *interventor* had been replaced by a second, Leopoldo de Amaral. A young dentistry student from Minas Velhas by the name of Luiz Mineiro was attending school in Salvador when this happened. Luiz Mineiro was a personal enemy of Morais and, by exploiting certain contacts in the capital, managed to get an "in" with people close to the new *interventor*. Mineiro was subsequently appointed mayor of Minas Velhas. He returned home and demanded the keys to the town hall from Morais. The latter complied and Mineiro began to run the local government. A short time later, however, he was obliged to return to Salvador in order to continue his studies. Before leaving, he appointed his brother, Izidro, a brass-smith by trade, to take his place. Izidro, unacquainted with the rudiments of bureaucratic procedure, mounted an uneasy throne while his brother went back to Salvador to become a dentist. Just about this time Vargas and Amaral, the *interventor*, parted ways. Juracy Margalhaes appeared in Salvador to take the latter's place.

This was the opportunity for which Morais had been waiting; for he had a friend, Judge Mafra, who was a friend of Juracy. Morais hurried to Salvador, met with Judge Mafra, and the two of them talked personally with the new *interventor*, explaining that Minas Velhas was being run by an illiterate brass-smith. When Morais returned from his visit to the capital he was by decree once more the mayor of Minas Velhas.

Again Morais's position was only as secure as the position of his sponsor in the state capital. Under the constitution of 1934 Juracy was elected governor of Bahia and Morais stayed on as mayor. But Juracy and Vargas parted ways in the revolution of 1937. Still another *interventor*, Fernandes Dantas, took his place. Now just as Morais had taken advantage of Juracy's rise, someone else from Minas Velhas was waiting to take advantage of his fall.

This was Joao Azevedo, a successful businessman who owns an interest in the town's largest store. Azevedo, starting out as a brass-smith, had amassed a considerable fortune by buying gold in the interior and selling it in Salvador. He married into the Bomfim family and moved to Salvador where he opened a second store. With wealth and good family connections, all that he lacked to make his success complete was political power.

Being a resident of Salvador considerably improved his chances of becoming the mayor of Minas Velhas! He busied himself with intrigues, and even before Juracy was evicted from the state government he had already established contact with Dantas, the newest *interventor*. Working steadily in Salvador, Azevedo arranged to have his sister's husband appointed mayor. A year later when his business permitted, Azevedo himself returned in triumph to Minas Velhas and completed his success story by becoming mayor of his home town.

In 1944 Vargas's regime collapsed and provisionary governments were appointed in all the states. In Minas Velhas the local government was presided over by a judge who was supposed to maintain order until elections could be held. Azevedo relinquished his post and prepared to fight it out with Morais in the campaign for mayor. Since Azevedo had to return to his business in Salvador he chose not to run himself but sponsored a man in his place. Azevedo was now formally allied with the political party known as the PSD while Morais represented the UDN (National Democratic Union). The judge who was supposed to maintain order until the elections was himself a partisan of the PSD. During the campaign certain members of the PSD attempted to efface the propaganda placards of the UDN. The UDN took similar measures of its own and in the ensuing confusion Azevedo persuaded the judge to call in a troop of soldiers. Morais, who once again was in Salvador trying to get this judge replaced, hurried home. Under his directions, the UDN amassed an armed force of its own. A tense period followed, but no outbreak of fighting actually occurred. Finally, the work Morais had been doing in Salvador bore fruit. The PSD judge was replaced by a UDN judge and the elections were held, if not in tranquillity, at least without serious violence. Morais won by a narrow margin.

These local political parties have a formal organization. The principal leaders are appointed by the state bosses and they in turn gather about them local adherents. Regular meetings of the local *Diretorios* (committees) are held in which campaign tactics are developed. The local parties thus keep in contact with the state organization. They adhere closely to the party line and distribute party propaganda in the form of leaflets and posters.

One of the many leaflets distributed by the PSD in 1950 reads in part as follows:

October 3rd nears as the golden presage of a day of light and sun. If our dear Lauro Farani [1] disappeared in the middle of the battle in a dignified and intense campaign, now rises the favored name of Regis Pacheco as candidate for the governor of Bahia. Let us march to the urns then, taking courage from our patron saint whom Lauro Farani so greatly exalted in his speech.[2]

Let us not forget our party obligations and, like the Pessedistas (PSDers) that we are, let us take to the urns the names of Christiano Machado, Regis Pacheco, and Adonias Cardoso for President of the Republic, Governor of the State, and Mayor of Minas Velhas, respectively.

This leaflet was written and signed by Padre Goncalves, who, in addition to being the priest in Minas Velhas, is the president of the local PSD. It was printed in Minas Velhas on a press owned by the president of the PTB (Brazilian Workers' Party). Another press, owned by Jose da Silva, the UDN's candidate for mayor, turned out propaganda for the UDN. Part of a typical leaflet in which Morais endorsed this candidate as his official successor follows:

Dear friend,

This is not the first time that I have addressed myself to my fellow countrymen. In identical situations, animated by the same faith that animates me today, by the same confidence that stimulates me now, I have looked to you and found you firm and unyielding in your political convictions, lending me

[1] Lauro Farani de Freitas, candidate for the governor of Bahia, was killed in an airplane accident shortly before the elections.
[2] Both the PSD and the UDN candidates for governor briefly visited Minas Velhas.

the support of your votes that have always carried me to victory.

Now that October 3rd . . . is very close, the end of my term is close also, and for this reason it is time for me to come to manifest my sincere gratitude for the help which you have accorded me and to tell you that I need it again.

I am continuing and will continue to play an integral part in the Uniao Democratica Nacional and to take an active role in our politics with the same interest as ever. I would be an ingrate if I were to abandon my friends in this emergency.

Thanks to my direction and to the stable orientation of the leaders of our party, there has been chosen as candidate for mayor the illustrious citizen, Jose da Silva, who merits our complete confidence and who is capable of directing our destinies. Also as candidate for the Governor of the State is the eminent leader, Juracy Magalhaes, my personal friend, who has rendered such real and necessary services to our county. . . .

On October 3rd, my friends, go out to vote for the candidate of the UDN.

The ability of the local *chefes* to gain the patronage of key members of the state government as illustrated in the foregoing episodes depends, except for a few instances of genuine friendship or kinship, upon the structure of local, state-wide, and national political parties. At the level of the county the task of organizing the electoral campaigns for president, governor, mayor, senator, and deputy falls to the local political leaders. Campaigns for local political offices are conducted simultaneously and in conjunction with these state and national campaigns. Thus in 1950, the UDN's mayoralty campaign in Minas Velhas was closely linked with that of Juracy Magalhaes for governor, while the local PSD worked as much for the gubernatorial candidate, Regis Pacheco, as for the office of mayor. A third political party, the PTB, organized in Minas Velhas for the first time in 1949, campaigned almost exclusively for the presidential cindidate, Getulio Vargas. The PTB had no candidate for mayor and in regard to local offices entered into a halfhearted alliance with the PSD.

Patronage is the binding force in party structure.

The local *chefes* promise votes for the state bosses; the state bosses promise assistance in all matters requiring mediation between the county and the state. State funds for roads, schools, hospitals, health posts, etc., are always more available to those counties whose current leaders are allied politically with the state regime. Such assistance is valuable both to the local regime and to the state-wide organization in terms of perpetuating or increasing popular support. In the administration of funds and materials there is also, of course, the opportunity for direct pecuniary gain. In Minas Velhas, however, these factors have been of secondary importance since the poverty of the county and its small electorate have effectively cut it off from substantial state aid, regardless of which party happens to be in power. But another and perhaps more effective mechanism of patronage has made the link between local and state power a deadly serious fact. Some of the best jobs in the community are contained in the state bureaucratic structure. Table 27 is a list of remunerative positions in the county of Minas Velhas under the control of the state government.

Most of these jobs are in one way or another under the thumb of various central bureaus located in Salvador. The present State Tax Collector, Lucrecio Bomfim, who is an ardent supporter of the UDN, received his post as a direct result of Morais's friendship with Juracy. While laws have since been passed making the appointment and dismissal of the tax officials subject to more rigid processes, powerful arbitrary effects still emanate from the central office. Thus, the result of the 1950 election was that the UDN was victorious locally, while the PSD swept the state. Joao Azevedo, the leader of the local PSD, almost immediately contrived to have the State Tax Clerk, a suporter of Morais, transferred from his post in Minas Velhas to one in a distant county. This move was calculated to bring hardship to the Tax Clerk and his family, who are natives of Minas

TABLE 27. STATE BUREAUCRACY IN MINAS VELHAS

OFFICE	MONTHLY SALARY (IN CRUZEIROS)
Tax Collector	4,000
Tax Clerk	2,400
District Attorney	3,800
Civil Catalogue Clerk	Fees and Costs
Court Clerk	1,150
Notary Public	Fees and Costs
Official of Registrations of Land Sales, etc.	Fees and Costs
Process Servers (2)	650
Porter of courthouse	650
Civil Register Clerk (births, deaths, marriages)	Fees and Costs
Justice of the Peace	Costs and County Bonus
Assistants to the Justice of the Peace (12)	Costs
Official of Registration of Deeds, Mortgages, and Contracts	1,450
Sargento of State Militia	1,450
State troops (2)	800
School Directress	1,400
District Teachers (14)	1,100
Teachers, Minas Velhas (7)	1,100
School Inspector	1,600

Velhas. The Tax Clerk of Vila Nova, who supported the PSD, was to take his place.

Azevedo further contrived to have the directress of the county's schools demoted. This woman is an outspoken partisan of the UDN camp. The question of her ability to run the local school system was not the least at stake. Everyone agreed that she was extremely capable; in fact, the new directress, one of Azevedo's sisters-in-law, burst into tears when she was informed of her appointment. "What am I going to do?" she sobbed to the old directress, "you'll have to help me."

Azevedo went from one bureau to another in Salvador, setting up the political axe for his enemies back home. In rapid succession the police sergeant and the court clerk followed the tax clerk and teacher. More shifts were in prospect when field work terminated. Travel between Minas Velhas and Salvador is at a maximum in the months directly preceding and following elections. At such times there are perhaps a dozen townspeople touring the various government offices in the hope of gaining audiences with actual or potential benefactors.

On the level of the county itself there are also a host of remunerative positions available as spoils. Most of these are included in the table of expenses for the county (Table 25). In addition there are from forty to fifty persons who work for the county during the year on the various construction projects.

Many of these posts are handed out by the victorious local party to the most active partisans. The reader should not be misled by the relatively small sums of money which seem to be involved. The duties of most of these jobs are easily performed in addition to some other regular form of employment. While many of the salaries involved are insufficient to live on alone, in combination with other sources of income they often spell the difference between a marginal and submarginal standard of living for an entire family.

The disposition of spoils is alone capable of generating intense, at times violent, party allegiances. With this power at his command, the local *chefe* has the means by which to surround himself with a core of dedicated partisans. But leadership depends ultimately upon the ability to finance a campaign in a manner acceptable to the state bosses. It is generally agreed that without money and a willingness to part with it, political prominence is impossible. The aspiring local politician must be able to afford frequent trips to Salvador. He must have sufficient time free for other trips into the various districts of the county. He must entertain a steady stream of guests at his house, hold dances, and receive the other candidates of his party when they visit Minas Velhas. Thus, in the 1950 campaign, Azevedo is said to have expended 20,000 cruzeiros out of his own pocket. This money went for printing propaganda, rewarding especially zealous lieutenants, political outings, entertainment, and for buying votes.

The motivation behind men like Morais and Azevedo is essentially that of gaining prestige. From time to time better educated men than either of these two have viewed the mayoralty and local political leadership primarily as a stepping stone to political careers in the state and national government. The former mayor of Vila Nova, for example, is now a state deputy. The same was true of Afonso Soares. Neither Morais nor Azevedo can look forward to such careers. Neither of them has finished primary school, and Morais finds writing tedious and difficult. Azevedo started out as a brass-smith and lacks the polished manners which would mark him as suitable material for an important bureaucratic post in the state government. Both men are outclassed by the really important figures in state politics. When Azevedo is not calling on the big city politicians he can be seen waiting on customers in his wholesale dry goods store in the Cidade Baixa (lower half of Salvador). But in Minas Velhas both men enjoy considerable prestige. In his store in Salvador, Azevedo works in his shirt sleeves; when he is in Minas Velhas, he is never to be seen without a coat and tie in which is set a conspicuous diamond stud.

In the local campaigns there is no question of opposing party platforms or dedication to specific reforms. Personalities are the only visible issues. The contest between the *chefe* and his challenger inevitably assumes the aspect of a struggle for power between two personal enemies. Indeed, before Azevedo made his money, he was an active partisan of Morais's forces. As a young man he had driven Morais through the county in an automobile rented for the campaign in 1934. But as Azevedo's monetary resources multiplied, so did his political ambitions. A personal enmity grew up between Azevedo and his former chief. Morais came to look upon Azevedo as an ingrate while Azevedo thought of

his onetime benefactor as a tyrant. In addition, great
bitterness grew up between Azevedo and certain members of his wife's family, especially that branch of which
the present State Tax Collector, Lucrecio Bomfim, is the
foremost representative. Lucrecio's father and Azevedo
were partners in a lucrative gold buying and selling
business at the time when Azevedo married one of
Lucrecio's cousins. The elder Bomfim was the representative of the Bank of Bahia in Minas Velhas. He
had heavily mortgaged his property to the bank in order
to buy gold. Azevedo thought that he detected a discrepancy in the receipts and abruptly pulled out of the
partnership, terminating the business. Both sides
threatened court actions. Meanwhile, the bank fore-
closed on Bomfim's property and put it up for sale.
Azevedo got all his money together and purchased the
bulk of his former partner's estate. As an additional
bitter pill for the Bomfim family, Azevedo replaced
Bomfim as the agent for the bank—a position which he
held until moving to Salvador, at which time he handed
it over to a political cohort in Vila Nova. Morais naturally supported the Bomfims throughout this altercation.
Lucrecio Bomfim and he were long-standing friends, and
it was Morais who, by using his influence with Juracy,
had secured Lucrecio his job as Tax Collector.

Azevedo's wife's branch of the Bomfim family remained loyal to the PSD. In 1950 one of her cousins
was the PSD's condidate for state deputy, and he and
Azevedo collaborated to the fullest extent. When Lauro
Farani, the gubernatorial candidate, and his entourage
visited Minas Velhas, they dined at Lucrecio's uncle's
house. Lucrecio himself studiously avoided this dinner
as well as the dance which followed.

It is often hard to tell whether people are enemies because they belong to different political parties or
whether they belong to different parties because they are
enemies. Townspeople with specific grievances against
each other seem to identify with the opposite camps.
In this way social snubs and hundreds of interpersonal

and interfamily frictions eventually come to be seen as part of the political struggle.

In 1946 a man beat a dog that had been chasing his pigs. The owner of the dog tried to stab the owner of the pigs. When the principals testified before the police, the incident was explained in the following way:

Question: Before this, was the plaintiff an enemy of the accused?
Answer: Yes.
Question: Was this unfriendliness due simply to their being political adversaries?
Answer: No. They were already enemies a long time ago.

In both camps there are partisans who look upon the opposition as people without honor. This conflict between personal enemies compounded with the struggle for spoils is sufficiently widespread to involve the whole town. The party line bisects the heart of Minas Velhas like an open wound.

Throughout the interior of Bahia, the extent of political partisanship is a constant source of surprise. Passengers on a flight from Salvador to Bom Jesus da Lapa will see an impressive sight as they approach a small mountain town called Macaubas. A plane lands here only once or twice a week, but when it does it has the choice of two separate airfields located on opposite sides of the town. One airport was built by partisans of the UDN and the other by partisans of the PSD. When our field group landed in Macaubas, we had to wait for the mail to be turned over to the pilot. Shortly after the plane landed, a truck full of townspeople drove up amid a swirl of dust. These were the airport's partisans. Fifteen minutes later, a lone figure carrying the mail pouch trudged into view. This was the mail clerk who, unfortunately, was of the opposite party and had to walk. In this same town there are two separate public address systems. Loudspeakers placed on opposite sides of the squares and streets simultaneously blare out propaganda for the respective political parties. One barber cuts only UDN hair, another only PSD hair; one bar wets only UDN throats, another only those of the PSD.

The political schism in Minas Velhas has yet to reach such extremes. There are, after all, but one bar, one loudspeaker system (UDN), and only half of an airport. But there are two barbers, and a lot of people get shaved according to political preference. The store an individual chooses to buy from is very likely to be determined by the owner's political preference. No self-respecting member of the UDN would buy at Azevedo's store. No *Pessedista*, on the other hand, would buy from Lucrecio's Bomfim's sister's store.

The town's police records show a score of incidents in Minas Velhas and other districts of the county which were precipitated by a combination of political zeal and personal antagonism. With a sophisticated appreciation of the power of the police and judicial authorities to settle disputes, most offended individuals seem to prefer to put their grievances in writing rather than engage in personal combat. (A suit and a counter-suit charging slander were recently submitted to the Court Clerk.) One dark night, for instance, a group of UDN partisans were setting off firecrackers near the Clube Social. A *Pessedista* named Luiz, who owns a small store in the Praca do Jardim, happened by and was jeered by the group. They crowded around him and called him a "thief and an ass." He claimed that he was pushed about and insulted right up to the door of his house. In the morning Luiz went to the police with three witnesses from his party and demanded that a criminal action be instituted against two of the men who had molested him. He submitted a written statement as follows:

The assignee, businessman in this city, wishes to bring to this *delegacia* (police station) a charge against Srs. E. J. and C. A., for their having yesterday at 11 o'clock in the night, accosted him in the street with insults and shoving, accompanying him to the very door of his house. There also arose out of these acts serious discomfort to his aged uncle and to his sister, who is with child.

One of the accused answered these charges as follows:

The plaintiff has named as witnesses Srs. F. C., J. C., and M. B., but it is well known that these persons besides being my political adversaries are my personal enemies. At the proper occasion I will argue against them with reference to their moral character. Despite the fact that the plaintiff calls himself a businessman, he is really only the proprietor of a little shack [*vendola*] with a capital of not more than 500 cruzeiros . . . furthermore, he runs a lottery, making the tickets himself, with which he exploits the children of this city . . . besides this, he has a way of exhibiting himself that disgusts me, and it is the general opinion that he is making this complaint because of the instigation of others. This is obviously the case because his petition is written in the hand of F. C., composed without technical ability and with gross errors in Portuguese.

This case, like a dozen similar ones on the records, never got further than the testimony at the police station.

The political schism has some effect on almost every aspect of town life. Even churchgoing has its political facet. The current priest of Minas Velhas, Padre Goncalves, is an ardent *politico*. He was formerly the mayor of a neighboring county. Now in Minas Velhas he is president of the PSD and a member of the town council. Not a few members of the UDN stay away from church on this account. Azevedo was a bitter enemy of Padre Goncalves's predecessor and was instrumental in having him replaced. Many people still remember the feud between the political boss of Minas Velhas early in this century and the man who was priest at that time. During the celebration of *carnaval* in 1916, an effigy of the priest was burned in the main square. It is said that once when the priest was interrupted by the loud talk of his enemy in church, he stepped down from the altar and pronounced a curse to the effect that the other would die of cancer, his fortune be dispersed, and his children grow insane. The struggle between these two figures was largely responsible for the ruin of the town's second church, do Rosario, and the decline of the Negro brotherhood connected with it. The two men sought to oust each other from the committee (*diretoria*) in charge of maintaining the church and managing the brotherhood. When the building began to show signs of decay, the *diretoria* was unable to agree on a course of action for repairing it.

The organization of the Society of the Poor was also to a large extent induced by political ambitions. The president of the newly formed PTB envisioned a working-class electorate taught to read and write in a night school run by the Society. He counted on Getulio Vargas's strong appeal to factory workers and the underprivileged to lend impetus to a third party in Minas Velhas. The night school, however, was poorly attended; it was finally abandoned when the school directress began a night school of her own designed to head off the instruction of possibly hostile voters.

Political campaigns afford the townspeople a great deal of welcome *movimento*. The principal stores serve as informal party headquarters where the men gather in the evening to listen to the news bulletins and campaign speeches on the radio. As the elections draw near, the crowds are larger and politics are discussed from morning to night. The UDN's public address system (owned by Morais's brother) maintains a long broadcasting day consisting of political propaganda interspersed with music. The official campaign songs and jingles are played on records distributed by the party. School children quickly learn the words and march up and down the streets singing them at the top of their lungs. Both parties organize *comicios* (rallies) which take place in the various district towns. Partisans from Minas Velhas are transported to these rallies on rented trucks. On the occasion of the *festa* of the patron saint of Gruta, two trucks carried over a hundred supporters of the UDN to a rally in that town. Candidates from both parties made speeches, printed propaganda was distributed, and hundreds of rockets were set off. The people on the trucks have a good time shouting *vivas* for their party and its candidates. They sing the campaign songs with lusty enthusiasm and do not seem to mind the dust that soon envelops them from head to foot.

In Minas Velhas itself, there are torchlight parades with music supplied by the town band. Dinners are given in honor of the candidates followed by a night of dancing and incessant bombardments of fireworks. The 1950 campaign was especially rich in *movimento* for the townspeople because for the first time in the history of the city both candidates for governor of the state together with extensive entourages made brief personal appearances. These occasions brought the largest number of automobiles ever seen in Minas Velhas. Juracy's caravan in addition brought with it a motion picture projector, and after the speeches one of the few movies ever shown in Minas Velhas was presented on an outdoor screen. In preparation for the arrival of the PSD's gubernatorial candidate, Azevedo dispatched a number of trucks into the district towns and villages accessible by road. Several hundred partisans were collected in this manner, most of them farmers. After the speechmaking on the steps of the church, the politicians and the crowd repaired to the house of Azevedo's sister-in-law, Eloisa Bomfim, where food and drink were served first to the dignitaries and then to the other people. A dance followed. This was the first occasion in twenty years for which Eloisa Bomfim had thrown her house open to the public. Never before were so many *gente da roca* (rustics) permitted into this strictly upper-class setting. A number of townspeople attended the festivities merely to take advantage of the opportunity to see what was inside the Bomfim mansion. The *tabareu,* however, were pretty well confined to one room, and few of them dared to dance with the local girls. Even so, it was rumored the next day that Eloisa Bomfim had been shocked by the low types Azevedo had rounded up from the villages and that she was determined never to undergo a similar ordeal again.

Prior to the elections of 1950, voters from a wide area were required to vote in Minas Velhas. Villagers and townspeople from the other districts came to the county seat by horse, mule, and on foot. All vehicles in the county were requisitioned in order to provide public transport. Election day thus used to be one of the city's brightest and most exciting moments. This procedure was changed for the most recent elections when separate local balloting centers were established throughout the county.

As election day nears, tension mounts between the two camps. Walls and sidewalks are painted during one night with campaign slogans and names only to have them crossed out and replaced with contrary slogans and names the next night. Posters are put up, torn down, put up again. Firecrackers and rockets are set off almost without letup. Sometimes small bombs are thrown onto the roof tiles of houses of particularly active partisans. The house of the school directress received this treatment prior to the last elections. Election eve of 1951 had several tense moments. Larger crowds than usual milled about in the stores and paraded up and down the dark streets. Every man was armed with at least a knife. The public address system, featuring exclusively UDN propaganda, was attacked by unseen members of the PSD—a stone at the end of a string was thrown at the wires—but the damage was quickly repaired. Despite this tension, with everybody armed, drinking *cachaca* and beer, parading up and down in a hostile manner, and making inflammatory speeches, no outbreak of violence occurred.

After the actual balloting, which is usually conducted in a tense, hushed atmosphere, there are still many exciting days to come. First come the victory celebrations when the results are announced—parades, dances, speeches. Then there is the big day when the new mayor takes office. From all over the county the members of the winning party flock to Minas Velhas to be on hand for the inauguration ceremonies in the town hall. On this day the new mayor is expected to provide food and drink to everyone who appears at his house. Sr.

Jose da Silva, the UDN's winner in 1951, played host to a horde of hungry partisans on the day of his inauguration. From early in the morning until late at night a continuous stream of people flowed in and out of his house. No sooner was one spot at the improvised tables vacated than the place was taken by someone else. The mayor's exhausted wife estimated that when it was all over she had served over a thousand people.

The end of balloting does not bring an end to political strife in Minas Velhas. Tension may even increase if, as was the case in 1951, the victorious local party cannot also claim victory in the state-wide elections. When it was announced that the PDS's gubernatorial candidate, Regis Pacheco, had won the governorship of Bahia, many local *Pessedistas* believed that the new UDN mayor would be ousted from his post in short order. After the elections, Azevedo retired to Salvador and persistent rumors followed to the effect that the PSD's candidate for mayor had received a telegram from his sponsor telling him to be ready to take over from Jose da Silva. Azevedo's brother asserted that it was no more than right for the UDN to relinquish its hold on the town hall because a city whose mayor was inimical to the governor of the state could not expect any help from the state government.

Even Jose da Silva's victory celebration was marred by the refusal of the *Pessedistas* to accept his election as final. When the results became official, a general meeting of the UDN's followers took place after dark in front of Morais's house. The town band arrived, lanterns and flares were ignited, and about three hundred people started down the Rua do Clube toward Praca da Grama, shouting, "Viva Artur Morais and Jose da Silva." Accompanied by the usual energetic efforts of the musicians, much shouting, and fireworks, the parade cut across the Praca da Grama and returned toward the Praca do Jardim via the Rua da Pensao. This brought the procession abreast of Azevedo's store where about one hundred *Pessedista* diehards were gathered. The

Pessedistas had fireworks of their own which they now ignited while lustily shouting the name of the new governor. The UDN group broke into its old campaign songs for Juracy and continued on its way while the other group remained on the corner, trying to sing still louder. At the other side of the square where it is joined by the Rua da Ponte the victory parade had to face a second group of *Pessedistas* who likewise assailed them with catcalls, boos, and *vivas* for Regis Pacheco.

The new mayor was waiting on the steps when the parade finally got to his house. The school directress then made a speech in which she named Morais forever the protector and chief of Minas Velhas even if he were no longer to be the actual mayor. Then everybody crowded into the house and a dance began. The party had been underway for less than an hour when a breathless figure pushed its way in from the street and whispered in Morais's ear, "The *Pessedistas* are coming." The word spread, and everyone ran to the windows. Down the street the full force of the *Pessedistas* were chanting the name of Regis Pacheco and marching toward the house. People dashed up and down the steps and milled about the hallway saying that there was going to be trouble. A fight seemed imminent, but the *Pessedistas* were met by some relatively neutral individuals who persuaded them to stop short of Jose da Silva's house and to finish their victory celebration in another part of town.

"These horrors could only be perpetrated by people absolutely void of shame," commented Morais's wife.

"We don't expect them to join us in our *festa*," said the Tax Clerk. "If Azevedo had won, the UDN might not have have followed along in their parade, but we would have at least shown some respect and let them hold their *festa* in peace."

The UDN finished its celebration without further incident, but the atmosphere in Mayor Silva's house was not as joyous as it might have been. While the UDN's victory celebration was considerably more elaborate than

that of the PSD, everyone was well aware that Joao
Azevedo would soon be making his tour of the government bureaus in Salvador.

One of the most serious consequences of political
strife in Minas Velhas has been the paralysis of the Cooperative Mixta, an agricultural cooperative organized
in 1943 for the purpose of aiding its members through
the collective storing and sales of products, and low-cost
loans. Two hundred and fifty people joined this organization, and it functioned long enough to furnish its
members with about 100,000 cruzeiros worth of small
loans. From the outset, however, the cooperative's *diretoria,* an elected body, was unable to agree upon a workable policy for collective buying and selling. The cooperative has in effect never been anything more than a
small bank. With the intensification of political an-
tagonisms prior to the elections of 1946, Azevedo accused certain UDN members of the *diretoria* of faulty
accounting and contrived to have even these banking activities suspended until a state accountant could ex-
amine the books. While this was being done, Azevedo,
followed by some of his partisans, renounced his mem-
bership. From 1946 to 1949 the cooperative functioned
lamely with a new *diretoria,* confining its activities to a
few small loans. In 1949 it again came to a complete
halt when the lawyer who was its most competent ad-
ministrator moved to another county. At the time of
field work the society lacked both a president and a general manager and had suspended all activities. According to the State Tax Clerk, who is the acting secretary,
no effective cooperation can be expected as long as the
organization is administered by an elected body. "The
only way the cooperative can be successful," he says, "is
by paying disinterested technicians to run it. The few
people we have in our midst who are capable of serving
on the *diretoria* are likely to quit after a short time
simply because of political issues."

The school directress's husband, who, like many
others, is waiting for the cooperative to reopen so that

he can cash in his shares, explains the malfunctioning in a similar way: "Here in Minas Velhas this kind of thing will never work. Politics make it impossible for those who join to cooperate in spirit. In fact any measure for the common good is difficult in this city because of politics. Why some of the *Pessedistas* have even stopped going to the Clube since Lucrecio became president." *So far the analysis is pluralist...*

Little of this excitement penetrates to the villages. The lower literacy rate in the rural zone reduces the electorate and keeps the villagers' interest in politics down to a minimum. None of the candidates is likely to make personal appearances where voters are so scarce. The villagers have no radios by which the national campaign can be followed. Most of them are ignorant of the name of the president of the nation as well as that of the governor of the state. Furthermore, nobody's job in the villages will be affected by the outcome of the elections and little in the way of spoils can be expected. In contrast to the townspeople, the overwhelming majority of the villagers are simply indifferent to the entire political process.

Each village has at least one *chefe* of its own who does become involved in politics. Ademar Sabino of Serra do Ouro, for example, is a *Pessedista*. During the last election he tried without success to stir up interest in his village on the basis of a promise reputedly received from Azevedo that if the PSD were to win, within an hour construction would start on a road between Serra do Ouro and Minas Velhas.

The villagers' indifference to politics can be traced to a fundamental difference in attitude toward the government. *O Governo* for the rural farmer is a present menace and not at all a potential benefactor. For the rural farmer, government means one thing—the tax collector. He pays taxes on land, produce, transportation, and irrigation which are swallowed up by some distant maw from which there is no return. These payments are looked upon as a form of arbitrary, meaningless tribute. Civic improvements of the type sponsored in Minas Velhas and the other towns of the county are simply lacking in the villages. Instead of roads there are mere trails; schools operate intermittently or not at all with inadequate buildings and poorly trained teachers. Decades of paying municipal taxes so that the townspeople could have sidewalks, public gardens, jails, and courthouses have left the villagers with a deep distrust of anything that has to do with bureaucracy.

Thus in Serra do Ouro the fieldworker's connection with the state government was found to be a serious handicap in establishing and maintaining contact with informants. In the town the exact opposite was true. Even in a lower-class home the explanation that these strangers represented the state's desire to help improve living conditions was enough to put the average urbanite at ease. This explanation seemed plausible to most people in Minas Velhas except perhaps to some members of the bureaucracy itself, who felt that they were being investigated for political reasons and that their jobs might be in jeopardy. In the villages, despite a concerted effort to portray the state Department of Health and Education as interested solely in helping the people, every attempt to gain information pertaining to basic subsistence was met with dogged resistance. Questions as to the amount of acreage, land use, total product, etc., in particular elicited expressions of great fear and hostility. In the villager's experience these questions were inextricably bound up with the evil machinations of the State Tax Collector, and it was not long before word had spread that the state government, no longer content with its annual tribute, was about to seize the land outright. Other villagers, fearing military conscription, refused to divulge the number of young men in their family. These reactions should be compared with those elicited by the Bubonic Plague Control agent who is refused entrance to the village houses on the grounds that he provides food for the rats. *a very interesting analysis of linkage politics, but no analysis of the local power structure or local decision making...*

RELIGION 6

THE BROADEST and perhaps most significant generaliza-
tion that can be made about religion in Minas Velhas is
that the Catholic Church does not produce an effective
synthesis of the schismatic economic, social, religious,
and political forces which act to reduce dangerously the
esprit de corps of the community. The cohesive inte-
grating influence sometimes exhibited by Catholicism, as
during the Middle Ages or in the contemporary folk cultures of Yucatan,[1] is in almost complete absence. It is
not possible, considering personality structure, social
structure, economics, politics, art, or any other point at
random in the total culture, to work back along a continuous interconnecting system of folkways to a central
religious theme. Furthermore, there are no important
permanent religious groups in Minas Velhas (except, of
course, the Catholic congregation itself.) *Irmandades*
(religious brotherhoods) which under other conditions in
Brazil have been shown to provide one of the principal
frameworks of social organization, exerting strong political influence,[2] are in Minas Velhas senescent and uninfluential. Even the cults of *candomble* which flourish in
the large cities on the coast do not exist here.

RELIGIONS OTHER THAN CATHOLICISM

In addition to Catholicism, spiritualism and Protestant-
ism are also represented in Minas Velhas. Spiritualism,
including such variants as esoterism, magnetism, occultism, and mentalism, is the more important of the two.
Were it not for the fact that its chief mode of propaga-
tion depends upon a more or less strenuous reading effort, it probably would be even more important. The
principal source of the spiritualist literature is the O

[1] Robert Redfield, *The Folk Culture of Yucatan.*
[2] Eduardo Galvao, " The Religion of an Amazon Community "
(Ph.D. thesis, Columbia University, 1952).

Pensamento Publishing Company of Sao Paulo, which mails out a steady stream of catalogues and books to the interior.   Next to school texts and newspapers, these publications constitute the most-read literature in the city.   They are circulated among a small group of disciples who profess varying stages and branches of training.   Of the five men in Minas Velhas who are the most faithful readers, two are storekeepers, two are peddlers, and the other is a student.   Of these five, it is interesting to note, the most serious have been or still are victims of incapacitating diseases (probably syphilis and tuberculosis).   Spiritualism offers the hope of gaining freedom from the malevolent forces which they think are plaguing them.   In addition, spiritualism offers the possibility of bettering their immediate material as well as spiritual welfare.   This is a point to be kept in mind when considering spiritualism as a religion that has to compete with Catholicism.

Also important in this respect is that spiritualism permits the disciple to deal directly with occult forces, a desire which in Catholicism must be satisfied in everybody but the priest by simple prayer.   There is room for but one official priest in Minas Velhas.   This monopoly is absolute and cannot but engender deviations in certain individuals whose personalities incline them to seek a priestly role.   Particularly relevant to this basic tension point in Catholicism is the fact that no women in the community are regular readers of the spiritualist literature.   The adepts are all men who continue to profess their allegiance to Catholicism.   All of them, however, have little use for Catholic rites administered by the priest; they scarcely ever even enter the church and none of them confess.   When the adept is questioned as to how he feels about the fact that the Church forbids the study of spiritualist literature, he is apt to reply that what he is learning already is known to the Church.   Odilon Viana, for example, maintains that the Church is bent upon keeping man ignorant of the powers which God is willing to make available to him.   "The word of Christ says that all men are entitled to learn the ways of God and are entitled to do good works with that knowledge," he says.

All of the disciples claim that their knowledge has given them supernatural powers. Odilon Viana attempts to "dissociate the essential from the manifest." He is thus enabled to know the *Essential* "I am I" for a few moments. During these rare intervals he can read people's thoughts, cure diseases, bring a galloping horse to a dead stop, etc. "If I could maintain this state for longer intervals, I could raise the dead. Christ had this contact with the *Essential* all his life."

Another of the spiritualists claims to be a medium. He is fairly well frequented by people who want to find out whether distant relatives are alive and in good health. Occasionally he obliges by forcing the relative to come back home. None of the services performed, such as reading the future from cards or palms, curing sicknesses, or locating lost objects, are rendered for a fee, probably because competition from the *curandeiros* (folk doctors) is too great. Some sincerity must also be accorded, however, to the assertion that fees would corrupt the purity of the spiritualists and diminish their power.

In recent years several amateur seances have been held by some young people who seem to have learned the practice in Salvador. They put the letters of the alphabet in a circle on top of a table and their fingers on top of a glass in the center. They invoke an "Angel of Light" and are told what they want to know by the moving glass. The real disciples, some of whom have been "studying" for more than fifteen years, look upon these amateurs as profane meddlers and predict bad ends for them all. They regard the *curandeiros* with the same bitterness: "These people are ignorant," one spiritualist declared. "Occasionally, in spite of their interference, a sick person whom they are treating gets better, and they think they have done it. They do not know that God has done all the work."

Protestants are known as *crentes* (believers); they are distinguished in the popular mind by the fact that they are supposed neither to drink nor smoke, must give one tenth of their incomes to their church, are baptized two times, and sing pleasant songs instead of going to mass. In Minas Velhas a Presbyterian sect is represented by a single family of about ten persons, including children, that emigrated a number of years ago from a town called Ponte Novo where the father had been indoctrinated at the American mission located there. This family maintains normal relations with its neighbors and suffers no difficulties in the community at large. Contact with the missionary group is maintained by the receipt of an occasional tract. A small amount of money is solicited when from time to time a pastor appears in Minas Velhas. On his arrival, the missionary holds a meeting in the *crente*'s house. About twenty persons are attracted, mostly out of sheer curiosity. They stand outside and look in at the proceedings through the windows, appreciating the intervals of singing and the words if not the text of the pastor's sermon, since Protestant clerics enjoy a reputation for exceptional fluency in Portuguese. Molestations are rare; the listeners for the most part are distantly respectful.

FORMAL CATHOLICISM

At best, the people of Minas Velhas exhibit but a mediocre concern for the formal aspects of their religion. The priest and the rituals he performs inside the church —confession, communion, mass—are regarded with emotional disinterest. On any given Sunday, the majority of adult townspeople do not attend mass. Church attendance over the period of a year is shown in Table 28.

Considering that twenty days in the year are special feast days, the attendance average for all groups combined—42—is quite low. The figures also reveal a significant difference between the attendance of the various socioeconomic strata, which, of course, is as much a factor in the low score as the failure of the community as a whole to see churchgoing as a vital activity. The two factors go hand in hand nonetheless; if a large part of the middle and lower economic strata stay away from church because of the difficulties of dressing properly, or through lack of leisure time, it is because regular churchgoing is not defined as an absolute necessity.

TABLE 28. CHURCH ATTENDANCE BY SEX AND CLASS PER YEAR

GROUP	AVERAGE, MALE	AVERAGE, FEMALE	COMBINED
Group A^1	59	71	65
Groups A^2–B^1	33	48	42
Group B^2	20	31	27
All Groups	34	47	42

There is also a significant difference between male and female attendance. At a typical novena, the ratio is about four females to one male—about 160 to 40. In religious processions, the ratio is 400 to 200, at communion 60 to 10. Moreover, the males include a higher ratio of children than among the women. At Sunday mass, the majority of the adult males stay near the rear of the church; some are really more outside than in. A few devout men station themselves in the space in front of the women near the altar. The women form a compact body in the center and it is only the women who have prayer chairs, of which there are about 250. About twelve women can be seen with prayer books, but the only male who reads during the services is the priest. The choir is exclusively female.

In Minas Velhas the men expect to see the women in church, and the women do not expect to see the men there—much as it is the women who wash clothes and carry things on their heads and not the men. This difference in roles is perhaps rooted in the symbolic structure of Catholicism. Psychologically, Christ, the central figure in the pantheon, would appear to be of little use to the male in Minas Velhas. He represents qualities which in real behavior the culture classifies in a hundred different ways as effeminate. His ministers are denied the male function. He is the idol of the meek and the poor—groups which simply are not idolized in the urban context where the rich and the powerful and the unmodest inherit the visible earth from generation to generation. Moreover, the story of the Crucifixion, the Western world's great tradition of suffering and redemption, is meaningful to the women in a sense in which it is not equally meaningful to the men. Among the men, even among the economically marginal, a sense of oppression does not exist. As long as he has a wife and children, there is an excellent chance that the male's dominating domestic role more than compensates for whatever oppression he may experience at the hands of others. The women, however, do often exhibit a sense of oppression, and are in fact subject to greater and more frequent duress than their husbands, especially if one considers the prolific rate at which they keep bringing children into the world.

Thus, confession for the male is a thoroughly nonfunctional rite. It is consequently a very rare phenomenon. Most townsmen confess once at first communion, once at marriage, and never in between or thereafter, except perhaps at death. A sense of guilt is a weakly developed trait among the townsmen. The male is permitted a relatively free hand in sex; his socialization is accomplished mostly by the argument that authority has force behind it; where physical punishment cannot reach, there is a strong sense of shame, which if anything, however, destroys rather than produces a useful function for confession, since the ideal model against which he is to measure his behavior consists of masculine motifs, while contrition is meant for women.

The role of the priest further reduces the ability of the menfolk to see the church as the center of their religious life. Rather than invest the priest with an air of holiness, the condition of celibacy only creates an air of suspicion. The men automatically associate duplicity with this requirement, and in many instances in the past their suspicions have been justified. A former priest of Minas Velhas, for example, is widely known as the father of three children—a fact which he made no great effort to conceal. The present priest is notably free from these accusations, but the standard conception is a greater force by far than the immediate example. The issue is greater than the priests who have come and gone in the community; an unfavorable stereotype exists from which it is difficult for the individual priest to escape. The stereotype is a man who is licentious, avaricious, and hypocritical.

A surprising number of stories known and told by the people of Minas Velhas feature a *padre* as the antagonist. These stories seem to be European in origin and attest to the great depth and continuity of the concepts involved. A typical example follows:

Once there was a padre who had a maid named Bibiana who was also his mistress. One day the padre left for a mass in a distant city. He came to a river which was swollen because of the rain and wondered whether he could get across. On the other side he saw a small boy. "Can the river be passed?" he called out. The boy shouted back, "It's easy. My father's mules just crossed over."

The padre urged his horse into the river which swirled up higher than the head of the horse and he was almost drowned. When he finally got to the other side, all wet and out of breath, he told the boy to kneel because he was going to bless him. The boy only laughed and ran away. Presently he returned with his father who offered the padre lunch. After the padre had eaten, he turned to the boy and said, "Tell me how it is that your father's mules cross the river so easily?"

"Come with me and I'll show you," the boy answered. He led the padre to his father's corral and pointed to the flock of ducks inside. "You fool!" the padre shouted, "these aren't mules."

"I know," the boy responded, "but my father isn't a padre and these are the only kind of mules that he can afford."

The padre went back to the boy's father and said, "I have taken a great liking for your boy. If you give your permission I will take him back to the city with me and give him a good education. ("The padre wanted to beat him—that was the 'education' he was thinking of," commented the narrator.) The father consented and the padre took the boy back to the village with him. When they got to his house the padre said that he was going to teach him a few things. He pointed to his cat. "What's this?" he asked the boy.

"It's a cat."

"Wrong," said the padre. "It's 'Papaostra,' " and began to beat the boy heavily. The next day the padre pointed to his maid and asked, "Who's this?"

"Your maid," the boy responded.

"You're wrong," said the padre. "It's Bibiana," and gave him another beating. The next day the padre sent the boy out to look for his mule. "If you're not back by two o'clock, you'll get another beating." The boy went out, found the animal, and returned before two o'clock. The padre pointed to his watch which he had set an hour ahead and said, "You're late," and beat him again.

That night the boy saw the padre and Bibiana making love. He caught the cat, attached a paper balloon to its tail, lit it, threw the cat into the room, and quickly locked the door. The cat jumped on the padre and began to claw him. The padre screamed for help and the townsfolk came running. They found the boy outside the room and asked him what was happening. The boy told them that the padre and Bibiana were making love.

"Steady there, Padre," the boy called out, "in the arms of your Bibiana. There's your Papaostra with a balloon on its tail to light up the way for you."

In another story a priest kills an old man and runs off with his wife. The priest blames the murder on Pedro who is traveling to his home after a long absence. Luckily, however, Pedro has cut out a piece of the priest's cassock while the latter was making love to the woman. Just as the hero is about to be hung, he produces the cloth and matches it with a hole in the priest's garment, proving the latter's guilt.

In another story, a husband discovers that his wife is a frequent hostess to a priest at night. The twist to the story depends on the fact that the priest is not what he is expected to be by the husband and listener. For a change he turns out to be the man's long-lost brother.

In still another story a priest attempts to force himself on a girl. When she refuses, he orders his slaves to kill her and bring him a piece of her heart. The slaves show him a piece of chicken heart instead, and the girl escapes. Later she returns and tells her father what happened. Her father kills the priest.

It will be a rare priest who will not have the edge taken off his enthusiasm by these prejudices. Padre Goncalves, for example, a former priest in Minas Velhas, showed little interest in the spiritual welfare of his parishioners. He had long since passed the stage in which other than pecuniary factors figured strongly in his willingness to administer the layman's spiritual needs. Since the priest's income from the parish of Minas Velhas shares the humble level with which commercial enterprises are generally afflicted in the community, it is not surprising therefore that Padre Goncalves wanted to leave the town. He frequently complained about the injustice of the fate which placed him in one of the poorest parishes in the country. His dream was to be located in Rio de Janeiro, which he found more attractive than the Bahian interior not only from the monetary standpoint but also because of the "greater freedom" which the capital affords. "Everyone does not know everyone else's business there," he used to say. Padre Goncalves was quite familiar with life in Rio de Janeiro. He was a priest for a short time in one of the suburban parishes, and he also served on the police force of that city for eight years prior to taking the cloth.

Padre Goncalves's life, as he used to tell it, was marked by two great misfortunes. The first was his dismissal from the police force in Rio—he had planned to become a chaplain in the army after becoming an officer; and the second was the loss of the parish of Sincora—the county which borders Minas Velhas to the north. The first incident would take us rather far afield, but the second is quite pertinent.

Sincora was a much more satisfactory parish, not only because the income there was considerably higher, but also because Padre Goncalves had managed to become the mayor. (In Minas Velhas he succeeded in being elected to the town council, but his political allegiance was with the minority party.) His loss of the parish of Sincora came about in the following manner: Padre Emanuel, who was in Minas Velhas at the time that Padre Goncalves was still in Sincora, dedicated the picture of a saint in the house of Sr. Azevedo, the present chief of the local PSD. This was at the time when Azevedo was mayor of Minas Velhas. That night Azevedo's wife decided to hold a dance to celebrate the occasion. The dance was held in the room where the picture had been hung. The following Sunday in church Padre Emanuel publicly censured the woman for having profaned a solemn event. Sr. Azevedo considered this a great insult to his wife and began a long series of attempts to force the priest to leave Minas Velhas.

At last a satisfactory pretext arose for direct action. There was an old woman named Maria who was always last to receive communion, waiting until the others had gone before her. One day Padre Emanuel held mass in a nearby village. After everyone who had visibly demonstrated a desire to partake of the communion had been attended, he called out if there was anyone else. Maria, whose devotion had carried her into the rural zone, made her usual belated bid and started to move forward through the crowd. The Padre saw who it was, became exasperated, and instead of waiting for her, turned back to the altar and went on with the service. Maria arrived back in Minas Velhas bitterly complaining that the Padre had denied communion to her. Padre Emanuel called her to his house and told her to correct her manners in church.

Meanwhile, Azevedo kept his eyes open. Maria also

had the habit of kneeling with the men very close to the altar during services. Padre Emanuel warned her several times that he did not like to have a troublemaker like her kneeling so close to him since he had to remain without rancor in his heart in order to give the service properly. Sr. Azevedo was informed of this development and seized the opportunity by telling the woman that she could kneel any place she felt like in the church and that no one could stop her. One morning before mass, Padre Emanuel entered the church and found Maria kneeling in the forbidden spot. The Padre remonstrated, "How many times have I told you that I don't want you kneeling up here." She responded, "Sr. Azevedo told me I can kneel wherever I want." At this the Padre seized her and attempted to force her down the steps. A brief struggle ensued during which the woman's sleeve caught on a chair and was torn. She rushed out of the church and ran straight to Azevedo's house. The latter notified the police and an investigation was commenced with a charge of assault against the Padre. Later it was shown that the woman had suffered no bodily injury. Azevedo refused to let the matter drop, however, and kept after the police to keep the inquiry alive.

At last, exhausted by the continuous persecution, Padre Emanuel went to Caetite and talked the bishop into letting him take over in Sincora—a post which was temporarily vacant since Padre Goncalves had gone off for a visit to Rio de Janeiro. When the latter returned to Bahia, he found himself stuck with the parish of Minas Velhas.

Relations between these two priests were markedly uncordial for a long time. The situation was complicated by the fact that Padre Emanuel began to suffer from a disease of the throat which prevented him from speaking coherently. Padre Goncalves obtained permission to say mass at Sincora for all the important holidays. But the sick priest tried his best to prevent the other from taking over in his stead.

A typical incident in this struggle took place for the *festa* of Coracao de Jesus. Padre Goncalves had made preparations for going to Sincora the day after the *festa* in Minas Velhas. The sedan for which he had telegraphed at a distant city was already on its way to Minas Velhas to pick him up when he received a telegram saying that Padre Emanuel had gone ahead and held the *festa* without his assistance. Padre Goncalves attributed this behavior to the especially lucrative prospect which the *festa* of Coracao de Jesus in Sincora usually entailed. "Now I'm not only going to lose the money from the *festa,* but I'm going to have to pay for the sedan," he lamented. "There's nothing left to do but complain to the bishop again."

The priest's income derives principally from baptisms, marriages, funerals, and special masses. The fees for these services are variable and depend upon the amount of pomp involved and/or the degree of inconvenience to which the priest is subjected.

The fee for an ordinary marriage performed inside the church during the daytime is 70 cruzeiros. Of this sum, 5 cruzeiros belongs to the bishopric and another 5 cruzeiros to the sacristan. If the marriage takes place at night inside the church the cost is 150 cruzeiros—of which 120 cruzeiros is for the priest, 20 cruzeiros for the bishopric, and 10 cruzeiros for the sacristan. If the night marriage takes place inside a private house rather than the church, another 50 cruzeiros must be added for the bishop's dispensation. Marriages between cousins entail a 20 cruzeiros license under all circumstances. On a scheduled visit to the outlying districts—including *festas*—the priest's fee per marriage is the same as for those performed in the city. If, however, he is called to an outlying settlement, the charge may be as high as 300 cruzeiros, depending on the difficulties of transport. Baptisms start at 15 cruzeiros and also vary with distance. For officiating at a *festa* his fee is between 300 cruzeiros and 400 cruzeiros, depending on the resources of the *festeiro* (organizer of a *festa*). Occasionally he may be called to help out the priest in Vila Nova for the same price. The tendency in the villages is to plan marriages and baptisms for the special feast days when the cost of the priest's trip has already been assumed by the *festeiro*. On a patron saint's day he may have as many as one hundred baptisms and twenty marriages waiting for him. It is clear why missing the *festa* in Sincora should have been the source of such impassioned feelings on the part of Padre Goncalves.

Funerals in which the priest accompanies the corpse to the cemetery vary from 50 cruzeiros to 200 cruzeiros, depending on the number of times the procession stops on the way and the number of prayers recited. Other burial fees belong to the church itself, are used for the maintenance of the burial grounds and other church property, and do not form part of the priest's income. The base rate is 20 cruzeiros, which reserves a final resting place for a maximum of four years. After this period the bones may be disturbed. Fifty cruzeiros rents an above-ground crypt for the same period. A permanent site may be bought for 500 cruzeiros.

Special masses are bought as *promessas* (in fulfillment of a vow) or as memorials to deceased relatives on both the seventh day and the first month after death and on each subsequent anniversary of the death. Masses are available in a varied price line. The basic rate is 20 cruzeiros for a basic performance at 7:00 A.M. To this may be added, if desired, 10 cruzeiros for ringing the bells, 10 cruzeiros for burning incense, 10 cruzeiros for using a black cloth, 10 cruzeiros for a special *encommendacao* (prayer), etc. Time is also a commodity since the priest gets hungrier as the morning progresses. Hence the basic fee advances with the hour. At 8:00 A.M. it is 30 cruzeiros; at nine, 40 cruzeiros; at ten, 50 cruzeiros; at eleven, 100 cruzeiros. It is possible if the hour is sufficiently advanced, enough bells rung, incense burned, and prayers read, for a special mass to cost as much as 300 cruzeiros.

In the memory of the community, however, it is unknown for a priest to confine himself to an income derived exclusively from religious functions. Some sold religious pictures, others were rich landholders, almost all of them were important financiers for the local gold miners. Throughout the old mining region, priests are associated with real and legendary mining activities. The priest, while not the richest man in the community, enjoys one of the highest regular cash incomes, and cash is the *sine qua non* of serious mining. Padre Goncalves used to be active if not successful in this line. He invested 6,000 cruzeiros in a river pool into which the water always managed to flow back faster than it could be thrown out. This ill-fated speculation, incidentally, did not help to increase Padre Goncalves's susceptibility to the charms of Minas Velhas.

It is not strange, therefore, that the men of Minas Velhas do not place much importance upon having their sins absolved by the priest. They do not feel sinful and the priest is scarcely the person who can convince them that they should. The situation may be summed up by the words of Sr. Paulo whose attitude is thoroughly typical. The last time Paulo confessed was in preparation for his marriage eighteen years ago. "The *padre* asked me how many women I had slept with. I told him, 'Excuse me, I can't tell you. I've traveled a great deal.'" Asked why he had never confessed since, he replied, "Why should he know the secrets of my life. I don't know his."

In keeping with the weak role of official Catholic dogma, the concepts of heaven and hell are not vital issues to the average townsman. The threat and promise of otherworldly rewards make little impression upon the sophisticated, materialistic urbanites. Some of the perfunctory performance of church ritual is undoubtedly maintained, especially among the men, by force of this dogma. In most instances, however, the threat is too ironic, and the promise too remote, to really make an impression on anybody. Eunice, a townswoman deserted by her husband and left alone to bring up six small children by working in a leather shop, expressed the viewpoint typical of many of the inhabitants of Minas Velhas: "I am not afraid of hell," she said, "because I am in it right here and now. I don't believe there is any place where you suffer more than you do on earth."

The ascetic spirit does not exist in Minas Velhas, except among a few individuals—mostly women—who are considered to be fanatics and a little queer. But Catholicism has more to offer than otherworldly heavens and hells. The townspeople are only mildly concerned about the spiritual future, but the material present is of vital interest to all. Hence, wherever Catholicism brings its promise to the present, therein is to be found its greatest affective force in both town and country.

INFORMAL CATHOLICISM

The principal agency available to the villagers and townsmen by which a religiously mediated influence may be brought to bear upon the immediate material world is individual prayer. The belief that events may so be influenced is held by most townspeople and all villagers. Miracles are accepted by the villagers as not only possible but also as relatively frequent; the townsmen regard them as possible but rare. It is this accessibility of supernatural assistance which marks the vital core of Catholicism in Minas Velhas.

The efficacy of prayer depends upon the devotion and faith of the suppliant. It is the general tacit assumption of both townsmen and villagers that the efficacy of prayer does not depend upon a pure moral condition or upon formal religiosity. Anyone who has good reason to be heard and who manifests enough devotion may be successful. In the villages and to a lesser extent in the town, this devotion usually exists as a long-established relationship with a saint, i.e., the deity most likely to be appealed to is the individual's patron saint. This relationship is marked by pictures or images representing the saint which the suppliant keeps in his house; by the observance of the saint's day as a holiday, on which he does not work, has paid for a novena, and perhaps sets off some skyrockets; and possibly by the name of the saint which he has been given by his parents and which he, in turn, will pass on to his offspring: In the villages, much more than in the town, it is an intimate, straightforward relationship practically without formalized ritual. As many people express it, the images and the pictures are the saint; the saint is present in the house, always there with them. In sickness, economic crisis, and danger, the aid of one or more of these *santos de devocao* is invoked. In extremely critical situations this usually takes the form of a *promessa*.

A man whose wife is sick, for example, prays to his favorite saint: "Misericordia. Hear a humble voice. Grant my wife health and I will set off a half-dozen skyrockets in front of the main door of the church on your day." If the wish is granted, the man carries out his promise. This is the basic type of *promessa*—a prayer which contains a bribe in the form of a promise to express devotion and gratitude if the prayer's wish is granted. The suppliant may promise to give a novena, set off fireworks, carry the *bandeira* (saint's standard) to take up collections, give money to charity, or make a trip to a shrine. If the last is to be in thanks for the curing of an illness, the pilgrim frequently makes or has made a waxen figure representing the part of the body which was cured.

In addition to this traditional type of *promessa,* there are two other kinds of procedures in Minas Velhas and the villages which are also called *promessas*. These involve: (1) the execution of the promise before the fulfillment of the prayer, and (2) the execution of a reward for the beneficent behavior of a saint which was not specifically solicited.

Here are two examples:

Several years ago, a poor townsman was accused of breaking into his neighbor's house and stealing some money. He prayed to Bom Jesus da Lapa and promised that if he were shown to be innocent, he would walk to the city of Bom Jesus da Lapa with a pot of water on his head from which neither he nor anyone else would drink. He made the trip and several months after his return to Minas Velhas the real thief is said to have confessed.

During a thunderstorm the roof tiles crashed down into the room where a brass-smith's children were sleeping. When the debris was pulled off the bed, the children were found to be unhurt; one of them, in fact, was still sleeping. The father decided that a miracle had been performed by his patron saint, Bom Jesus. He had a photograph taken of the children in the ruined bedroom and said he was going to leave it at the shrine of Bom Jesus.

While no reliable statistical count of the relative frequency of appeal to patron saints among villagers as compared to the number of appeals by townspeople can be offered here, it was the writer's impression that the relationship between patron and suppliants increased in emotional intensity as one moved away from the "elite," down to the town's lower socioeconomic stratum and out to the villages. Conversely, as one moves away from the villages and toward the town's "elite," formal church attendance was found to increase. Thus the average number of visits to church among 170 adult villagers was 32.3 times per year, whereas the average number of visits for the townspeople was 42 per year. The home cult of the saints, in other words, may be regarded as strongest where formal churchgoing is weakest.

As Table 29 shows, a great many different saints are represented in the home cults of Minas Velhas. Generally speaking, children adopt the patron saints of their parents, especially if the transmission of a name is involved. Pictures and images, also inherited, tend to maintain uniformity in the family line. The system, however, is only partially hereditary since there is considerable room for pragmatic innovation. Donna Clara,

TABLE 29. HOUSEHOLD PATRONS

PATRON SAINTS	HOUSEHOLDS	PERCENT
Bom Jesus da Lapa	25	26
Santissimo Sacramento	12	12
Senhor de Bonfim	6	6
No. Sra. das Gracas	6	6
Sao Jose	5	5
No. Sra. da Conceicao	5	5
No. Sra. do Perpetuo Socorro	3	3
Sao Benedito	3	3
Senhora Santana	3	3
Seo Joao Batista	3	3
Santo Antonio	2	2
No. Sra. do Livramento	2	2
Coracao de Jesus	2	2
Divino Espírito Santo	2	2
Todos os Santos	2	2
Anjo da Guarda	2	2
Santa Marta	1	1.1
Coracao de Maria	1	1.1
Santa Rita de Cassia	1	1.1
No. Sra. do Rosario	1	1.1
Sao Sebastiao	1	1.1
Sao Cosme e Sao Damiao	1	1.1
Menino Jesus	1	1.1
N. S. Jesus Cristo	1	1.1
Sta. Tereshina do M. Jesus	1	1.1
Sao Francisco de Assis	1	1.1
Santa Luzia	1	1.1
No. Sra. do Garmo	1	1.1
Sao Pedro	1	1.1
Santa Helena	1	1.1
Total	97	100

for example, prayed to St. Benedict to cure her sick child, but without result. A friend of hers suggested that she try St. Joseph. This time her prayers were answered; now St. Joseph belongs to Donna Clara's pantheon and she is now trying to exchange the picture of St. Benedict with someone who has a picture of St. Joseph.

Most of the houses in Minas Velhas have at least one holy picture on their walls. In the display of these pictures, especially in town, it is usually the case that two other factors in addition to that of devotion are present: one decorative, and the other fetishistic. The decorative element is clearly shown in those houses where the pictures take their places in arrangement with advertising posters for headache powders, family potographs, calendars, pictures of bathing girls from magazines, and other pictorial elements that are judged to produce an aesthetically enhancing effect upon the bare walls. At the same time, the saints' pictures are felt to have magical powers against evil, much as the cross worn around the neck is at once both decorative and protective.

Table 29 reveals the high degree of individuality and specialization which we have grown accustomed to expect of Minas Velhas. The fact that Bom Jesus da Lapa has fully twice as many devotees as Santissimo Sacramento, the city's official patron, helps to demonstrate the low level of participation from which most formal aspects of Catholicism suffer.

In Minas Velhas the *festa* of Santissimo Sacramento is one of the least frequented of all, despite the fact that it is organized by a commission appointed by the priest and also receives monetary assistance from municipal funds. Very few persons are attracted from outside the city; the auction is less animated and shorter than the *festa* of the Divino Espirito Santo which precedes it by two weeks. The *festa* of Santissimo Sacramento is referred to as the *festa da igreja* (*festa* of the Church), whereas that of Divino Espirito Santo is referred to as the *festa do povo* (*festa* of the people).

The failure of the majority of townspeople to identify their own personal protector with the official protector or guardian spirit of the town may be considered as another instance of the failure of the individual to identify his own personal well-being with the fate of the community as a whole.

Bom Jesus and the pilgrimage to the shrine at Lapa,

about two hundred miles from Minas Velhas on the banks of the Sao Francisco River, loom large in the religious and economic life of the community, as well as that of the region, and the phenomenon deserves special mention. An intricate complex of motives is responsible for the movement. From ten to fifteen persons from Minas Velhas make the trip to Lapa each year. Most of the town pilgrims now go by truck. Many pilgrims from the rural areas go by animal or walk. From Minas Velhas, the majority of pilgrims are peddlers who are commercially interested in the fair; there are also one or two townsmen who have *promessas* to perform, or who simply want to pray at the shrine; and lastly, there are always one or two persons who go along simply to see the sights. A townsman who was planning to make the trip explained his motivation: "My father was there. My son has been there, too. I have heard about Lapa all my life, and so I want very much to see what it is like."

Despite the hardships involved in crossing the state to the Sao Francisco River, the truck ride to Bom Jesus is considered the pleasure high point of the year. If the trip is negotiated without a breakdown, Bom Jesus da Lapa is two full days by truck from Vila Nova across a zone which in July and August (the day of the *festa* is August 6, but the movements begin in July) is a veritable inferno of heat and dust. The pilgrims crowd in, men, women, and children, forty-five to fifty on top of wooden benches, and are burned by the sun, pounded by the truck, and choked by the dust for hour after hour without mercy. Lapa itself is hot and dusty and filled with noise and confusion; the pilgrims must pay 200 cruzeiros just for a room—meals, water, and showers are extra during the peak week. And yet when the pilgrim and peddlers get back to Minas Velhas, hungry, dirty, and near exhaustion from lack of sleep, they have always had a wonderful time. "There was a great deal of *movimento* there," they report, and those who stayed behind wish they could have gone.

Bad as the truck ride is, walking is infinitely worse. Within the last ten years no townsman has walked to Lapa, although most of the peddlers still go by mule. Every year, however, hundreds of pilgrims from the rural areas of the county walk all the way. They trudge slowly into Minas Velhas and stop briefly in the market place to light a fire and cook some food before resuming their ordeal. Women with suckling babies are no rarity. Most of the townspeople regard these walking pilgrims with a good deal of scorn. A brass-smith who stood watching one group of returning pilgrims that had taken fifteen days to walk from the shrine expressed a more or less representative urban opinion: "They look very poor, but I bet they left a conto (1,000 cruzeiros) at Lapa. Poor fools! When they get to heaven, their heads will get in but their behinds will stick out."

RELIGIOUS FESTIVALS

The religious *festas* of Minas Velhas vary in scale and content, according to the traditional importance attached to the given day and according to the zeal and the financial resources of the person or persons responsible for their organization. A *festa* is judged good or bad depending on the quantity of fireworks set off, the amount of music heard, the number of people who come to the city from the country and neighboring towns, the quantity of free alcohol dispensed, and the general intensity of the *movimento* generated by all these factors in combination. The expressed understanding is that the greater the noise and excitement, the more the saint is honored. For most people the *movimento* is more important as an end in itself than is the homage thereby rendered.

Most *festas*, notably those of Sao Sebastiao, Divino Espirito Santo, Sao Benedito, Nosso Senhora do Rosario, and Senhora Santana, depend for their celebration upon an individual—the *festeiro*—chosen by lot annually after the mass on the saint's day (many, however, lapse for years because of the absence of the designated individual). For all *festas* except the Divino Espirito Santo, Coracao de Jesus, and Corpus Christi, any individual, who because of a *promessa* seeks to become the *festeiro,* is granted his desire and the process of choosing by luck among a list of volunteers is waived.

The *festa* of the Divino Espirito Santo is maintained by a fixed list of volunteers known as *Juizes, Mordomos, Mordomos da Capa,* and *Mordomos da Vara* with an obligation of contributing five, ten, twenty, and twenty-five cruzeiros respectively toward the expenses of the *festeiro.* Here the festeiro can be chosen only from their ranks; no special devotions are sufficient to waive the process of chance selection. Each year the names on the fixed list are sorted by luck so that some of last year's *Juizes* may become *Mordomos* this year. Names may be dropped or added to the list at the recommendation of the *festeiro* and the approval of the priest. The list at present has about 160 names, all of which are eligible to be chosen *festeiro.* Many of the names are those of low income individuals who ordinarily would find it impossible to give a *festa.* Because of its broad appeal to the middle and lower classes, the *festa* of Divino Espirito usually shows a profit. Contributions from the people are exceptionally liberal because of the tradition that it is the *festa do povo.*

The *festas* of Coracao de Jesus and Corpus Christi are given by the brotherhood of Coracao de Jesus and by the brotherhood of Santissimo Sacramento, respectively. The *festeiro* is chosen by lot from among the ranks of the members. The *festa* of Corpus Christi has no *festeiro.* The priest, as president of the brotherhood, appoints a commission which is responsible for its organization. This procedure, excluding individual initiative and creating the impression of an aristocratic church function, accounts for the comparative lack of enthusiasm exhibited by the bulk of the population, despite the fact that it is the *festa* of the city's official patron, Santissimo Sacramento.

Despite the latter-day omission of several traditional

features, Minas Velhas's *festas* continue an ancient pattern, consisting typically of seven distinct elements which occur in the following sequence: (1) *Saida da Bandeira,* (2) Novena, (3) Auction, (4) Mass, (5) Procession, (6) Blessing, and (7) *Entrega da Bandeira.*

(1) *Saida da Bandeira* (Emergence of the Saint's Standard): Nine days before the saint's day a group of men sometimes committed by a *promessa* and sometimes hired on a percentage basis leaves the city and begins a tour of the principal rural areas, taking up a house-to-house collection which will be applied toward the expenses of the coming *festa.* They carry with them a small facsimile of the saint's flag. A particularly ambitious *festeiro* may have the group leave two weeks to a month before the *festa* and carry on the solicitation of funds in every corner of the county, and occasionally even travel into the neighboring counties. The Sunday before the *festa* the group returns to the city and the official *saida* takes place. For the canvas in the city, the *festeiro* always accompanies the standard, though if he is anxious enough about the fund raising there is nothing to stop him from accompanying the rural canvas as well. The town band calls for the *festeiro* at his house; the group that emerges—the *festeiro,* the *porta-estandarte* who carries the *bandeira* (the real one this time that has been kept in the *festeiro's* house throughout the year), one or two girls who receive the donations, and sometimes a secretary who records the receipts—marches through the town with the band playing and begins the house-to-house canvas. All the houses are visited except those in Mud Alley, which, despite their being no more than thirty yards from the next street, get their chance to honor the saint's standard later on with the rural zone, when there are no women in the group.

(2) *Novena:* An atmosphere of expectation is gradually built up by the novenas, which are better frequented as the day of the *festa* approaches—almost exclusively, however, by women. The *novenarios* are

chosen by lot like the *festeiro* at the preceding year's mass, and sometimes go to considerable expense to provide illumination and decoration for the church and also for fireworks which are released in quantity after each night's services.

(3) *Auction:* After the last novena which is the eve of the saint's day, a long table is set up outside the church on the front apron and it is soon heavily laden with fruits, sweets, roast pork, stuffed chicken, wine, cakes, etc. These articles are in part donated by the people and in part furnished by the *festeiro* himself. The auctioneer (*leiloeiro* or *gritador*) is contracted by the *festeiro* and is destined to receive a 20 percent commission on total sales so that he goes about his business slowly and with great tenacity. The town band seats itself on improvised benches, and its members work diligently throughout the night to provide as noisy a background to the scene as possible. The auctioneer slowly circles through the crowd with the item to be sold in his hands, which he thrusts insinuatingly at the faces of those who feign disinterest. The small space in front of the church extending to the limit of the lamplight is given over to a tightly packed crowd of young people who divert themselves by walking up and down in such a way as repeatedly to cross each other's paths with collisions and noisy encounters. From time to time the church bell, accompanied by the indispensable and incessant bombardment of firecrackers and rockets, adds its voice to the confusion, celebrating bids which have risen out of proportion to the normal value of the item concerned.

The bidding for the most part is frugal, though there is the constant expectation among the crowd around the table that a competition between two committed parties may take place. Mild forms of competitive situations are sometimes produced artificially such as happens when one individual "offers" another the article he has won and the other has to reciprocate with an article that ought to have equal or greater value, or a group of men will secretly agree to contribute toward a fixed bid which is thereafter used in an attempt to force individual bidders up to extremes. These impromptu syndicates are common among the young men of the lower socioeconomic strata who thereby gain an opportunity to be heard bidding impressive sums at little cost to themselves.

For the most part, the auction simply provides an opportunity to display economic rank. The amount of money bid corresponds to the relative financial capacity of the bidder so that under ordinary circumstances, when a bidder of the middle group is outbid by an individual of the upper, no loss of prestige is involved, since the high bidder has merely confirmed his known social position. In situations where the bidders are of the same class or where the status of one is in doubt and where their simultaneous desire is motivated by anything greater than whim or fancy—be it a desire that has been expressed by a friend, a relative, or more disastrously, a fiancée—the competition is likely to become intense. Take, for example, a much talked-about case involving a young mulatto teacher who remained only marginal to the upper class and who was engaged to marry a white girl. The auctioneer held up a single rose; the man began to bid. It was obvious at once that he was going to present the flower to his fiancée. Another man, white and definitely of the upper class, began to bid against him. The bidding rose by leaps and bounds until the teacher, thinking ahead, as he afterward expressed it, that he would spend every cent he would make that year if necessary, jumped the bid from 100 cruzeiros to 400 cruzeiros. This gesture of defiance made the auctioneer's eyes bulge and the crowd hold its breath. The contender made no response, and the teacher emerged victorious at the cost of a month's salary. The man who had bid against him could afford to let reason prevail over pride; the man of lower rank could not and would have gone on until he had placed himself in debt. The keen interest accorded the auction depends upon the ever imminent possibility that a man who has social pretensions is likely to be challenged and put on trial.

It is usually well past midnight when the last article goes under the hammer and the *filarmonica* is free to march to the bar and take some much needed refreshment, in preparation for the morrow's activities.

(4) *The Mass:* The mass on the saint's day is the religious climax of the *festa*. There are usually two, one at eight o'clock for communion and another at ten o'clock. The latter is the better frequented. The band crowds into the balcony where there is also a female choral group, and the well-filled church reverberates with loud and frequent music. Outside, loud tolling of the bell and formidable barrages of fireworks punctuate all the important points in the ritual. As an added feature, the priest delivers a sermon which in its meandering course touches on a great many subjects, from the danger of Communism to the necessity of going to church more often, including along the way mention of the glories of the saint whose day is being celebrated. Afterward, the names of next year's *festeiro* and *novenarios* are pulled from an urn and publicly proclaimed. As the congregation leaves the church they are met with such a terrific barrage of fireworks that they are forced to seek shelter by hugging the walls of the building.

(5) *The Procession:* During the day the image of the saint has been displayed in front of the altar, strewn with flowers, and in one case—Santissimo Sacramento—attended by a two-man guard of honor. At about four o'clock the image is placed on a stretcher-like platform (*andor*), shouldered by four persons, usually including the *festeiro* and *novenarios,* and carried outside. Two long files are formed, starting in front with school children, followed by women, and brought up in the rear by the men. At the very end is the town band, slightly in front is the standard, and immediately ahead of that is the image, flanked by children dressed as angels. The priest takes his place about halfway up between the men's files. At the very head of the procession go three

boys in red robes carrying silver lanterns. As the bell tolls and the band plays, the procession, representing about two fifths of the city's population (between 550 and 750 men, women, and children including, however, persons from the rural zone), starts off on a slow march through the principal streets. The long file of silent marchers casts a slowly moving centipede-like shadow across the square. This solemn scene represents the most thoroughly collective act known to the community.

(6) *The Blessing:* The procession completes its circuit and returns to the church; the image is brought up between the waiting files amid loud applause, *vivas,* and fireworks, and placed once more before the altar. Usually at this point a second priest, brought in perhaps from Vila Nova, delivers another sermon. The visiting priest never fails to eulogize the congregation in the name of the glorious tradition of gentility and piety for which it is renowned throughout the area. The congregation kneels, the blessing is administered; afterward the standard is taken out of the church and carried back once more to the house of the *festeiro.*

(7) *Entrega da Bandeira* (Retirement of the Standard): The new *festeiro* meanwhile has spent the time ever since his name was called out during the morning's mass in feverish activity finding extra chairs, glasses, and lanterns, and buying food and drink in preparation for the crowd which will descend upon his house in the evening. At about eight o'clock the *filarmonica* is heard once more in the streets moving swiftly toward the circle of lights which mark the old *festeiro's* house. In a moment the old *festeiro* emerges with the flag, lanterns appear, and the tireless musicians start off for the house of the new *festeiro.* More lanterns and more people join the crowd which rolls like a disorderly wave toward the house of the new *festeiro.* At the door the people stop and crowd around; the priest raises his hand for silence (he does not get it), and makes a speech thanking the old *festeiro* and all the people for the fine celebration that has taken place. The old *festeiro* steps forward

and hands the flag to the new *festeiro* who also makes a speech, vowing to guard the flag throughout the year with love and devotion, and promising to give as good a *festa* next year as this one was. Everybody who can swarms into the house, including the members of the *filarmonica;* wine is served, and later, coffee and cakes.

When it is all over, the *festeiro* has laid out a sum which varies between 2,900 cruzeiros (approximately $97 U.S.) at the minimum, and 6,800 cruzeiros (approximately $223 U.S.) at the maximum. A breakdown of minimum and maximum expenses per item is shown in Table 30.

TABLE 30. MINIMUM AND MAXIMUM EXPENSES
FOR A TYPICAL FESTA

ITEM	MINIMUM (CR.$)	MAXIMUM (CR.$)
Fireworks: including greater quantity, more elaborate colors, picture of saint	300	1,500
Priest: extra *padres,* including cost of transport	300	1,500
Music: more *passeiatas,* more playing, necessitating frequent replacement of musicians	700	1,200
Illumination: more candles in church	300	500
Flowers (artificial): more flowers, particularly for the *andor*	400	600
Sacristan: (labor for decorating church and lighting candles)	150	150
Auction: articles to be sold	200	300
Cachaca and wine to be dispensed to visitors to the *festeiro's* house	150	200
Lunch for the musicians on the saint's day	100	200
Decorations, streamers, masts	100	200
Games and diversions (all or some of the following: *Bumba meu boi, Quebra pote, Pao de sebo, cavalhada, marujeda*)	200	500
Total	2,900	6,850

The *festeiro* meets these expenses from the sources listed in Table 31. By cutting all expenses to the minimum and by exploiting the receipts to the utmost, it is quite feasible for the *festeiro* to make a profit of from one to two thousand cruzeiros. Theoretically any such profit ought to be handed over to the church to become part of its operating funds (*patrimonio*). There are many well-known instances where the *festeiro* has publicly proclaimed a loss, but where it was quite obvious that the contrary was the case. From time to time a *festeiro* appears who is determined to have a good *festa* despite the risk of losing money. The rule, however, is that the *festeiro* tries to break even. There is no established pattern of using the *festa* as a vehicle for the honorific consumption of wealth. The *festeiro* proceeds for the most part with a liberality commensurate with his real economic status.

TABLE 31. SOURCES OF INCOME FOR A TYPICAL FESTA

SOURCE	MINIMUM (CR.$)	MAXIMUM (CR.$)
Saida da bandeira (rural zone and other cities)	800	1,500
Saida da bandeira (Minas Velhas)	1,200	1,500
Auction (discounting percentage of auctioneer and cost of goods to *festeiro*)	900	1,500
Total	2,900	4,500

In the villages there is but one important religious event, the *festa* of the local patron. Village *festas* present many features not found in the city. Baixa do Gamba, for the *festa* of Sao Sebastiao, the village patron, begins preparations long in advance. The small adobe church is cleaned and repaired; the area surrounding it is cleared of brush; many persons repair and freshly whitewash their homes in expectation of visitors. The *festeiro* begins to stock up on food and *cachaca* since it will be his obligation to provide food and drink for many of the hundreds of persons who are due to arrive. The novenas are held without the benefit of the priest but are well frequented by the women, who seat themselves on the floor on top of grass mats. The men gather outside in the darkness where they build a fire, talk, and listen to the women singing. About a week before the *festa* the construction of small temporary three-walled huts of interlaced boughs is begun in the clearing surrounding the church. These will serve as stalls where food and drink will be sold. Four or five days later, the *festeiro* moves from his house to one near the church. In the past this house was unused throughout the rest of the year but recently it began also to serve as the village schoolhouse. The *festeiro*'s house is cleaned, repaired, and ornamented; during the week it is the scene of several impromptu dances with music provided by a couple of guitars and a tambourine. On the day before the *festa* an ox is slaughtered to provide meat for the influx of people from the surrounding area which begins in the evening. The stalls open up for business, and the quantity of *cachaca* consumed by men, women, and children down to unweaned babies rapidly rises to the exceptionally high level at which it is maintained until the end of the *festa*.

The village auction commonly sees both bidders and auctioneer quite drunk; in contrast to the town auctions, every bid is hotly contested and there are frequent remarks to the effect, "I will have to sell a cow," or, "I will have to sell some land," in order to make good on the bids—statements which in many cases are likely to be the truth. In the villages, it is five or six o'clock in the morning before the auction is over, while in town the auction rarely lingers on much beyond 1:00 A.M.

The day of the mass finds a tall pole erected in front of the church. On top of this mast there is a wooden sign bearing the name of the patron saint and the year of the *festa*. The pole is greased, and while the crowd waits outside for the priest to arrive from Minas Velhas it is entertained by small boys who try to climb up to the top and twirl the sign. The priest usually arrives tired and hungry from his trip and is likely, before holding mass, to chastise the assembled congregation for their having built the stalls that sell *cachaca* too close to the walls of the church and for failing to maintain proper silence within God's house. After the mass the priest performs the accumulated baptisms and marriages and hastily departs.

A dance begins in the *festeiro*'s house; after the *entrega da bandeira,* it is resumed in the house of the new *festeiro* and is apt to continue all that day, that night, the next day, and the next night, slowly losing intensity as fatigue, the depletion of the supply of *cachaca,* and the departure of visitors make themselves felt.

The *festeiro* of Baixa do Gamba is not chosen by lot. The dance which takes place in his house after the mass requires a supply of *cachaca* that can only be accumulated during a long period of saving. No one in Baixa do Gamba is expected to have enough cash on hand to buy the customary quantity at a moment's notice; however, in contrast to the town, the village *festeiro* does not expect to make up his expenses from solicited donations. Hence, about six months before the *festa,* the old *festeiro* chooses from among a group of volunteers the man who is to be his successor. The priest has tried, rather ineffectually, to change the manner in which the holiday is celebrated, especially with reference to the emphasis on drink. Recently he tried to appoint the new schoolteacher, a devout old lady from Minas Velhas, as *festeira.* The man who had been chosen by the regular process protested the usurpation bitterly, claiming that he had already gone to considerable expense to prepare for the *entrega da bandeira.* The priest was not impressed: "Bring what you have bought to my house, and I will refund what it has cost." The aspiring *festeiro* could not very well accept the offer since his principal expense had been for alcoholic beverages. He continued to protest, however, and the priest finally gave up the idea of a schoolteacher *festeira,* threatening not to return the following year if the people did not change their habits.

It must be remembered that by far the most important *festa* in the yearly round of the townspeople is Carnival. This holiday is not only absolutely secular but, in a sense, anti-religious as well.

Since official Catholic policy is opposed to the celebration of Carnival, during the three days of gaiety, parades, and dancing the priest feels obliged to absent himself from the town. The priest spends the holiday in a neighboring county where he does not have to witness the disobedience of his flock. In Minas Velhas, Carnival is the longest and most eagerly awaited *festa* of the year. In total, more money, time, and effort is spent in preparing costumes, buying perfume sprays and decorations, and learning songs than for any other occasion. It will be recalled that Carnival is the most critical time of the year for interclass tensions and that the rallying point of the founders of the Sociedade dos Pobres was the issue of exclusion from the Clube's masquerade balls. In contrast to the town, the villages do not celebrate Carnival. A handful of country people make the journey to town, but most of the villagers spend the three days working in the fields.

RELIGIOUS BROTHERHOODS

There are two extant religious brotherhoods in Minas Velhas: the Irmandade do Santissimo Sacramento and the Irmandade do Sagrado Coracao de Jesus. The former is composed of about two hundred members, all male. Its organization, on paper at least, is elaborate. There is a board of directors (*diretoria*) consisting of chairman (*Provedores*), treasurer (*Tesoureiros*), secretary (*Secretarios*), and twelve other members. The by-laws call for monthly meetings in the church, but these never take place. The real direction of both brotherhoods it assumed by the priest, but there is nothing much to direct. Each member contributes five cruzeiros per year, producing a balance that is insufficient to meet the expense of the *festa* which is the *irmandade*'s chief living function. Every Thursday there is a mass dedicated to Santissimo Sacramento, and it is the obligation of all the brothers to attend. Less than ten of them, however, can be expected to appear.

The Irmandade do Coracao de Jesus consists of about 240 women and 60 men. Its *diretoria,* similar in organization to the other, is exclusively female and similarly enjoys but token functions. The annual dues are two cruzeiros. New members receive a red ribbon with a silken heart in the middle which some of them wear around their necks for important religious events. The chief function of this *irmandade,* like the other, is the organization of a *festa.* There is also a special mass the first Friday of every month, which, because of the preponderance of women, is better attended than that of Santissimo Sacramento.

In former times three other *irmandades* used to exist which are now extinct. These were the Irmandade do Rosario (1800–1920), Irmandade das Almas (1920–40), and Irmandade de Santana (1800–1885). It is more probable, however, that there never were more than two *irmandades* functioning at the same time.

The Irmandade do Rosario consisted mostly of Negro members. It was responsible for the maintenance of a church in the Praca da Grama. The church itself fell into disrepair as the *irmandade* declined, and was finally torn down so that today scarcely a trace of its former existence is visible.

The Irmandade de Santana was responsible for the initiation of the construction of Minas Velhas's third church, which was never completed and which stands today as a monument attesting to the death of the *irmandade.*

The brotherhood of Santissimo Sacramento itself passed about one hundred and fifty years in a state of suspended animation. It was only with the arrival of Padre Goncalves in Minas Velhas that it was brought to life again. At the same time, the Irmandade das Almas, a creation of Padre Emanuel, came to the end of its brief career.

Considering the town's total cultural edifice, we can safely say that Catholicism, even in its folk aspects, is not the keystone in the arch. Far from constituting an important cohesive force, formal religion itself suffers from a series of internal tensions that result from its inability to be reconciled with the institutions which provide its setting. It is at a tangent to the whole complex of masculinity and hence is deprived of the full support of the sex whose participation would be most important in this outspokenly male-dominated culture. It is partisan to the leisure class, maintaining economically based criteria of association which tend to exclude at least one quarter of the population from active participation. Its priests have been caught in the web of political intrigue and have been forced to choose among the local political parties. Its forms of religious association are senescent and secondary to political parties and purely social clubs. The entire edifice is impregnated with a type of philosophy sufficiently materialistic to convert its holy days into occasions for making money.

FOLK BELIEF

MOST OF the people of Minas Velhas believe in ghosts, demons, magic, and the curative powers of certain herbs and roots. There are many townspeople who are skeptical about specific manifestations of ghosts or the ability of a particular herb or magic performance to get results; but on the whole, the principle behind these beliefs or superstitions is rarely denied in a categorical fashion. The fact alone that Minas Velhas is characterized by a less scientific world view than, let us say, Sao Paulo, is quite irrelevant to the strength or weakness of the urban ethos in either city. As we shall see, it would be as much of a mistake to confuse urbanism with science as to confuse urbanism with industrialism.

Among the folkways found in Minas Velhas we may distinguish two different categories: those which pertain to a supernatural, occult realm, i.e., to the magico-religious aspects of the culture in the absence of a rigorous empirical method; and those which, while only slightly prescientific, belong to a rational, nonoccult realm which we shall call folk science.

In the first category there is an emphasis upon the mysterious, the uncanny, the supernatural, and the supernormal. It includes practices and beliefs connected with gods, ghosts, demons, magic, and sorcery. In the second category there are those beliefs and practices which are performed as part of a daily routine, without reference to any supernatural or mysterious conditions. Dietary taboos, various explanations of natural phenomena, and curative and preventive medicine insofar as they neither relate to nor involve supernatural practices belong in this category. Upon reflection, the reader will see that the distinction made here is part of a larger distinction consisting of what can be called the sacred and secular aspects of the culture. In this broader sense religion itself belongs in the first category, and everything that is not intimately connected with magico-religious traits belongs in the second. One of the basic urban characteristics of Minas Velhas which should be apparent from the preceding chapter, and all that went before it, is the overwhelming emphasis placed upon the secular. The daily routine of making a living and the practice of social grouping and daily consociation are almost entirely devoid of religious overtones or sanctions. In this chapter it will be further shown that even on the level of folkways the secular behavior and beliefs prevail. In addition, as in every other aspect of the culture, many significant differences between the town and the villages may be distinguished with regard to both sacred and secular folk patterns.

FOLK BELIEFS

In Minas Velhas, supernatural beliefs and practices have given way to modern ideas to a much greater extent in the town than in the villages. In order to find out about ghosts, demons, and magic, the ethnologist must now perform the peculiar antiquarian ritual known as "collecting." Beliefs which perhaps at one time were founded upon direct common experience have now become legends. The townspeople tell stories about other people seeing ghosts, but one must search diligently in order to find the people who actually saw them. When the townsmen talks about ghosts, magic, and sorcery, he prefaces his remarks with the word *dizem* (they say), thus, "They say there are many ghosts abroad during the last week in Lent. I don't know. I've never seen them myself. But, *they say* it is so . . ." By patiently inquiring from one person to the next—the older, poorer, and less well-educated the better—it is possible to build up a considerable body of data on the sacred folklore of Minas Velhas. Such a collection includes beliefs in all stages of use and disuse, and is of only minor value in a description of the everyday dynamics of town life. In the villages, on the other hand, the same folk beliefs are likely to be held, experienced, and practiced to a much greater extent. Informants are more apt to say "I saw a ghost near the river," or, "I don't go out at night during Lent."

The differences between townspeople and villagers in this realm of culture are, like those pertaining to religion, largely a question of emphasis, intensity of feeling, and degree of use. In this sense, the townspeople, in an apparent paradox, may be said to have folk beliefs. There is no greater paradox involved, however, in an urban community with a largely prescientific pattern of belief than in an urban community with a preindustrial technology.

Several townspeople have seen or felt the presence of ghosts and almost everybody can cite cases which are said to have happened to relatives or friends. Ghostly manifestations usually take place at night, in lonely places, near the graveyard, or in houses which the deceased once inhabited. Some of the ghosts are associated with given individuals, others—the majority—are anonymous, forming a company of lost souls who have no known specific history and who are likely to turn up anywhere. These are sometimes called *espiritos sem luz* (spirits without light); they have died in mortal sin and need somebody to pray for them. The presence of ghosts is most frequently indicated by indirect evidence—a horse shying, a dog whimpering, a colored light, a ball of fire, a groaning sound, footsteps, etc. Rarely does the ghost appear in human form. Among the villagers, almost any unexplained sight or sound, especially at night, may be ascribed to the machinations of an *espirito*.

By and large the circumstances with which most ghostly appearances are connected in Minas Velhas, however, are those in which gold is concerned. According to many of the townsmen who have panned for a living during hard times, gold itself is an enchanted entity. Unlike other metals, it cannot be moved by water (this is the principle of placer mining with a *batea*), hence it does not move in the stream bed. And yet gold does go from place to place. It walks glittering in the air; it flies from one mountain to another in a flash of light. Moreover, all the gold that a man finds has an owner (*dono*), the individual to whom it "belongs." Thus, a hundred men will dig in the same spot, but only one, the "owner," will find the gold. No one else will find it because it is not "waiting" for him. The relationship between the owner and his gold is said to persist after death, especially if the owner dies after putting it back in the earth once more. Hence, it is to be expected that the ghost of the owner will continue to claim his possession.

A complementary belief, widespread among the townspeople, is that *os antigos,* the early miners, buried large quantities of gold in and around Minas Velhas. The belief in buried treasure is much more common than belief in the ghosts which are said to emanate from it. These treasures are said to be hidden under the foundations of old houses, in the walls of the back yards, under floors, under old tree roots, in caves, and in open fields. Scores of townspeople know of a place which contains or once contained buried treasure. Probably there is a certain amount of basis in fact connected with some of these claims. In the absence of banks and vaults, some of the metal extracted during the eighteenth century which remained in the hands of the local inhabitants, especially the part which was kept illegally to avoid the royal taxes, must have been consigned to the ground as the most convenient form of protection.

A few townspeople insist that they know where there are fortunes to be dug up, but refuse to do so because the moment they start digging the ghost of the owner shows up. Monteiro, a tinsmith whose house is situated on land once owned by a rich priest, began to execavate a mound in his back yard. His wife said she saw the ghost of the priest hovering over the mound one night and begged her husband to stop. Monteiro gloomily gave in and has not touched the mound since. Raimundo, a blacksmith, lives in a house which he claims is plagued by all sorts of ghost-produced phenomena. He and his family hear strange knockings, rappings, and whistling

sounds. Occasionally there are loud footsteps as of someone walking in wooden sandals. "I once chased them
from one room to another, but couldn't find anything,"
Raimundo says. A certain old relative from Gilo who
visits the house from time to time wakes up in the middle
of the night screaming that someone is beating him with
a whip. Raimundo is convinced that there is gold some-
where under the foundation. Someday, he says, he will
take the house apart down to the last brick and find it.

According to some accounts, there have been those who
have disregarded the ghost of the owner and gone on to
find riches. Pericles knows a story about a man who saw
a flame appearing and disappearing on his back-yard
wall and who tore out the bricks and found a fortune in
old coins. Others tell of a ghost that appeared to a wood
carrier and pointed to a spot on the ground. The man
refused to go near the place, but a friend in whom he
had confided returned and dug up the treasure. This,
according to some, is supposed to have been the origin of
the wealth of an important family in Vila Nova. No one
in Minas Velhas, however, is said to have got rich this
way.

Streaks of light, balls of fire, and tongues of flame are
among the strange phenomena which miners are said to
encounter as they draw near a rich vein or a heavily
laden fluvial deposit. Sometimes these are interpreted as
the ore seen in its wandering from place to place.
Pericles says that he himself once heard the cry of an invisible cock, and he used to know someone who once
came upon a serpent ringed about by a wall of flame. A
few other townspeople say that the enchantment is sometimes expressed by a beautiful golden-haired girl who
hovers in the spray above swirling river pools, dressed in
a bridal veil and gown; or again, it may be a swarthy
miner, similar to the man with his sleeves rolled in the
dream cited below, who is present one moment and gone
the next.

Perhaps three fourths of the townspeople believe that
the souls of the living as well as the dead occasionally

make use of dreams to communicate information, that a relative is sick, a death has occurred, the dreamer is in danger, etc. Dreams are also said to be a favorite medium by which the owner of a buried treasure reveals its whereabouts. In such cases, the ghost which appears may or may not be known to the dreamer. Carlos, the blind artisan, says that in his youth he had a dream in which a small dark man with his sleeves rolled up appeared and asked if he wanted money. He replied affirmatively, and the mysterious figure conducted him to a spot in the woods where there was a sack of charcoal. The man rubbed his index finger on the ground, opened the palm of his hand (signifying great quantity), and disappeared. Later, Carlos claims to have recognized the place and seen the sack of charcoal. He never did anything about it because it is on someone else's property. Sr. Paulo says his father had a dream like that also. Paulo's grandmother appeared, pointed to a spot on the wall, and begged to have a mass said for her. After having the same dream repeated on three successive nights, Paulo's father said that he opened the wall and found a purse full of old coins. "There was enough for the mass and some left over."

While dreams are thus occasionally interpreted by the townspeople as revelatory phenomena, it must be emphasized that the large majority of dreams are simply ignored. For example, Sr. Paulo in recounting his dreams about marrying a beautiful woman and becoming a landlord in a distant place felt that there was no meaning here. "It is nothing at all," he said. "It's just *bobagem* (stupidity). Dreams always have a lot of *bobagem* in them." Sr. Rogaciano, the coin beater, also says that most dreams are just nonsense. But he adds, *"They say* that if you are gold mining and you dream about an orange-colored cow, a blond girl, or a grain of rice, you are going to get rich soon." With similar reservations, several other townspeople can give additional interpretations of dream symbols: "They say that if you dream about finding money, you are going to lose it, but if you dream about finding excrement, you are going to find some money." Dreaming about a marriage means that someone is going to die; about illness means you are going to be healthy; and if you dream about laughter you are going to cry. All such dream interpretations have a very limited distribution among the townspeople and are generally regarded with more skepticism than belief.

The townspeople are acquainted with a few malevolent spirits also. The Devil, like God, is represented mostly in abstract terms and is unimportant both in the town and in the villages. One townsman who frequently goes hunting claims to have seen the Devil near the waterfall, "red-mouthed, with a tail, like a big monkey." Beyond this, the Devil serves principally as material for invectives. Other demon spirits which are known in both town and country are *caipora* and the *mula sem cabeca* (headless mule). A sprite called *caipora* inhabits the bush and remains invisible. Some hunters from Minas Velhas say that they know they had encountered the *caipora* one day when their dogs began to whine and came running back from the chase with their tails between their legs. Hunting is discontinued after such encounters. In contrast to the villages, many urban school children do not know what *caipora* is and have never even heard of it, let alone come in contact with it.

Many of the villagers claim that they have seen the headless mule. Jose of Baixa do Gamba, for example, says that he saw it the night before Good Friday: a huge black headless animal galloping through the streets with sparks flying out from its hooves. The apparition is said to be the ghost of a priest's mistress, and it will trample anything that gets in its way. In contrast, while all of the townspeople have heard of the headless mule, none of them claim ever to have actually seen it.

The same is true of the werewolf (*lobishomen*). During Holy Week the prospect of encountering this man-beast that runs on all fours, furious, dripping saliva, and that attacks people with its teeth, kills pigs and eats them raw, is in many rural homes a strong argument for not venturing out after dark. Jose can name two individuals, both deceased, who were supposed to have been werewolves—persons reputed to have been conceived on Good Friday. No one in Baixa do Gamba at the present moment is suspected, and yet the idea and the fear connected with the werewolf are still maintained in considerable strength. In town, however, the werewolf is rarely mentioned except in order to frighten children into going to bed. The same is true of a certain type of witch (*bruxa*), a girl, the seventh child or only daughter, who enters houses through keyholes, breaks pots and pans, drinks up all the liquor, and overturns the furniture. No one in Minas Velhas can name such a case in the past. The concept still has a certain living currency as an idea, though it is obviously on its way to extinction.

In considering the urbanite's willingness to believe in ghosts, it must be borne in mind that ghosts have both conceptual and functional parallels in formal Catholic dogma. Ghosts are sinners according to ecclesiastical definition; they want absolution by prayer. In addition, the headless mule is an accomplice to the violation of ecclesiastic law, and the werewolf is the result of another such violation. All the activity of the folk spirit world reaches a climax during Holy Week, concurrent with the most solemn period in the Catholic calendar. Ghosts and the concept of an immortal soul are, after all, integral parts of formal Catholicism. The appearance of a soul on earth is a miraculous event, subject to careful verification, but possible nonetheless.

The connection of the folk beliefs about ghosts with formal Catholicism is shown by the rite called *encomendacao das almas* (prayer for the souls). This rite has not been performed in Minas Velhas for at least fifty years, but it still takes place regularly in Serra do Ouro and other villages. During Lent a dozen or so of the villagers dress up in white sheets and go out late at night to pray. One of the group carries a wooden instrument called a *matraca* which, when struck, emits a weird hollow sound. They wait until the village is quiet and there are no lights showing. Then they begin to pray for the souls in purgatory and for those in mortal sin.

> Brother mine who is awake
> Awaken him who is asleep.
> Let us remember our souls
> And those of our departed brothers.

The men in white sheets, late at night, making fearful sounds, are dramatizations of souls come back to earth. Everyone must be off the streets and neither child nor adult will look out to see them because even the sight is dangerous.

"These *gente da roca* do strange things," commented Pericles upon witnessing the rite for the first time.

MAGIC

In both the town and the villages, most people know a few magic rites and formulae. A more complete knowledge of these subjects is restricted to the *curandeiros,* the folk specialists in magic and herb cure. The essential point in this matter is that magic neither in town nor villages forms as essential part of any economic routine. Neither agriculture nor the handicrafts require special magical practices in the course of the daily or seasonal routine. During droughts, the villagers may take special measures such as pouring water at the foot of a cross, but normally planting and harvesting are carried out only with reference to purely natural phenomena. The magical performances with which the average townsman and villager is acquainted present in addition an extremely ragged coverage of subject matter, as though the ideas were torn from context or were remnants of some once larger and more coherent system. Magic, like the folklore connected with ghosts and demons, is comprised largely of esoteric bits which few people, especially among the townsmen, ever actually use. A number of townsmen, for example, can recite a word formula for curing broken limbs:

A virgin thread—previously unstitched—is passed through the eye of a virgin needle—previously unthreaded. The needle is then pushed back and forth through a piece of cotton.

> Broken flesh, twisted nerve
> Join together.
> As God's power is great
> I sew them together.
>
> Ave Maria (one time)
> Santa Maria (one time)

But a townsman would be considered out of his mind if he ever tried to cure a broken arm by such measures alone. The recognized way to treat a broken arm is to go to Vila Nova and have the doctor set it. After this is done, in some instances the injured party might, in addition, call upon a *curandeiro* who would use the above formula or one like it. The use of the *curandeiro* is much more likely among the villagers than among the townspeople, however.

Other examples of magical acts which are known to both villagers and townspeople, but which are hardly ever used by the latter are: A piece of snake hide worn under the belt will cure a backache (snakes being immune to disturbances of the vertebral column). A child will grow up to be a priest if its umbilical cord is buried near the church, to be a businessman if it is buried near a store, etc. Such obvious instances of magical symbolism are comparatively few in number. More often the relationship has become obscure with time or never was clear to begin with. A grain of rice or a coffee bean thrown under the bed will cure the mumps. A green leaf behind the ear helps indigestion. Turning a dog over by its tail cures it of worms. Turning up the footprints of a cow cures it of worms. A woman who dislikes her husband can be made to love him by having her step three times over a black dog.

The impression created by the meager quantity of such acts, the small number of people who know about them, and the even smaller number, especially among

the townsmen, who make use of them is that they are
instances of "survivals." The same is true of benign
magic which depends upon charmed objects, of which
there are but a few examples: the universal Christian
cross; medals of saints; palm leaves which have been
blessed; *arruda,* a weed that guards against the evil eye:
the cattle stone, a magic stone found in certain charmed
cattle that can be used to domesticate wild animals; and
another stone from snakes which is widely used among
the villagers to cure snake bites. The effect of the magic
snake stone is said to depend upon its ability to suck
out the poison from the wound. When applied to the
puncture made by the snake's fangs, it remains in place
and will not fall off until the poison is extracted.

During the field team's residence in Serra do Ouro, a
woman was bitten by a poisonous snake while working
in a bean patch. Three or four villagers offered the use
of their magic stones, but no attempt was made to get
the woman to the doctor in Vila Nova. The stone was
applied, and the woman promptly died the next morning. Her husband explained, "The stone won't work
unless God wills it." Despite the townspeople's fear of
snakes, which is as great as if not greater than that of
the villagers, no one in town owns a magic snake stone,
although many people have heard of it.

Like benign magic, the inventory of disease- and mis-
fortune-producing sorcery is not very well developed and
is rarely practiced. Some examples given by townsmen
follow: Cut a piece of leather into a fire and chant repeatedly, "Fulano's life will progress like the leather
that is burning in the fire." Steal a hat or a pair of
pants belonging to the victim and throw them into the
river—as they go downstream, so will the victim's fortune. A fingernail slipped into a drink of *cachaca* will
produce a state of madness. In addition, various manip-
ulations can be practiced upon the victim's footprints—
rubbing them out, driving nails into them, and spitting
on them, for example. Salt and tobacco have a variety
of sinister uses. Hung above the stove in the victim's

kitchen in a little cloth sack, they may bring a steady decline of health and fortune. Thrown into the gravel being worked by a miner, they will ruin his day. Salt mixed with red ink and thrown into the fire while calling out the victim's name is said to produce boils on his face. Other acts of sorcery are concerned with such things as: stopping dogs from vomiting (link right and left index finger), making cattle fall to the ground (cut a leather cord into water), making a snake keep chasing somebody (put fingers in nostrils), and destroying the power of a *curandeiro* (bury an unformed chicken egg near his house). All of these seem to be esoteric bits that no one actually uses.

Since sorcery is popularly known as *porcaria* (dirty, messy), any individual who practices it is felt to be unclean. Even the *curandeiros* who boast about their skill in the practice of other forms of magic are always quick to assert their total ignorance of sorcery. Hence, while there are about fifteen townspeople and many villagers who claim to have been at one time or another victims of *feitico* (acts of sorcery), there are only a very few who admit to knowing anything about producing it.

Many of the instances of alleged sorcery among the townspeople are concerned with love triangles, composed of two women and a man. The parties most likely to be accused are the town's prostitutes. A husband may be made unfaithful by the use of the following techniques: a pin stuck in his shirt; the length of his penis measured with a string, the string tied into a knot and worn next to the woman's skin; eating a cake made from eggs which have been beaten up, poured over the woman's head, and caught between her legs; a love letter wrapped around with a lock of the woman's hair and a black chicken feather, and hidden inside the man's pillow; and stealing one of the man's undergarments and wearing it next to the woman's skin.

There is no reason to believe that these measures are employed by more than one or two of the townswomen. There is one case in Minas Velhas of a man who says he used sorcery to gain his wife. The man is a mulatto and his wife is quite white. He claims that he pressed a piece of tobacco into her hand over which he had said a prayer (*Salve Rainha*) substituting her name for that of Jesus. Another townsman claims that his inability to find a wife for a long time was caused by a prostitute who made him appear impossibly ugly to every woman in town. A storekeeper traces the pains in his legs to a similar source. One blacksmith who has suffered from temporary impotence believes that a prostitute gave him a tea made from *catuaba* bark stripped downward (stripped upward, *catuaba* is considered to be an aphrodisiac). A shoemaker who went crazy on his wedding night and slept in the woods instead of with his bride was said by Pericles to be the victim of one of the many other girls who had their own marital hopes fixed on him. The town's most accomplished spiritualist attributes his malady (which appears to be advanced syphilis) to a visit he paid to his intended in-laws fifteen years ago. He claims that they gave him a tea so powerfully charmed that even fifteen years of intensive study of these matters has not led him to discover a satisfactory antidote. The remaining cases of townspeople who claim to be victims of sorcery consist of people who were treated by *curandeiros*. The latter frequently explain disease as due to *porcaria* on somebody's part. There is no reason to believe that the number of persons practicing sorcery is at all proportionate to the number of their alleged victims. At any rate, even the number of alleged victims is relatively small, and black magic can certainly not be said to be a common practice in Minas Velhas. In this respect, between the town and the villages there is little difference.

If we consider the number of people who believe that any kind of magic really can produce results, there is only a slight difference between town and country. The rural population concurs unanimously, while approximately 10 percent of the urban population categorically dissents. People like the mayor, the tax collector, some storekeepers, and most of the teachers openly express disbelief. "Superstitions of the people," they say. The rest of the townspeople believe that, if performed by a skilled *curandeiro,* many magical results are feasible. Nonetheless, a considerably larger number of towns-people than villagers live out their lives without them-selves resorting to such magical acts and without calling on a specialist to do the act for them.

FOLK SCIENCE

Probably the greatest emphasis of the entire magico-religious system of Minas Velhas and the villages is on the prevention and cure of disease. The *promessas,* the prayers, the formulae, the acts of sympathetic magic that are performed in order to combat sickness seem to far outnumber those that are performed for all other rea-sons combined. Yet strictly speaking, it is not in the realm of the occult that the disease-conscious towns-people make their strongest bid for health. In case of sickness and in all matters regarding health, the average townsman is much more likely to rely on a patent remedy from the drugstore, a herb remedy, a dietary regimen, or some other nonoccult procedure rather than rely on a prayer to his patron saint, magical acts, or other measures involving the supernatural or occult.

The use of herb remedies is clearly recognized as an order of behavior different from magic. There is no sentiment that an occult operation is involved and there is no attempt at secrecy. Although even benign magic is likely to bring down the accusation that one is prac-ticing *porcaria,* the person who suggests an herb cure is entirely free from such charges. Unlike magical acts, herb cure is regarded as a completely normal cause-and-effect physical process. There are no mysterious lacu-nae, and the curative process is entirely congruent with effects of ordinary ingestion upon the body.

The great arsenal of folk medicine in the struggle against sickness is the *gerais,* the enormous rocky wilder-ness of shrubs and gnarled trees that surrounds Minas

Velhas on all sides. Most villagers know how to collect
the roots and leaves of the plants which have medicinal
value. The average townsman, however, does not know
how to identify most of these plants. He must rely on
the villagers who sell them at the fair or who will accept a commission to find a particular one. A great
variety of species is collected and distributed to the
townspeople in this manner and made into teas, brews,
and potions. The villagers themselves have a more extensive herb lore and make readier use of the plants
than the townspeople. Every village household always
has some favorite roots on hand. In the villages they
are usually stored in a special leather bag (*patua*) which
hangs from the rafters of most rural houses. The townspeople, while more inclined to rely on drugstore remedies, also make considerable use of herbs. It can safely
be said that not a single household in Minas Velhas
passes a year without making use of one or two of the
following folk medicines:

Alcacuz	an expectorant
Angelim	a vermifuge
Arruda	a vermifuge; roasted and made into powder, it is dusted on wounds
Cabcludinho	infantile colic
Cainana	colds and grippe, necessitates a forty-day *reaguardo* of abstention from green vegetables
Carqueija	a purgative
Condomba	kidney disorders
Cangusiu	sobers up drunks
Contra-erva	colic
Fedegoso	irregular menstruation
Gamba	rheumatism
Guine	rheumatism
Herva de bicho	stomach aches
Imbuaba	syphilis
Jacare	rheumatism
Losna	indigestion
Marao	aphrodisiac
Orelha de Onca	grippe

Papacohna	postnatal treatment
Perdisse	irregular menstruation
Pimentinha	toothache; indigestion
Quina	fevers
Raiz de Cascavel	snake bite
Roxinha	"like milk of magnesia"
Santa Maria	gonorrhea
Sassa	good for young children
Teu	snake bite
Umburana	headaches, colds, grippe
Unha de Anta	with toasted salt—sore throats; with cobwebs—increase of mother's milk

Despite the fervor with which one person will designate the curative value of a particular drug for a particular disease, another person will often maintain the same fervor for the same drug for a different disease. At one time or another all of them except the purgatives get described as "good for everything"; but since purgatives themselves are prescribed for practically all symptoms, the prevailing ambiguity holds for them also.

Some other substances occasionally used by the townspeople and more frequently by the villagers should also be mentioned. Cobwebs have already been cited. Roasted lizards ground up to make a powder and drunk with water are said to be good for syphilis. Lampblack is an important ingredient in combination with *fedegoso* in treating menstrual disorders. Powdered deer antlers are said to be good for those who suffer "epileptic" fits. Watermelon seeds crushed and served with the white of an egg are widely used by villagers and townspeople to treat infantile colic. Even sugar is thought to have medicinal properties, especially in the villages where it is too expensive to be consumed regularly and is considered a luxury. Probably the most widely used remedy of all is *cachaca*. Burned, with crushed *perdisse* added, it is used by many townswomen during menstruation. Taken pure it fortifies against colds, destroys germs, and increases potency. It is also used as a sort of "booster" for practically all of the herb remedies. Several storekeepers in Minas Velhas have on hand a selection of bottles containing *cachaca* in whose respective murky depths there are the following ingredients: *teu, quina, roxinha, pimentinha, unha de anta,* and *umburana.* Sr. Antonio, who keeps a full supply of such medicinal *cachacas* on hand, readily acknowledges that the admixture of such substances is prohibited by the state sanitary code. "But I have tried every one of them myself," he says. "They are all good, none of them can do any harm. Besides, I'm being very humane; all of these roots contain a large percentage of water. If you put them into the *cachaca,* they dilute the alcohol. The *cachaca* becomes weaker and is less harmful. Generally speaking, people are inclined to drink too much at one time anyway."

Food taboos, in addition to herb remedies, are secular folkways related to the prevention and cure of disease. Just as medicine lore involves the concept that the best way to cure a disease is through the ingestion of beneficial substance, so too the majority of health-maintaining taboos involve a concept that the digestive tract is the first line of defense against disease. In this way they are eminently secular and natural. There is no air of mystery connected with the idea that certain substances are good and that others are bad, and that the good foods ought to be eaten and that the bad foods ought to be avoided. Many of the food taboos which pertain to special occasions during the life cycle have already been dealt with. Some more general food taboos remain to be mentioned: Few townsmen will eat oranges after midday. In the villages this idea is regarded with great fear, and it is said that if it has been raining and the afternoon is far enough advanced, death will result. Most townspeople consider any fruit that has been warming in the sun a great menace and will not eat it for fear of getting headaches and colic. All townsmen agree that *cachaca* should never be drunk after eating eggs. Mangos and milk are never eaten at the same meal; the same is true of milk and pineapple and of pineapples and bananas. Few townsmen will eat meat and fish at the same meal for fear that their future children will be born deformed.

Pregnant women also abstain from eating fish and meat at the same meal for fear of having an abortion. All townspeople agree that nothing hot may be followed by anything cold, as for example, coffee followed by water.

It must be emphasized that for the most part these taboos are unconnected by any generalized theory greater than the one which holds that there is a relationship between food and health. Taboos which have religious rationales are also known: hats must be removed in the church, no work can be done on a saint's day, sexual intercourse is prohibited on Good Friday. *But there are no food taboos derived from religious concepts.* Nor are there food taboos whose sanctions depend on concepts of moral uncleanliness. Most of them are derived from isolated, self-contained folk-science theories which state the consequence of violating the taboo in terms of the specific pathological states that may occur. Moreover, the people of Minas Velhas are always prepared to prove the truth of these theories by appeal to empirical evidence: "Jose drank milk after eating a mango. He had to stay in bed three days before the pains in his stomach went away." "Maria ate a watermelon that had just been taken out of the sun; she went crazy and had to be locked in a room." Even when the theory does not specifically indicate the results of infraction, it is always stated or understood that the forbidden food or combination *faz mal a saude,* is "bad for your health."

In both town and villages there are many secular health taboos which do not center upon the digestive tract. The townsmen view with great alarm the sight of someone washing his face immediately after eating. It is said that paralysis of the facial muscles will follow such foolish behavior. In addition, one should not read after eating; the risk is "cerebral congestion." There is a tremendous fear connected with getting wet by the rain, especially on the head. Townspeople believe that one should never go without a hat when there is precipitation, even if the precipitation is only the dew. Few townspeople would venture out into even a slight rain without a hat or umbrella. To warm oneself by a fire indoors is also considered extremely risky; an unexpected draft may cause paralysis. The same is true of exposing oneself to cold air after drinking or eating something hot.

An extreme but nonetheless suggestive example of the difference in intensity between townsmen and villagers with respect to most of these taboos is that of Pedro, the old villager from Gilo who claims the spirits whip him at night. Pedro's superstitions are a great source of amusement to the townspeople. He made the mistake of revealing that his fear of cold winds includes other people's breath. Now an hilarious pastime has been developed by the town's children which consists of sneaking up on Pedro and blowing in his face. Pedro reacts violently and tries to hit the rascals with his stick. "The other day I had just finished my hot coffee when one of these ruffians came and blew his cold breath right on my neck," he explains. "They shouldn't do that to an old man like me, I am likely to catch cold from all that blowing."

In addition to these ideas which are more or less common to townsmen and villagers, there is another group of folk-science beliefs which is known by most villagers and hardly at all by the townspeople: a drunk cannot be injured by snake bite; a male child is born when mother and father reach climax together, a female when orgasm is separate; water snakes are born from human hair; the cobwebs fall from the ceiling before it rains. As the moon waxes, many variable phenomena are thought by the villagers to increase in strength and intensity; as it wanes, these phenomena manifest their weaker aspects. Thus it is said in Serra do Ouro that all pains wax and wane with the moon. Heavy rains come at full moon, and a snake bite after full moon is less dangerous because the poison is weaker—at full moon it is almost always fatal. A child born as the moon is waxing is likely to be born a boy, the stronger sex; as the moon wanes, the probability of a girl, the weaker sex, increases. Pigs and horses are castrated after full moon because the danger of infection is less. The best time for a woman to wash her hair is during the new moon. And the best time for planting is at full moon.

The wealth of folk belief associated with health and disease requires specialists for its most efficient utilization. These are called *curandeiros,* the folk doctors who serve the townspeople and villagers in return for monetary compensation. There is one *curandeiro* in town, one in Baixa do Gamba, and two in Gilo. Three or four others nearby in the zone also occasionally visit Minas Velhas. Some of the *curandeiros* have clients— both townsmen and villagers—who seek their services from as far away as ten or twenty miles. In the villages the *curandeiro* is usually called for by the sick person or his family. In town, however, the *curandeiros* show up when they learn that someone is sick who is likely to make use of them. Much greater use is made of *curandeiros* in the villages than in the town. In the urban sample 33 percent of the households admitted having used a *curandeiro* at least once; whereas for twenty-four households in Serra do Ouro, the number was sixteen, or 75 percent; in Baixa do Gamba every household at one time or another has been treated by Joaquim, who is also the acknowledged *chefe* of the village.

The *curandeiro* employs elements both of folk science and of the magico-religious system identical with or similar to those already discussed. In addition all *curandeiros* depend heavily upon the facilities of the local drugstore. On a Saturday afternoon after the fair, Joaquim can often be seen stuffing well-known patent medicines for diseases of the liver, menstrual disturbances, and colic into his saddlebag to take back to the village with him. If a common ailment is diagnosed, the *curandeiro* will usually prescribe a medicine made from herbs and roots taken from the *gerais* or purchased in the drugstore. Only if the first results are unsatisfactory or if the disease itself is hard to diagnose will he include magico-religious performances. Under these conditions the *curandeiro* can cure at a distance. Sick people in Serra do Ouro, for instance, which has no *curandeiro,* received treatment from the *curandeiro* in Gilo by correspondence. A description of the symptoms of the sick person is taken by messenger and the *curandeiro* sends back a packet of roots or herbs, sometimes a bottle of some potion, or sometimes merely the name of a patent medicine to be bought in Minas Velhas together with directions for taking same. For a prescription of this sort, the fee is 10 cruzeiros.

When the symptoms consist of obscure pains, inexplicable lethargy, or nervous aberrations, the diagnosis is usually made in person and often involves sleight of hand and various divinatory devices such as knives, coins, and books. In addition to herbs, the treatment in such cases usually also involves prayers and other magical performances. One of Councilman Waldemar's sons, Edilson, for example, is a peddler who often could not bring himself to get started on a selling trip. On the day that he was supposed to set out, he invariably woke up with a weakness in his body, sharp pains in his feet, and a strange desire to go back to sleep. Joaquim, who had treated Edilson before, heard about his new sickness and came to town. He made a diagnosis using a knife and a set of old coins, which he said represented seven different spirits. The *curandeiro* traced the outlines of Edilson's foot with his knife. After Edilson removed his foot, the *curandeiro* made a five-pointed star next to the outline, a cross inside, and encircled it with one of the coins. Next he had the patient place his foot back inside the outline, told him not to be afraid, and threw the knife into the floor, barely missing Edilson's toe. Then he attempted to balance the coins on top of the knife one by one. At last a coin stayed on top. The diagnosis was over—he had found the responsible spirit. As usual in such cases, he declared that Edilson was the victim of sorcery. He next began to tap the knife with the balanced coin until it fell over. Taking the coin and encircling the patient's head and body with it, he proceeded to utter a magic prayer under his breath:

In the name of the Father, the Son, and of the Holy Ghost. In the name of St. Bartholomew, St. Augustine, St. Caetano, and St. Andre Avelino, I confront you, evil angel, that seeks to enter me and seize me. By the power of Christ's cross, by the power of His divine wounds, I cast you out, evil one, so that you may not tempt my divine soul. Amen.

A group of twenty townspeople who had consulted *curandeiros* were interviewed to determine their symptoms. The majority of them demonstrated vague symptoms like those of Edilson. As reported by the patients and their relatives, these were as follows: (1) "paralysis of the legs," (2) pains in the legs, (3) violent fits, (4) insanity—stays in the house, keeps to himself, speaks incoherently, (5) irregular menstruation and enlarged stomach, (6) pains in leg, headaches, (7) "syphilis," (8) alcoholism, (9) despondency, attempted suicide, (10) lethargy, (11) inability to work due to weakness in the body, (12) headaches, toothaches, could not move arms, somnolence, and inability to work, (13) somnolence, pains in body, (14) skin rash, painful menstruation, headaches, (15) three successive miscarriages, (16) "unluckiness," (17) headaches, "something eating her inside," (18) sore foot, (19) emitting worms, (20) "crazy."

It is generally assumed that all *curandeiros* of merit are capable of practicing black as well as white magic. Hence, the term *feiticeiro* often is used as a popular synonym for *curandeiro,* though the former term more properly means one who concentrates on the practice of black magic. There is a popular saying that all *feiticeiros* are more with the Devil than with God. The professional pose of the *curandeiro* requires that he deny ever having used his power to do evil, all the while darkly hinting that he could if he wanted to. Most of them always refer to God and Christ as the indispensable agents of their cure and warn that they cannot help unless the patient has faith. Edilson, in order to explain his use of Joaquim, cited the following story:

There was a man who used to laugh at a certain *curandeiro*. One day the *curandeiro* pointed out two pigeons flying high and fast toward the south. "Do you see those pigeons?" he said. "Well, they're not really pigeons at all. They're two rattlesnakes that are flying to Minas Gerais to kill an enemy of mine there." The man merely laughed at this. So the *curandeiro* stared at the birds. They came lower and lower. Finally they reached the ground, but instead of the pigeons they were now two rattlesnakes. One bit the man on the left leg and the other bit him on the right leg. Then they turned back into pigeons and flew away.

The attitude of most of the townsmen toward the *curandeiros* is of this nature. The *curandeiro* is not to be laughed at since he knows things that ordinary people do not and can do things that ordinary people cannot do. In spite of this cautious esteem, *curandeiros* are uninfluential in town life, are excluded from the Clube Social, and remain essentially "hicks" to the majority of townsmen. In the villages, however, the *curandeiro* is likely to become a dominant figure.

In Baixa do Gamba, for example, Joaquim has successfully held his position as *chefe* of the village for many years. He exercises a strong hand over the affairs of the community, arbitrates disputes, and is spokesman for the group before the political powers in Minas Velhas. His position is given semiofficial recognition since, for forty years, he has been the police inspector, an office for which he qualified by virtue of having been for a long time the only one in the village who could read and write. Joaquim capitalized on his literacy in other ways; he has done his best to make the people of Baixa do Gamba believe that reading and writing are magical accomplishments, claiming that he learned the art on two successive Sundays by making *promessas* to Sr. Bom Jesus. For many years people used to come from miles around to have him read their letters. It is only recently that this service has ceased to stimulate the awe which the villagers used to feel toward a person who has mastered the art of writing. It is not surprising, therefore, that one of the chief opponents of the municipal school in Baixa do Gamba was Joaquim, who like a true visionary correctly equated a reduction in illiteracy with a reduction of his own powers over his neighbors.

There is a *curandeiro* from the village of Gilo who is more often called a *feiticeiro* than the others. This is Mario, the snake caller. Mario enjoys a tremendous reputation in the rural zone for his ability to clear farms of snakes. Many farmers regularly engage his services and pay his fee of 50 cruzeiros with open satisfaction. Mario recently had a chance to display his powers in a demonstration which took place right in town. Pericles's son was killed by a snake. His wife brooded about the boy's death, feeling especially melancholy because the snake which had killed him was still alive. Mario said that for 50 cruzeiros he would find the snake and destroy it. One day he came to the city and told Pericles to wait in the back yard and not to leave under any circumstances because the snake would come that day. He himself, however, could not wait (only a few townsmen thought there was anything strange in this) since he had to go to Vila Nova. About an hour after Mario left, a snake was seen crossing the river by some women who were washing clothes. Others claimed to have seen it climbing the wall of the back yard and several others were on hand when the snake reached the spot where Pericles was waiting to kill it.

Some of the *curandeiros* specialize in curing animal diseases. Miguel, the *curandeiro* who lives in the city, makes a specialty of curing sick pigs, chickens, dogs, and cattle. It is to the last, however, that he is most devoted, especially to the art of making maggots fall off. The maggots cause spreading sores in the skin of the animal; if not treated, it is believed that the cattle will eventually die. Miguel charges two cruzeiros per head, and does not even have to be near the diseased animals, many of which are roaming about in the *gerais* and

could be located only after a lengthy search. Of all the
occasions when a *curandeiro* is used by the townspeople
this seems to be the most common. The disease can be
treated very successfully with creolin, but almost without exception those of the townsmen who own a few
head of cattle employ *curandeiros* rather than make a
search for the animals. Miguel's treatment involves
"counting":

Assim como cai o tronco dos bracos do Nosso Senhor Jesus
Christo, assim tambem cairao os bixous desta bixeira de um a
um, de um a dois, de dois a tres, de tres a quatro . . . de oito a
nove, de nove a dez, de dez a nove, de nove a oito . . . de dois
a um. Bixeira, bixerinha.

As the body of Christ fell away from his arms, so will the
bugs fall from this beast, from one to one, from one to two,
from two to three, from three to four . . . from eight to nine,
from nine to ten, from ten to nine, from nine to eight . . .
from two to one. Big animal, little bug.

[This is repeated three times in its entirety.]

Sr. Braulio, among the least superstitious of the townsmen in Minas Velhas, expressed this dilemma: "I never
used to believe it. I had Miguel try it once, and the
damn *bichos* fell off. Since then it has never failed, so
I have to believe it now."

Rivalry between *curandeiros* parallels the rivalry between priests except where disciples are concerned
(Miguel was taught by Joaquim, for example). Between
Joaquim and Chico, a *curandeiro* from a neighboring
county, competition is very keen and one continually
derides the ability of the other. A favorite tactic in the
struggle for prestige is to spread the word that one has
called in the other for consultation. Chico arrived in
Minas Velhas in a great hurry one day and said that he
was on his way to visit Joaquim. He said that Joaquim
had fallen victim of sorcery and had asked for his help.
Later Joaquim reversed the story and insisted that the
other had voluntarily come to him to be treated for a
pain in the chest.

There is no doubt that the *curandeiro* is an established figure in the urban as well as in the rural scene. In order to determine the importance of the *curandeiro*, however, we must consider him in relation to the town drugstore. The incidence of the use of the *curandeiro* in the town sample was 33 out of 100 households. The 33 households report using a *curandeiro* a total of 117 times, or about 293 times for the town as a whole. This figure represents a lifetime total. In one year, however, the number of purchases made by the people of Minas Velhas at the town drugstore is at least three times this number.

The drugstore in Minas Velhas is a cultural feature many times more important and more firmly established than the *curandeiros*. The stock of patent remedies kept on hand is enormous. The owner reports that he has in stock thirty different types of medicines for colds alone. The store contains a selection of eight different vitamin complexes, ten different cough medicines, a large supply of the sulfa series of antibiotics, penicillin, verious sedatives and barbiturates, and twenty different kinds of tonics. Since there is no doctor in Minas Velhas, scarcely more than seventy-five medical prescriptions are filled each year. The rest of the huge turnover in medicine depends upon the druggist's advice, the *curandeiros'* prescriptions, or the townspeople's own idea of what is good for them. The townspeople exhibit a rather remarkable preference for medicines which can be taken in intravenous injections. Three of the townsmen, including the druggist, know how to use a hypodermic needle and all three of them are kept busy throughout the year. One of these, Sr. Alvaro, the State Tax Clerk, is highly regarded by the community for the unselfish way in which he has administered injections. Sr. Alvaro is frequently called upon late at night to tend to some sick person on the other side of town. Accustomed to keeping records in the Tax Office, Sr. Alvaro has kept a record of his activities as a doctor. In the typical year of December, 1945, to December, 1946, this record shows that Sr. Alvaro gave 126 injections to 112 different townsmen. He gave 53 injections of 10 different patent medicines for colds and grippes; 25 injections of 11 different medicines for syphilis; 25 injections of 11 different tonics and vitamins and 9 injections of 4 different medicines for liver trouble. It must be remembered that these injections were given by one person and that there were two other men who administered at least another 100 injections during the same period. Moreover, at the same time, an even larger number of medicines which can be taken orally were bought at the drugstore.

The popularity of new vitamins and antibiotics among the townspeople deserves special note. As of 1950, every townsman had heard of penicillin. It was being used, sometimes in absurdly small doses, to cure everything from toothache to indigestion. The druggist himself, not too sure of how and when penicillin ought to be used, sells it to anyone who thinks that it will do him good. From December, 1947, the date when penicillin first appeared in Minas Velhas, to December, 1950, Sr. Alvaro reports that he injected 36 townspeople with 100,000 units of penicillin, 19 with 200,000 units, 2 with 300,000 units, one with 400,000 units, and one with 600,000 units. This makes a total of 59 persons who were treated by Sr. Alvaro alone since the drug's first appearance. During the same period, the other two "injectionists" were equally busy. Sr. Alvaro reports that the same sort of enthusiasm was shown for the sulfa series when they first appeared about a decade earlier.

Among townsmen afflicted with a recognizable disease, the drugstore is used before a *curandeiro*. Most townspeople begin the treatment of a disease by observing the various taboos and folk healthways. If the symptoms persist, they will subsequently ask the druggist to prescribe a patent medicine. If this is of no avail, the next step for those who can afford it is to visit the doctor in Vila Nova. If the disease still lingers on, prayers to a patron saint and consultation with a *curandeiro* are likely to be added to the treatment. Thus, in the urban context, the magico-religious treatment of disease is clearly secondary and supplementary to the abundant nonoccult practices.

An additional group of folkways which deserve special emphasis are those embodying certain paramount fears. The question, "Of what are you most afraid?" was asked of 38 urban school children. Their answers follow, classified into two categories.

TABLE 32. FEARS OF SCHOOL CHILDREN

WORST FEAR (NATURAL)		WORST FEAR (SUPERNATURAL)	
Thieves	8	The dead	3
Snakes	8	Spirits	3
Jaguars	8	Demons	2
Crazy people	2	Werewolf	1
Death of mother	1	Headless mule	1
	27		10

An intense fear of thieves, jaguars, and snakes is shared by adults as well as by school children, urban as well as rural. There can be no question that the fear of thieves represents a folk belief rather than the reality situation. In the last ten years there have not been more than three cases of robbery in Minas Velhas. None of these involved breaking into inhabited homes; none involved a case of armed assault. All were done by sneaks. In two cases a store was entered and some flashlights and hardware stolen; in the remaining case a radio was taken from the Clube Social. During the last twenty years, there has never been a case of anyone being physically molested by a thief. And yet the preoccupation with the danger of armed robbery is reflected in a ceaseless state of preparedness. The precautions against night intruders is all the more remarkable in the town where each house adjoins two others and where a shout from one can be heard by at least five or six neighbors. At night the door of every house in Minas Velhas, without exception, is not only locked but bolted. Every window is also bolted, and stones are wedged into the sills. Every townsman sleeps within easy reach of a variety of weapons including pistols, daggers, axes, and bushknives. After ten o'clock the city takes on the appearance of an armed camp awaiting the attack of a hostile army. A knock on the door after midnight is a terrifying experience for most townspeople. Late travelers arriving at the pension can gain entrance only after many minutes of indecision on the part of the proprietor as to whether it is a thief or a guest who stands outside.

Pericles tells of an incident which happened to him in the rural zone. He was returning from Gruta when he took the wrong trail and got lost. Night fell and it soon began to rain. After a considerable amount of wandering around in the darkness, he finally stumbled upon a house. When he knocked on the door, no one answered. Accustomed to the habits of his fellows, he waited patiently, knocking again at intervals. At last a light appeared inside the house and a voice asked him to declare his business. Pericles answered that he was lost and wanted to come in out of the rain. "I am alone," he said. "There is no one with me but my mule." After some more delay, the door opened a crack and the barrel of a rifle was poked out. When the man had made sure that he was alone, Pericles was permitted to come in out of the rain. Inside he saw that there were thirteen men sleeping on the floor. He learned that he was at a *fazenda* and that the men on the floor were hired hands who were working on the harvest. As Pericles came in they were all wide awake and had their hands ready on their bushknives.

The fear of jaguars has even less of a basis in fact than the fear of thieves. This animal is practically extinct; occasionally an isolated farmer will report that he has seen the tracks of a jaguar or that one of his cattle has been killed. Ninety percent of the townspeople have never even seen the tracks of a jaguar, much less the animal itself. In fact there is such a strong curiosity about what a jaguar looks like that the traveling circuses which pass through the zone from time to time count on this animal as one of their strongest drawing cards. Despite the rarity of the beast, it manages to infest an astounding number of different places at the same time. When a townsman or a villager travels he is constantly apprehensive about jaguars. All caves and thick woods are suspect and everything possible is done to avoid passing near them. If a detour cannot be managed, the traveler hurries past shouting at the top of his lungs, for it is said that loud noises frighten the animal.

The fear of snakes has, of course, some basis in fact. Scarcely a year goes by in the rural zone without a death caused by snake bite. Nonetheless, the intensity of the fear is disproportionate to the facts. Snakes are a minor cause of death; the horror and fascination associated with them, however, occur on a much larger scale. In the town one of the best ways to insure an interested audience aside from talking politics is to talk snakes. Snakes are looked for and expected everywhere, in the backyard, the kitchen, the dining room, among the rafters, under the bed, and in bed. In the villages the lore which centers around these reptiles is extensive. Hair becomes snakes; handling of a bird's egg in the nest "calls" snakes; snakeskins prevent backaches; snakes that climb trees yield magic stones. In the rural zone there is a belief that certain cases of anemia in children are caused by a snake having taken the mother's milk instead of the child; the snake comes at night, puts its tail in the child's mouth to quiet it, and the mother never knows the difference until it is too late. The fear of snakes extends to such great lengths that even in death they are considered dangerous. Their skeletons must be buried because to step on their bones is as bad as being bitten.

These folk fears may be interpreted as additional evidence that the primary emphasis of urban folk beliefs in general is upon secular elements. While the fear of thieves is as much a product of the imagination as the concept of ghosts, it still remains that thieves are of the order of natural phenomena and ghosts of the supernatural. In Table 32, the children's answers are grouped according to natural and supernatural categories, left and right columns respectively. Fully three fourths of the children associated the most fearful thing in the world with natural phenomena.

The children's answers are also significant from the point of view of omissions. No one gave Hell or the Devil as an answer. Children do not learn by the examples which their elders set that these are the things most to be feared. This is not to say that the formal Catholic demonology is unknown. When the question, "Are you afraid of the Devil?" was put to the same group of children, all but one answered affirmatively (the affirmation was unanimous for jaguars, thieves, and snakes). The level of response is different, however, having been elicited by suggestion. The concepts involved evidently exist largely as verbal abstractions for both children and adults.

Hence we see how on all sides the occult and the spiritual in Minas Velhas are overshadowed by the natural and the material, and how this is true within the body of folk belief itself as well as for the culture as a whole. Only in relation to health do the magico-religious techniques coincide with another central cultural concern and even here the various supernatural techniques are overshadowed by natural alternatives in the form of herb cures, drugstore remedies, and other elements of folk science.

The folk fears are also mentioned here because they seem to be related to a more general component of the urban complex: the isolation of the townspeople from their natural habitat. Although the same fears are shared by villagers and townsmen alike, there are other factors in village life which counterbalance their significance. The villagers are by and large much more familiar with the countryside than the townsmen. They know the back trails, the high peaks, and the streams. They know the names of the plants that grow in the *gerais,* know how to find the medicinal herbs and the wild fruits and berries. But beyond the gates of the city, beyond the little cluster of houses and rudimentary pavements, the urban resident looks out upon a scene with which he is familiar only to the extent with which one is familiar with a landscape—like a backdrop to a stage. It has only two dimensions. In detail, the third dimension is quite lost. Familiarity extends along the main roads; even then, only the road to Vila Nova is generally familiar. Off the roads only a few hunters and miners can serve as guides. The women of the city in particular live and die in complete ignorance of their natural surroundings. Even so great an attraction as the spectacular waterfall of the Rio das Pedras, less than two miles away from the city, has never been seen by at least 60 percent of the urban female population. This is true of perhaps one quarter of the male population also. Picnics—urban outings with lunch baskets and tablecloths and servants—are occasionally held near the waterfall. If anything, however, these outings tend to fix rather than augment the townspeople's knowledge of the countryside. No new spots are sought after and no exploring is involved. Fifteen miles to the north of the town there are at least two summits which no townsman has ever scaled. The land about these impressive peaks, rich in timber, water, and minerals, is virgin and practically unexplored.

The folk fears considered together with the urbanite's ignorance of the countryside and his contempt for farming form a fundamental motif of the urban ethos. For the city dweller the countryside is a no man's land, a hostile backdrop filled with predatory animals, thieves, and crude peasants. The town is the attempt to deny all this. By building houses close together, paving the streets, wearing suits and ties, the townsman creates his own environment. His empire lies on the coast, in the bustling cities with their automobiles and their tall buildings. It is for this reason, perhaps, that all about him, after two centuries of settlement, the wilderness still flourishes.

CONCLUSIONS

THE DICHOTOMY between rural and urban communities is an old one, recognized by scholars as long ago as the beginning of the Christian era.[1] Today in sociology and social anthropology the differences between "rural" and "urban" society have been discussed by many writers. It has been said, for example, that urban communities are generally larger and more densely populated than rural communities and that they tend to be more heterogeneous ethnically and culturally. They characteristically contain more social differentiation and stratification, show greater territorial and occupational mobility, and have more occupational specialization with manufacturing, trade, commerce, professions, governing, and other nonagricultural pursuits predominating. Urban populations work and live in a man-made world isolated from the natural environment.[2]

The rural-urban differentiation is also regarded as a special form of a more general distinction between societies and cultures which are more "folklike" and those which are more sophisticated or "civilized."[3] The world view of city dwellers is said to be more "secular" as against the "sacred" viewpoint of rural or folk societies. In urban communities interpersonal relations are dominated by impersonal institutions instead of by

[1] " In the history of mankind we find two modes of life, that of the city and that of the farm."—Marcus Tenentius Varro (116-27 B.C.). " One sees by this that the life of the city and that of the country are two states, each subject to natural laws."—Ibn Khaldun (1332-1406).

[2] Pitirim A. Sorokin, Carle C. Zimmerman, and Charles J. Gilpin, *A Septematic Source Book in Rural Sociology*, I, 238 ff. Additional texts, readings, and bibliographies in urban sociology are contained in Noel Gist, *Urban Society* (Thomas G. Crowell, New York, 1947); T. Lynn Smith, *The Sociology of Urban Life* (Dryden Press, New York, 1951); and Paul Hatt, *Reader in Urban Sociology* (Free Press, Glencoe, 1951).

[3] Alfred Kroeber, *Anthropology*, pp. 281 ff.

kinship or extended familial bonds. There are generally a greater number of alternative patterns of behavior available to the city dweller, "allowing a greater freedom of action and choice to the individual." [4]

City dwellers, furthermore, do not tend to identify themselves with their locality and are more subject to the changes and whims of fashion. Urban cultures do not afford their members full participation in their functioning. In contrast, folk or rural cultures

> invite and encourage such participation. . . . The relatively small range of their culture content, the close-knittedness of their participation in it, the very limitation of the scope, all make for sharpness of patterns in the culture which are well-characterized, consistent, and inter-related. Narrowness, depth and intensity are the qualities of folk cultures.[5]

These and similar differences between urban and rural societies are by now well accepted at least as working hypotheses.

Although some of the numerous criteria of urban society as distinguished from rural society apply to Minas Velhas, others do not.

Minas Velhas is a heterogenous, individualized, secular community. Occupational specialization, division of labor, differences in rank stratified into at least two sharply defined classes, and political schisms are the principal factors in this cultural heterogeneity. Closely linked with these factors are a strongly individualized sense of economic destiny, a low order of economic and political cooperation, a weak sense of community *esprit de corps,* a dominance of capital as the organizing factor in group labor, and a high incidence of impersonal transactions lubricated by cash rather than by family or friendship.

Secularization in Minas Velhas is evidenced by the almost complete absence of religious controls or motives in the daily regimen of making a living, the free and

4 Robert Redfield, *The Folk Culture of Yucatan,* p. 338.
5 Kroeber, *Anthropology,* p. 282.

abundant choice between magico-religious and purely natural modes of maintaining health and curing disease, and the absence of important associations dedicated to religious ends. It is evident also in the dominance of civil over ecclesiastical authority in local government, in the unfavorable attitude of the men toward the priest, the lower order of participation in formal church ritual, the commercialization and loss of religious meaning of sacraments and festivals, competition between household saints and formal religion, and in many other internal strains caused by class, sex, and political differentials in religious behavior.

Additional characteristics of the urban complex found in Minas Velhas are the predominance of manufacture, trade, commerce, and other nonagricultural occupations, a strong development of political institutions, and isolation from and an unfamiliarity with the natural environment.

It is only with respect to two major characteristics generally held to be universal for urban societies that Minas Velhas deviates from the usual definition of an urban culture. These are: degree of isolation and population.

In terms of geographic accessibility to metropolitan influences, Minas Velhas is even more isolated than many communities which have been characterized as possessing a folk culture. Tepoztlan, for example, a homogeneous, collectivistic community studied by Robert Redfield, lies only fifty miles from the great metropolis of Mexico City. Since 1910 a railroad has connected the two points and since 1936 a bus line has provided regularly scheduled public transport over a paved highway.[6] This should be compared with the complete absence of motor transport in Minas Velhas up until a very few years ago and the town's present-day lack of any scheduled transportation. The distance between Minas Velhas and the nearest railroad stop is as far as the distance

[6] Oscar Lewis, *Life in a Mexican Village*, p. 35.

from Tepoztlan to Mexico City. As for size, Tepoztlan
had a population of about four thousand at the time of
Redfield's study, which is more than twice that of Minas
Velhas. Cheran, a Tarascan village in Michoacan,
Mexico, studied by Ralph Beals, is characterized by the
complete absence of class or caste stratification, yet it has
a population of five thousand.[7] Moche, a similarly class-
less, homogeneous community in Peru, studied by John
Gillin, is slightly larger than the town of Minas Velhas.[8]
In terms of space and facility of transport and communication, Minas Velhas does not stand midway between
the villages and the city. The residents of the village of
Baixa do Gamba, for instance, live only one hour further away from Salvador, the nearest big city, than do
the residents of Minas Velhas. The town of Minas Velhas is ten times as large in population as the village of
Baixa do Gamba, but it in turn has only 1,500 people
as against the approximately 350,000 in the city of Salvador. Yet the sub-culture of Minas Velhas perhaps shares
more in common with Salvador than it does with the
sub-culture of the nearby rural villages.

The fact that Minas Velhas was founded as a mining
town, from the outset a food-consuming rather than a
food-producing community, an administrative, religious,
and educational center, profoundly different from the
rural villages, is apparently of greater account in determining its urban characteristics than its size or proximity to a metropolis. If Minas Velhas is at all typical of
the many hundred small Brazilian county seats, the
mere size of interior settlements or their distance from
the coast is not a reliable index of the degree of urbanization.

Although it cannot be maintained that a dense population and proximity to urban influences emanating from
a metropolis are alone sufficient to produce an urban
sub-culture, it is fairly certain that these two factors may
be counted on to intensify whatever urban characteris-

[7] Ralph A. Beals, *A Sierra Tarascan Village*, p. 98.
[8] John Gillin, *Moche*.

tics are already present. The effect of a population increase upon heterogeneity and individualization in
Minas Velhas would obviously be one of intensification,
while increased contact with Salvador or Rio de Janeiro
would also intensify many urban features including
heterogeneity, individualism, and secularism. Since
Minas Velhas and other small Brazilian towns are so
conspicuously urban, in spite of their isolation and small
size, they are in a sense even more urban than larger
and less isolated towns and cities. Londoners or New
Yorkers are certainly no more conscious of being city
people than are the inhabitants of Minas Velhas.

In Minas Velhas, we have seen that the contrast between town and village is an outstanding characteristic
of the local scene. The villagers live in settlements
which are almost distinct communities, although closely
related to the town. They are all farmers, and there are
no class distinctions among them. The villagers grow
the major share of their own food supply. They come
to town regularly as a distinct trading group, selling
food and buying hardware. Their speech, dress, and
manners are distinguishable from those of the townspeople. The villages have no public buildings; there
are no public gardens in which to promenade or that
need to be guarded against stray animals and no social
clubs in which to play billiards or dance. The villagers
are generally illiterate and unaware of national and
world affairs and their intimate familiarity with local
flora, fauna, and geography further distinguishes them
from the townspeople. Villagers are generally afraid of
strangers, disinterested in politics, and hostile to government. In the village, respect for familial relations is
more intense and the extended family is more firmly
rooted than in the town. In religion, the villagers are
more given to the household pantheon than to churchgoing. Health-insuring taboos are more numerous and
more closely observed among the villagers than among
the townspeople and villagers rely more on folk doctors
than drugstore remedies. Their religious festivals and

marriage festivals also differ from those of the towns-people. Both villagers and townspeople are aware of these many differences between the rural and urban way of life. In total and subjectively, they are sufficient to make a *vida do campo* (life of the fields) seem altogether different from a *vida do comercio* (life of the business district), causing the villagers to feel uncomfortable in town and allowing the townsmen to be scornful of the villagers.

Yet, it must be pointed out that objectively the social and cultural differences between Minas Velhas and its village satellites are not sufficient in themselves to account for the fervor with which townspeople maintain that they are different from country people. It is true that Minas Velhas is relatively more heterogeneous, more individualistic, and more secular than any of the villages. That the villages are, on the other hand, relatively homogeneous is unquestionable. But despite consistent differences in degree, the villages cannot be called either collectivistic or sacred except in relation to the town. As has been indicated, work patterns among the villagers are highly individualized; there is no cooperative labor and the village family is only slightly more cohesive than in the town. With regard to magico-religious beliefs and practices, it may safely be said that there are more similarities than differences between the two groups. This is not surprising in view of the fact that both groups are but segments of a single larger community which includes a town and its satellite villages and that both have sub-cultures which share many common patterns of Brazilian national culture. In the eyes of the townspeople, however, every objective contrast is seized upon and deliberately magnified. The entire urban complex is greatly admired and its elements are endorsed through an elaborate system of values. In Minas Velhas, urbanism is not a mere by-product of occupation or of population density, it is a quest, a vision, a whole ethos.

An urban ethos may be said to exist when a people,

consciously or unconsciously, abstractly or concretely, values, endorses, and seeks to perpetuate the various urban traits of its culture. The strength of the other characteristics of the urban complex is not necessarily an indication of the strength of the urban ethos. In Minas Velhas, for example, the desire to live in a city is probably much stronger than it is for the average New Yorker. In New York and other large metropolises a man's degree of success is often measured in terms of the distance he has managed to put between him and the city. A home in the suburbs, a home in the country, and a home in Florida mark successive stages of personal fulfillment. For the people of Minas Velhas, the exact opposite holds true. Ultimate success comes to the townsman when he can open a home in the center of some metropolis. This desire to live at the center of things is well expressed within the town itself by the preference for living on the most central streets and the love of noise and bustle.

It is also important to realize that the urban ethos is not subsumed by any single value such as the preference for living in town rather than in the country. Ethos is a complex of interconnected values: a major orientation. It consists of items like the high value placed on civic improvements, such as the town garden; the disapproval of agriculture and of menial labor in general; the high value placed on professions (doctors, lawyers, politicians, teachers); the high value placed on education, literacy, fluency of speech, formal speeches, and legal processes; the desire to wear "city clothes" such as neckties and suits; the awe associated with wealth in the form of cash; the love of noise, movement, crowds, and houses close together; the low value placed on knowledge of the countryside; the high value placed on knowledge of the coastal cities; the love of individualism and the low value placed upon communal conformity as seen in the indifference toward the community's patron saint, the proliferation of personal patron saints, the proliferation of stores and workshops and their resistance to merger, the individualistic work patterns, the political schisms, racial ranking, and in the very acceptance of class differentiation itself; the high value placed upon progress emanating from the city in the form of radios, automobiles, electricity, the sulfa drugs, penicillin, and patent remedies; and the willingness to accept impersonal government as the guarantor of security and the prime mover in progress. These are some of the interrelated values or forms of behavior stemming from values which, taken together, result in the urban ethos of the townspeople of Minas Velhas.

The list can scarcely be terminated. There are many more items, since each set of values determines innumerable minor choices and preferences expressed during the course of daily life.

The writer believes that Minas Velhas's urban ethos is of more than local or regional significance. Far from being an atypical feature, such an ethos is probably a fundamental part of Mediterranean and Latin American culture. Although mining is usually associated with intense urban characteristics, mining itself cannot be thought of as having *created* the system of urban values which we find in Minas Velhas. On the contrary, the very business of searching for precious metals already implies a culture with a peculiarly urban orientation. If there had not already been a fundamental and ancient distinction in Europe between food-producing and food-consuming sociocultural segments, the search for gold would have been not only impossible but also without sense or purpose. Mining does not create an urban civilization; but in settlements whose subsistence is based on mining, urban values and institutions are likely to reveal themselves in their purest forms. There are other types of settlements, of course, for which the same observation may be made. Settlements based on trading and commerce, such as ports and market towns;

towns which make their living from manufacture; and governmental and bureaucratic centers also encourage the development and expression of urban ways.

In the history of Europe, it is only since the last two or three hundred years that the highest expression of urbanism has come to be associated with manufacturing. Prior to the industrial revolution, most large cities were primarily commercial and governmental centers, though artisans were always present and important. The introduction of power-driven machinery intensified the urban characteristics of these cities and also created a great number of new urban settlements. The remarkable growth of cities since the eighteenth century in Europe, the United States, Latin America, and the rest of the world is undoubtedly everywhere connected with the advent of power-driven factories. A particular urban center may grow directly as a result of increased manufacture, or indirectly as the result of increased trade and the greater wealth, scope, and power of government. But industrialization is everywhere to some extent responsible for the contemporary general expansion and intensification of urbanism. It is this circumstance which accounts for the misconception that urbanism is strongest where industrialization is most advanced. The introduction of power-driven machinery has probably led to the formation of urban values similar to those found in Minas Velhas in many groups which never before possessed them. But from its present isolated, pre-power condition and from its specific history as a town, we know that the urban values found in Minas Velhas must to a large extent predate the industrial revolution. To trace these values to their ultimate source is beyond the scope of the present work. We would have to go back at least as early as the period of discovery and possibly as far back as the Roman Empire. The geographer Jean Brunhes notes that

Almost all the Mediterranean peoples, preeminently "urban," have grouped themselves in settlements with houses closely crowded together, so closely that they have the appearance of small cities, even when they are only simple villages.[9]

In presenting an historical explanation of the urban ethos or any other component of the urban complex, it should be pointed out that there are dynamic, functional factors which account for the persistence of these traits and for their apparently rapid and world-wide intensification. Once a society reaches the stage of technology and social organization in which a large number of people can be freed from food-producing activities and occupational specialization becomes feasible on a large scale, there is little likelihood of reverting to more homogeneous arrangements. Although the urban complex in Minas Velhas represents a cultural tradition, a social inheritance from one generation to the next, the tenacity of the tradition itself stems as much from functional as historical causes. In a broad perspective, the end of the gold-mining era in the mountain region did not signal the end of urbanism in Minas Velhas because it did not eliminate the possibility of economic specialization. As long as the region and the nation produced an agricultural surplus, the bureaucratic, commercial, and craft specialties lingered on, modified, it is true, to some extent, but preserving the emphasis on individualism and heterogeneity and inviting secularism. A specialized economy evidently tends to respond to a threat to its particular specialties by developing new specialties. Urbanism, in this sense, is a one-way road, from which, once having embarked upon it, there is no turning back.

The remarkable strength of the urban complex in Latin America has only recently begun to receive the attention it deserves. Statistical analyses of this phenomenon generally suffer from an inability to think of urbanism except in terms of population size and indices of industrialization. Davis and Casis make a significant contribution by recognizing that Latin American urban agglomeration does not bear the same relation to industrialization as it does in other areas.

[9] Jean Brunhes, *Human Geography*, p. 503.

In comparison with more industrialized areas, the Latin American countries do not seem at first glance to be highly urban. In the United States in 1940, for example, the percentage of persons living in places of more than 5,000 inhabitants was 52.7, and for Canada 43.3, whereas for most of Latin America it was only 27.1. But when one realizes that the difference in urban concentration is very much smaller than the difference in industrial development, and that as compared with nearly all other areas the Latin American countries have a very much smaller average density, the percentage of urban dwellers to the south begins to look fairly high. Indeed it seems to us that in view of its retarded industrialization, Latin America is urbanized to a surprising degree. In other areas the growth of cities has arisen from large-scale industrial developments, but in Latin America it has come from non-industrial causes.[10]

Thus, even when the totally arbitrary figure of 5,000 is used as the criterion of an urban community, it is evident that the number of people in such communities presents a puzzle. It must be made clear, however, that Davis and Casis are here speaking of the amount of urban concentration and only indirectly of the degree of urbanism. The term "urbanization" is widely used to mean both the increasing concentration of a population within cities and the culture change involved in the modification of a rural culture in the direction of an urban one. Increasing urbanization, i.e., greater concentration of population, is often accepted rather gratuitously as indicative of culture change. The sheer fact that cities are larger now than in the past is not by itself an indication of such change, except insofar as there is a limited correlation between size and the intensification of other urban features. In cases where the growth of cities is due largely to the immigration of rural people, culture change is still not necessarily a concomitant of the population shift. All that may happen is that a large number of individuals move from the small towns

[10] Kingsley Davis and Ana Casis, " Urbanization in Latin America," *Millbank Memorial Fund Quarterly*, XXIV, No. 2 (1946), 2.

and countryside to the city while the town and city sub-cultures remain essentially unchanged. *this is what is found.*

All Latin American subcultures are certainly changing under urban and industrial influences, and yet the differences between some of them may remain great for many years to come. The content of Peasant and Metropolitan subcultures in Europe has in both cases changed profoundly during the last five hundred years, but the differences between city folk and peasants in almost any European nation are still striking. In the future, certain subcultures may diminish in importance or entirely disappear as the people who carry them adopt other culture patterns. . . . But any such picture of progressive urbanization must take into account the possibility that as the subculture types change toward greater urbanization, most of them do not merge in content, but remain as distinctly defined as ever within the national context. This is true because throughout all the stages of the urbanization of a nation, the city subcultures are not static but rather continue to be the innovators of most of the new features.[11]

If, however, the ratio of rural to urban inhabitants shows a progressive advantage on the urban side we may, of course, from the standpoint of the nation as a whole, speak of a greater degree of urbanism even though neither the urban nor the rural sub-cultures in themselves show any significant modification.

Thus the statistics of urban concentration can be used as an index of national urbanizing trends when the rate of growth of cities is compared to the rate of growth of the rest of the population. According to Davis and Cassis, "The general population of Latin America is growing at an exceedingly fast pace, yet the cities are growing even faster, and the larger cities are growing with phenomenal speed."[12] In Brazil, between 1920 and 1940, the population increased 36 percent while the

[11] Charles Wagley and Marvin Harris, "Typology of Latin American Sub-Cultures," *American Anthropologist,* LVII, No. 3 (1955), 448.
[12] Davis and Casis, "Urbanization in Latin America," *Millbank Memorial Fund Quarterly,* XXIV, No. 2 (1946), 11.

population of twenty-two large cities for which a 1920 figure is available increased 61 percent.[13]

These figures permit us to conclude that Brazil as a nation is becoming progressively more urban. But, the question as to whether or not the urban and rural subcultures of Brazil themselves are becoming more urban is another problem. Its solution would have to depend on whether or not heterogeneity, secularism, and individualism are becoming more intense, whether the distinction between urban and rural facets is becoming more or less sharp, and whether an urban ethos is growing stronger or weaker. This problem is not one which can be answered simply by the statistics of city growth.

Davis and Casis show that the phenomenal growth of Latin American cities is due to migration from the rural areas. They answer the problem of why the cities are such big attractions to the Latin American people in terms of Spanish and Portuguese institutions coupled with factors in the Latin American environment.

Environmental conditions . . . offered formidable barriers to settlement, and the Spaniards hardly had hard work in mind. As a consequence the interior was not developed along the lines of homestead farming, but was given to large landowners who used native or slave labor and aimed at getting out from forest, field, or mine as quickly as possible a commercial product for foreign shipment. The market lay across the ocean. . . .

The interior, inaccessible and undeveloped, had little of culture or convenience to offer. . . . Nobody wanted to stay there any longer than necessary. To live in the city was every man's dream. Persons who owned enough land in the interior lived in the city, where they formed a class of absentee landowners, educating their children abroad, doting on Europe, and in general neglecting the interior from which their wealth came. . . .

The emphasis upon urban dwelling among the wealthy meant that . . . sanitation, education, utilities and amuse-

13 Hubert L. Dunn, "Demographic Status of South America," *Annals of the American Academy of Political and Social Science,* CCXXXVII (1945), 25.

ments were fostered in the city but not elsewhere. The resulting gulf between city and country, still noticed by travelers and amply documented in rural-urban statistics, served to reinforce the initial preference for the city as a place to live. The idea of a quiet home in the country, far from the urban crowd—an idea dear to the Anglo Saxon—was not prominent in the Latin American mind. . . .

In short, the rural-urban migration that has given rise to unusual urbanization has not been due to heavy industrialization, but rather to the preculiar institutions of the Spanish and Portuguese and the environmental conditions in their part of the new world.[14]

And Theodore Caplow, speaking of the slight suburbanization of metropolitan centers of Latin America, confirms the conclusions of Davis and Casis:

This phenomenon is certainly related both as cause and effect to the positive value attached to the urban way of life in this culture [Latin America] in sharp contrast to the depreciation of urban values elsewhere.[15]

It is hard to see why, as Davis and Casis suppose, the Latin American environment offered more formidable barriers to the Iberians than, let us say, North America did to European homesteaders. Brazil, at least, with its great regional diversity, has as much to offer a prospective homesteader as any other quarters of the globe of equal size. The remainder of the remarks of Davis and Casis agree substantially with the results of the present study. It should be clear from the case of Minas Velhas, however, that the special system of urban values which is necessary for the understanding of the growth of the big Latin American cities is no less necessary for the understanding of the little ones, in growth or decline, and that the rural areas are to be best understood in relation to the small urban communities which dominate them.

14 Davis and Casis, "Urbanization in Latin America," *Millbank Memorial Fund Quarterly*, XXIV, No. 2 (1946), 16-17.
15 Theodore Caplow, "The Modern Latin American City," in *Acculturation in the Americas*, p. 258.

The strength of urban culture traits, especially of the urban ethos, in the town sub-cultures of Brazil must be taken into consideration by those who are interested in improving living conditions in the Brazilian interior. The people of Minas Velhas are ready to accept radical cultural changes, especially as these pertain to technological innovations. Far from presenting any ideological resistance to technological progress, they desperately desire it in all forms, from automobiles and electric power, to modern housing and miracle drugs. Modernity is well-nigh a passion with them and the new is valued over the old in almost all situations where the townspeople are presented with a choice. This is true despite the fact that Minas Velhas enjoys a local reputation for being a "traditional" and conservative community.

Yet wishes alone, are clearly not enough to bring about the changes which the townspeople so greatly desire, and in many respects the very intensity of the urban complex is the greatest obstacle to the development of improved standards of living and of technology. The townspeople have adopted for their own, prestige standards derived from urban life, which cannot effectively be supported under the given techno-environmental condition of the town and its hinterland. The level of agricultural and industrial productivity is simply not high enough to support the intense individualism, competition, and conspicuous consumption which the urban model demands. By facing toward the coast, lured by the truly stupendous achievements represented by cities like Sao Paulo and Rio de Janeiro, the townspeople have in effect turned their backs on what is ultimately their only possible source of future betterment. They refuse to admit that they are of the country and hence the wilderness all but engulfs them. They despise the work of the peasant and see in him the destroyer rather than the creator of civilization. They take from the soil and give nothing back, not even their labor. When fortune comes, they desert the interior and take their skills and money to the coast. The "lion" whose absence Jao

Celestino bemoaned is the town itself. The townspeople are the logical media for organizing and improving the agricultural production. They have capital to invest; they have bureaucratic ability suitable for organizing and directing cooperatives; they go to school and are literate and could easily be taught scientific principles of soil management and crop production; they are ready to use machines and believe in progress. Yet there is not a teacher in Minas Velhas who knows the rudiments of agriculture or who does not despise farming as a profession. Agricultural interests are represented in the town by absentee landlords who desire from their land what their sharecroppers are able to produce for them, i.e., enough so that *they* need not touch the hoe. But the town is not really there in the backlands. It stands like a deserted fort in the wilderness. Its people are away, dreaming of the city.

REFERENCES CITED

Azevedo, Fernando de. A Cultura Brasileiro. Sao Paulo, Companhia Editora Nacional, 1944.

Beals, Ralph L. A Sierra Tarascan Village. Washington, Smithsonian Institute of Anthropology, Publication No. 2, 1946.

Brunhes, Jean. Human Geography, tr. by T. C. Le Compte. Chicago, Rand McNally, 1920.

Calmon, Pedro. Historia do Brasil. 1935.

Calogeras, Pandia. As Minas do Brasil e Sua Legislacao, Vol. 3. Brasiliana, Vol. 134, 2d ed. Sao Paulo, Companhia Editora Nacional, 1938.

Caplow, Theodore. "The Modern Latin American City," in International Congress of Americanists, Acculturation in the Americas, edited by Sol Tax. Chicago, University of Chicago Press, 1952.

Davis, Kingsley, and Ana Casis. "Urbanization in Latin America," Millbank Memorial Fund Quarterly, XXIV, No. 2 (1946).

Deffontaines, Pierre. "Mountain Settlement in the Central Brazilian Plateau," Geographical Review, XXVII (1937), 394-413.

—— "The Origins and Growth of the Brazilian Network of Towns," Geographical Review, XXIII (1938), 379-99.

Dunn, Hubert L. "Demographic Status of South America," Annals of the American Academy of Political and Social Science, CCXXXVII (1945).

Freyre, Gilberto. Casa-Grande e Senzala. Rio de Janeiro, Schmidt, 1936.

Galvao, Eduardo. "The Religion of an Amazon Community." Ph.D. dissertation, Columbia University, 1952.

Gillin, John. Moche. Washington, Smithsonian Institute of Anthropology, Publication No. 3, 1947.

Henderson, James. The History of Brazil. London, 1821.

Hutchinson, Harry W. "Vila Reconcavo." Ph.D. dissertation, Columbia University, 1954.

James, Preston. Latin America. New York, Odyssey Press, 1950.

Kroeber, Alfred.   Anthropology.   New York, Harcourt Brace, 1948.

Lewis, Oscar.   Life in a Mexican Village.   Urbana, University of Illinois Press, 1951.

Mawe, John.   Travels in the Interior of Brazil.   London, 1821.

Mintz, Sidney, and Eric Wolf.   "An Analysis of Ritual Co-Parenthood," *Southwestern Journal of Anthropology*, VI, No. 4 (1950), 341-68.

Nash, Roy.   The Conquest of Brazil.   New York, Harcourt Brace, 1926.

Peixoto, Afranio.   Historia do Brasil.   Sao Paulo, Companhia Editora Nacional, 1944.

Redfield, Robert.   The Folk Culture of Yucatan.   Chicago, University of Chicago Press, 1941.

—— Tepoztlan.   Chicago, University of Chicago Press, 1930.

Smith, T. L., and Alexander Marchant.   Brazil.   New York, Dryden Press, 1951.

Sorokin, Pitirim A., Carle C. Zimmerman, and Charles J. Galpin.   A Systematic Source Book in Rural Sociology.   Minneapolis, University of Minnesota Press, 1930.

Southey, Robert.   History of Brazil.   London, 1817.

Spix, Johann von, and Karl von Martius.   Atraves da Bahia, tr. by Drs. Piraja da Silva and Paulo Wolf, 3d ed.   Sao Paulo, Companhia Editora Nacional, 1938.

Wagley, Charles (ed.).   Race and Class in Rural Brazil.   Paris, UNESCO, 1952.

Wagley, Charles, and Marvin Harris, "A Typology of Latin American Sub-Culture Types," *American Anthropologist*, LVII, No. 3 (1955), 428-49.

Willems, Emilio.   Cunha.   Sao Paulo, Secretaria da Agricultura, 1947.

Wirth, Louis.   "Urbanism as a Way of Life," *American Journal of Sociology*, XLIV (1938), 1-24.

Young, George.   Portugal Old and Young.   New York, Oxford University Press, 1917.

INDEX

Absentee landowners, 286

African culture patterns, 113, 114

A.G., Sr., 22, 76; effort in behalf of professional school, 184; quoted, 29

Agricultural cooperative, paralysis of, 205

Agricultural workers, 76 ff.

Agriculture, 3, 46, 47, 76-80; crops, 26, 80; effect upon the economy of emphasis on, 94; hoe the universal implement, 82, 84; in Bahia, 26, 27; in mountain region, 15; in villages, 83-90; lack of local government assistance, 182 f., 184; markets, 26, 85; soil conditions, 27; urban standpoint, 94; see also Farmers; Farming; Landlords; Sharecroppers

Alvaro, Sr., activities as a doctor, 267, 268

Antojo (pregnancy desires), 170

Architecture, Minas Velhas, 30 ff.

Aristocracy, 101 ff.

"Artisan's Lyre," 133

Auction, 134, 143; at religious festa, 231, 237

Azevedo, Joao, 188, 189, 192, 193-205 passim, 217

Bahia, bureaucratic superstructure, 18; former mining centers, 15; gerais, 9; gold, 12 ff.; mineral resources, 9; motorized transport, 69; saturation and mismanagement of lands in mountain region, 90; settlements based upon mining, 4; social, ethnic, and economic factors, 23-30; topography, 6 ff.; vegetation, 8; see also Minas Velhas

Baixa do Gamba, chefe, 264; clamor for school, 139; corn stock deterioration, 84; dissection of land, 88; domiciles, population, 25 tab.; émigrés, 90; festa of Sao Sebastiao, 236 ff.; few whites in, 113; irrigation, 87; population, 277; superstitions, 248; use of curandeiro, 261

Bananal, domiciles, population, 25 tab.

Band, focus of rivalry, 133

Baptism, 152

Beals, Ralph A., 277

Behavior, actual interracial, 124-28; differences in, 97; inter-related forms which result in urban ethos of Minas Velhas, 281; patterns available to city dweller, 275 ff.; sub-cultural varieties, 96

Black magic, sorcery, 252 ff.

Blacksmiths, 49, 52

Blacksmith's forge, illus., 50

Blessing at religious festa, 234

Bomfim, Carlos, mayor of Minas Velhas, 187

Bomfim, Eloisa, 201

Bomfim, Gerolina, 104

Bomfim, Lucrecio, 76n, 128, 192, 196; quoted, 141

Bomfim family, 102, 104

Bom Jesus da Lapa, 61; pilgrimage to shrine, 226 ff.

Boom and bust, 12 ff.

Botequins (small stores), 72

Boys, in town and in rural zone, 156 ff.

Brancos-ricos (rich whites), 96

Brass-smiths, 50 ff.

Brass-smith's lathe, illus., 51

Braulio, Sr., 55, 58 ff. passim, 104, 150

Brazil, discovery of gold, 12; failure to perform mineralogical surveys in region of Minas Velhas, 75; gold cycle

Brazil (*Continued*)
draws to close, 14; population density, 3; population increase, 285, 286; regional diversity offered to homesteader, 287; a rural nation, 3 ff.

Brazilian Institute of Geography and Statistics, 22

Brazilians, agricultural people, 3

Brazilian Workers' Party (PTB), 190, 191, 200

Broken limbs, word formula for curing, 250

Bromado, 6, 9

Brotherhood of the Negroes, 133

Brotherhood of Rosario, class schism in, 133

Brotherhoods, religious, 239-41

Brumadinho, domiciles, population, 25 *tab.*

Brunhes, Jean, quoted, 282

Bubonic Plague Control Service, 142; agent refused entrance to village houses, 207

Bureaucracy, state, in Minas Velhas, 193 *tab.*; distrust of, 207

Buried treasure, belief in, 245

Caatinga, 8

Cachaca, 257

Capitalists, role of, 57

Caplow, Theodore, quoted, 287

Carnivals, 130; *preto-pobre*, 131, 239

Casis, Ana, and Kingsley Davis, 283, 284, 285, 287; quoted, 286

Catholic Church, absence of cohesive integrative influence in Minas Velhas, 208; attendance, 211, 212 *tab.*; basic tension point, 209; masses, 220

Catholicism, formal, 211-22; inability to be reconciled with local institutions, 241; informal, 222-28

Catholics, 113

Celestino, Joao, 52, 70, 71

Charmed objects, 252

Cheran, Mexico, 277

Childbirth, 164

Children, care and training, 155; fears of school children, 269 *tab.*; games, 157; godparents, 152 ff.; in local agriculture, 90; occupational preferences of urban school children, 175 *tab.*

Churches, Bahia, 25; Minas Velhas, 23; *see also* Catholic Church

Cities, growth of: causes of growth in Europe, United States, and Latin America, 282; in Latin America, 284 ff.

City dwellers, attitude toward country people, 141; behavior patterns available to, 275 ff.; countryside a no man's land for, 273; secular world view, 274; urban complex, 272

Civic improvements lacking in villages, 207

Civil service, 45

Class and race, 96-146; *see also* Race; Social classes

Clube Social, 128-30

Commerce, 46, 47; settlements based on, encourage development of urbanism, 281

Commercial establishments, 71-74

Communists' flight across Bahia, 176

Compadre system, 151 ff.

Concubines, 167, 168

Contract artisan, 64

Cooking facilities, 35

Cooperation, lack of well-developed patterns of, 64 ff.

Cooperative labor groups, 67

Cooperative Mixta, paralysis of, 205

Coracao de Jesus, *festa* of, 229

Corn, deterioration of stock caused by consumption of best cobs, 84

Corpus Christi, *festa* of, 229

Country people regarded as inferior by city dweller, 141

Countryside, folk fears and urbanite ignorance of, 272-73
Cousin marriages, 102
Craft interdependence, 62-64
Crafts, economic individualism, 64-68; past and future of, 69-71
Crystal mining, 75
Cultural change and population shift, 284
Culture, sacred and secular aspects, 242
Cultures, distinction between folk and sophisticated, 274-89; strength of urban traits in town sub-cultures, 288
Curandeiros (folk doctors), 261 ff.

Dancing, 159
Dantas, Fernandes, 188
Davis, Kingsley, and Ana Casis, 283, 284, 285, 287; quoted, 286
Deffontaines, Pierre, quoted, 4
Demon spirits, 248
Devil, 248, 272
Diamantinas, opulence became a memory, 14
Diamonds, 12, 13
Disease, folk belief associated with, 261-69; prevention and cure, 255
Divino Espirito Santo, *festa*, 226, 229
Doctors, folk, 261 ff.
Dreams as revelatory phenomena, 247
Drugstore, 267
Dwellings, *see* Houses

Eastern Highlands, 4
Economic conditions, *see* Standard of living
Economic gradient in class structure, 97
Economic group, actual and ideal distribution of racial types per, 136 *tabs.*
Economic individualism, 64-68
Economics, 44-95; agriculture, 76-80; agriculture in the villages, 83-90; craft interdependence, 62-64; distribution of industrial products, 59-62; economic individualism, 64-68; emigration, 90-95; entrepreneurs, 57-59; gold mining, 74-76; large farms, 80-83; leathercraft, 53-57; metalcraft, 48-53; occupational specialization, 44-48; past and future of crafts, 69-71; role of capital, 57; stores, 71-74
Education, 21, 111-12; highest grade completed, 111 *tab.;* years of schooling, 111 *tab.*
Educational gradient in class structure, 98
Elections, election day, 202; election eve, 200 ff.; literacy a requirement for voting, 98
Electoral campaigns, 191 ff.
Emanuel, Padre, 217 ff., 240
Emergence of the Saint's standard at *festa,* 230
Emigration, 90, 95; difference between rural and urban movements, 93
Émigrés, occupations of urban, 92 *tab.*
England, colonial investments in Brazil; treaty of Methuen with Portugal, 13
Entrega da Bandeira at religious festival, 234
Entrepreneurs, 57-59
Escarpment of central Bahia, 6 ff.
Ethnic groups, Bahia, 25
Ethos, what it is, 280

Fairs, 26
Family, and the individual, 147-78; cohesion, 147-51; elite, 101 ff.; intrafamilial bonds, 150; married life, 165-74; relationships more intense in village, 278; ritual kinship, 151-55; urban discontents, 174-78
Farani, Lauro, 190, 196
Farmers, 76 ff.

Farming, despised by towns-people, 289; irrigation, 87; *see also* Agriculture

Farming population, Bahia: cluster-type settlement, 24

Farms, large, 80-83; small, semi-subsistence, 83

Fazendeiros (plantation owners), 77

Fears, 269-73; of school children, 269 *tab.*

Feiticeiros (magicians), 263

Festa, religious, 228-39; expenses for a typical, 235 *tab.;* of Minas Velhas, seven elements, 230; sources of income for a typical, 236 *tab.*

Festa dos Reis (Festival of the Kings), 132

Festeiro, 228-39 *passim*

Festival, religious, *see Festa*

Festival of the Kings, 132

Field team, 75

Filipe (School teacher's husband), 173, 174

Folk belief, 113, 242-73; associated with health and disease, 261-69; fears, 269-73; folk science, 242, 255-69; magico-religious aspects, 242, 250-55, 279; secular behavior and beliefs, 243; supernatural beliefs and practices, 243-50

Folk community, 37; *see also* Rural

Folk doctors, 261 ff.

Food, corn, 84; percentage of income used for, 109 *tab.;* taboos, 242, 258 ff.

Food stores, 71 ff.

Formiga, 8

Frigidity, sexual, 169

Garden, town, 38

Gates, 24, 37

Gerais, 9

Ghosts, 242 ff.; parallels in formal Catholic dogma, 249

Gillin, John, 277

Gilo, domiciles, population, 25 *tab.*

Girls, in town and in rural zone, 156 ff.

Godparents of baptism and of marriage, 152 ff.; per head of household, 154 *tab.*

Gold, discovery of, 4, 5, 12; early prospectors, 16; effect upon course of European history, 13; ghostly appearances connected with, 244; taxation of crude, 17

Gold mines, dwindling of, 14

Gold mining, 74-76

Goldsmiths, 49

Goncalves, Padre, 199, 216 ff., 221, 240; quoted, 190

Government, and politics, 179-207; appropriation for a professional school in Minas Velhas, 185; lack of assistance to public health, agriculture, and industry, 182 f., 184; local, 179-86

Goyaz, 16

Gravata, domiciles, population, 25 *tab.*

Groups, social strata, *see* Social classes

Gruta, 8; *festa* of patron saint of, 200; landlords, 77; shortage of hired hands, 90

Harris, Marvin, and Charles Wagley, quoted, 285

Headless mule, 248, 249

Health, folk belief associated with, 261-69; taboos, 242, 258 ff.

Herb remedies, 255 ff.

Hoe, universal instrument of work, 84

Home cult of the saints, 222 ff.

Homesteader, regional diversity offered to, 287

Households, 106, 107 *tab.;* number of individuals per household, 147 *tab.;* three types, 147

Houses, types, 109 ff. *with tabs.*

Iberians, barriers to, in Latin American environment, 287

Inauguration ceremonies, 202
Income, monthly cash, per head of family, 108 *tab.*; percentage of, used for food, 109 *tab.*
Individual, and the family, 147-78; life cycle, 155-65
Industrialization, effect upon urbanism, 282, 284
Industrial products, distribution, 59-62; prices, 60; value of monthly exports from Minas Velhas, 60, 61 *tab.*
Industries, craft interdependence, 62-64; lack of local government assistance to, 183, 184; vulnerable to competition of metropolitan factories, 69
Industry, economics, 44-95
Institutions, duplication of, 137
Instituto Brasileiro de Geografia e Estastistica, 93
Intravenous injections, 267
Irmandade (Brotherhood) de Santana, 240
Irmandade do Rosario, 133, 240
Irmandade do Sagrado Coracao de Jesus, 239
Irmandade do Santissimo Sacramento, 239
Irrigation, 87
Izidro, Sr., 54

Jaguars, fear of, 269, 270
Joaquim, *curandeiro*, 261
John V, king of Portugal, splendor in court of, 14

Kinship, ritual, 151-55
Kitchens, 35
Kroeber, Alfred, quoted, 275

Labor, menial, degrading, 99
Land, diminishing ratio per individual, 88, 90; legal and use-defined ownership, 86; *see also* Property
Landlords, 76 ff.; absentee, 286
Language, Portuguese, 98
Lapa, pilgrimage to shrine at, 226 ff.

Latin America, environment offered barriers to Iberians, 287; increasing speed of urbanization, 285; rural-urban migration, 286; strength of urban complex, 283
Leathercraft, 48, 53-57
Life cycle, 155-65
Lima family, 102
Lisbon, effect of Brazilian gold upon, 13
Literacy, a criterion of rank; a requirement for voting, 98, 112 *tab.*
Living standard, *see* Standard of living
Lojas (stores), 71

Macaqueiros (laborers), 78, 104
Machine products, invasion of, 70
Mafra, Judge, 188
Mafra, Portugal, monastery-palace-barracks, 14
Magic, 250-55; sorcery, 252 ff.
Magico-religious system, 242-73, 279
Mandioca mill, 80
Manufacturing, occupations, 45 *tab.*, 47 *tab.*; urbanism associated with, 282
Marcelino, governor of Bahia State, 186
Marchant, Alexander, and T. L. Smith, quoted, 3, 4
Margalhaes, Juracy, 188, 191
Markets, 85; effect of inability to tap distant, 91
Marriage, 102 ff.; ceremonies, 160 ff.; godparents of, 152
Married life, 165-74
Martius, K. von, 17, 20, 21, 22
Mass at religious *festa*, 233, 237
Matto Grosso, 16
Mawe, John, quoted, 14
Medicines, 267; folk, 255 ff.
Men, attitude toward the Church, 212; attitude toward confession, 213; dominance of (*see* Married life); use of money prerogative of husband, 172

Menial services, 45, 47; low esteem of, 175

Menstruation, 157

Merchandise, see Industrial products

Metalcraft, four types of artisans, 48-53; raw materials, 61

Metal industries, electrically plated products a threat to, 69; quality degraded by struggle to produce in quantity, 70

Methuen, treaty of, between England and Portugal, 13

Minas Gerais, 4; gold, 16; sculpture, 12

Minas Velhas, and vicinity, map, 7; architecture, 30 ff.; back yards, 36; balance of the sexes affected by emigration, 93; class and race, 96-146; climate, 34; decline, 19 ff.; designated a vila, 16; economics, 44-95; educational standards, 22; exodus of workers, 90; family and individual, 147-78; feeling of superiority, 22; flower garden, 38; folk belief, 242-73; goldsmith's art and other metallurgical crafts, 17; government and politics, 179; government's failure to be concerned with welfare of, 184; heterogeneity, 279; historical background, 12-23; industry, 16, 44-95; isolation, 276; journey to, 6 ff.; judicial center, 18; mineral resources its only hope for future, 75; occupations of émigrés, 92 tab.; passion for modernity, 288; political importance lost, 29; population, 20, 93 tab.; ready to accept technological innovations, 288; religion, 208-41; religious festas, 228-39; roads and trails, 6 ff.; sacked by communists, 176; satellites, 28, 36; setting, 6-43; social and cultural differences between, and its satellites, 279; social cleavage, 128-46; streets, 36, 37; swinging gates, 24, 37; technological lag, 44; total number of households, 47; the town, 10, map, 31; town and country, 23-30; town flower garden, 38; townspeople turned backs on only source of future betterment, 288; urban activities, 39-43; urban ethos, 21, 23, 275, 279 ff.; urban scene, 30-39

Minas Velhas county, 18; expansion of school facilities, 139; expenditures 1949-50, 180-81 tab.; receipts, 183 tab.; remunerative positions, 192, 193 tab., 194; state bureaucracy in, 193 tab.

Mineiro, Izidro, 188

Mineiro, Luiz, 187

Minerals, Bahia, 9; chief asset of Minas Velhas, 75; concern with mineral wealth, 75, 76; found in vicinity of Minas Velhas, 75; see also Gold

Mining, associated with urban characteristics, 4, 281

Mining towns, sites deficient in food-producing soils, 15

Moche, Peru, 277

Modernity well-nigh a passion in Minas Velhas, 288

Money, use of, the prerogative of husband, 172

Morais, Artur, 187, 188, 195, 196, 203, 204

Morales, Sr., 95

Mountains, central Bahia, 6 ff.; saturation and mismanagement of lands in, 90

Mulatto, relative racial attributes, 120 tab.; relative racial rank, 121 tab., 122 tab.; social behavior, 113

Mule, headless, 248, 249

Nash, Roy, quoted, 5

National Democratic Union (UDN), 189, 190; public address system, 200; victory celebration, 203 ff.

Negro, attitude toward, 114 ff.; distinction between white and, 96; family structure, 114; measured by same yardstick as the white, 123; occasional, rises to high social level, 127; "quota" on proportion of, who may rank equal to whites, 135, 137; racial barrier resented by, 137; relative racial attributes, 120 *tab.*; relative racial rank, 106, 121 *tab.*, 122 *tab.*; social behavior, 113; social characteristics, 129; stereotypes regarding, 117
Negro-Caucasoid mixtures, 113
Negroes, Society of the, 131
Nickel, 62
Novena of religious *festa*, 230, 236

Occultism, 208, 209; *see also* Supernatural
Occupational gradient, in class structure, 98
Occupational preferences of urban school children, 175 *tab.*
Occupations, 106; distribution of, 47 *tab.*, 110 *tab.*; occupational specialization, 44-48; of émigrés in Minas Velhas and abroad, 92 *tab.*; variety of activities, 45
Orlando, Sr., 54
Osorio, Ataliba, 187
Otacilio, Sr., 54, 55
Ouro Preto, *see* Vila Rica

Pacheco, Regis, 191; governor of Bahia, 203
Parana, agricultural expansion, 90; occupations of émigrés, 92 *tab.*
Patent remedies, 267
Patron saints, 222 ff.; household, 225 *tab.*
Peasant seen as destroyers rather than creator of civilization, 288
Peddler, 59

Penicillin, 268
Pensamento Publishing Company, 209
"People of distinction," 100
Physical characteristics, no important groups determined by, 126
Physical types, resultant from race mixture, 118 ff.
Plains, 9
Plantation owners, 77
Plantations, 77 ff.; large, 80-83
Planting seasons, 83
Plants, medicinal, 255 ff.
Platibanda, 34
Plow, sharecroppers' refusal to use, 82, 84
Political campaigns, 191 ff.
Political parties, local, 189
Political power, despotic, 101
Political schism, 196 ff.
Politics, 151; government and, 179-207; indifference of villages to, 206; literacy a requirement for voting, 98
Poor, Society of the, 130-35, 200, 239
Population, shift of, and cultural change, 284
Population density, Brazil, 3
Portugal, effect of Brazilian gold upon, 13; treaty of Methuen, 13
Portuguese Empire, dwindled into insignificance, 14
Positions, occupied by all racial types, 123; remunerative, in county of Minas Velhas, 192, 193 *tab.*, 194
Postnatal taboos, 165
Praca da Grama, church, 240
Prayer, efficacy of, 222; for souls in purgatory and in mortal sin, 249
Precious metals, search for, implies urban orientation of culture, 281
Prenatal taboos, 163
Presbyterian sect, 211
Prestes, Carlos, 176
Pretos-pobres (poor negroes), 96

Priests, income, 219 ff.; role of, 213; stories about, 214 ff.

Procession at religious *festa*, 233

Professional school for minors, appropriation for construction of building, 185

Professions, 45, 47

Promessa, 223

Property, average value, 107 *tab.*; range and distribution, 108 *tab.*; see also Land

Prostitution, 158, 166 ff.

Protestants, 211

PSD (Social Democracy Party), 185, 189

PTB (Brazilian Workers' Party), 190, 191, 200

Public health, local government's lack of concern with, 182

Public works, 181

Purgatory, prayer for souls in, 250

Quince, 85

Race, actual interracial behavior, 124-28; as a diagnostic of class, 137; cleavage in social life, 128-35; distribution of racial types, 113; distribution of racial types per economic group, 136 *tabs.*; factor in social tension, 134-40; intermediate or mixed types, 119, 123; physical types resultant from race mixture, 118 ff.; a ranking gradient in middle strata, 105, 106; a ranking gradient in social structure, 100, 112-24; relative attributes, 120 *tab.*; relative rank, 121 *tab.*; relative rank as seen by each group, 122 *tab.*

Rains, 84

Rank, criteria, 96-100

Rapadura (crude sugar), 82

Raparigas (loose women), 167, 168

Raposo, Sebastiao, 16, 17

Raw materials, 61

Reconcavo of Bahia, 67

Redfield, Robert, 276

Religion, 113, 208-41; formal Catholicism, 211-22; magico-religious aspects of the culture, 242; religions other than Catholicism, 208-11

Religious brotherhoods, 239-41

Religious festivals, 134, 228-39

Retirement of the Standard at *festa*, 234

Rio das Pedras, 8; marginal lands, 27

Rio das Pedras Falls, 8

Rio de Janeiro, florescence, 14

Robbery, fear of armed, 269

Roceiros (farmers), 77

Roman Catholic Church *see* Catholic Church

Royal Highway, 16, 19

Rural, term, 3

Rural groups, Bahia, 24 ff.; physical homogeneity, 25; social and economic disadvantages, 28

Ruralism in Brazil, 3

Rural or folk cultures, qualities of, 275 ff.; sacred viewpoint, 274

Rural settlement, a one-class community, 140; see also Villages

Rural-urban differentiation, 274-89

Sabino, Ademar, 206

Saida da Bandeira, at religious *festa*, 230

Saints, household, 225 *tab.*; patron, 222 ff.

Salvador, population, 277

Samba, 114

Samba em roda, 163

Santissimo Sacramento, *festa* of, 226, 229; procession, 233

Sao Joao, *festa* of, 152

Sao Paulo, 4, 16; agricultural expansion, 90; occupations of émigrés, 92 *tab.*

Sao Sebastiao, *festa* of, 134, 236 ff.

Satellite villages, agriculture, 83-90

Schoolteacher and her husband, 173, 174

Sculpture in cities of Minas Gerais, 12

Secular, emphasis placed upon the, in Minas Velhas, 243

Seed selection, 84

Serra do Espinhaco, 12

Serra do Ouro, climate, 35; distrust of fieldworker's connection with state government, 207; distrust of strangers, 142; domiciles, population, 25 *tab.;* émigrés, 90, 91, 93; farming, 84; few Negroes in, 113; prayer for souls, 249; streets, 37; timidity of women, 174; use of *curandeiro,* 261

Services, 45

"Seven-day sickness," 155

Sex, important ranking principle, 156

Sexual codes and practices, 158 ff., 166 ff.

Sharecroppers, 76 ff., 82; on a large farm, 80; share of yield, 89

Shoemaking, description of, 55

Silva, Jose da, 80, 95, 150, 190, 191; inauguration as mayor, 203; refusal of *Pessedistas* to accept his election as final, 203

Sin, prayer for souls in mortal, 250

Slate mining, 75

Slave labor, 23; effect upon sugar plantations, 14

Smelting house, 17

Smith, T. Lynn, and Alexander Marchant, quoted, 3, 4

Snakes, fear of, 269, 271

Snake stone, magic, 252

Soares, Afonso, 186, 195

Social classes, class and race, 96-146; class structure, *fig.,* 97; cleavage between town and village, 140-46; criteria of rank, 96-100; elite, 100-104; *maca-*

queiros or submarginal group, 104-5; middle strata, 105-6; race as a diagnostic of, 137; racial ranking gradient, 100, 112-24; rank and the standard of living, 106-12; rift between, 128-46; social cleavage, 128-46; tensions, 134-40; two groups, 96

Social Democracy Party (PSD), 185, 189

Social life, Clube Social, 128-30

Sociedade dos Pobres, 130-35, 200, 239

Sociedade dos Pretos, 131

Societies, differences between urban and rural, 275-89

Society of the Negroes, 131

Society of the Poor, 130-35, 200, 239

Soils, sites of mining towns deficient in food-producing, 15

Sorcery, 252 ff.

Southey, Robert, 12

Spinsters, 102

Spirits, malevolent, 248

Spiritualism, 208 ff., 242

Spix, J. von, 17, 20, 21, 22

Standard of living, indices of economic, occupational, and educational gradients, 106-12 *with tabs.;* of whites and Negroes, 136

State bureaucracy in Minas Velhas, 193 *tab.*

State Tax Collector, hostility of villagers toward, 207

Storekeeper, conspicuous role of the chair, 73

Stores, 71-74; failure of small, to effect mergers, 73

Sugar industry, senescence of Brazilian, 14

Sugar mill, 81

Sulfa remedies, 268

Supernatural, belief in, 114, 208 ff., 242; *see also* Folk belief

Taboos, health, 242, 258 ff.; postnatal, 165; prenatal, 163; religious rationales, 259

Tax, royal, on crude gold, 17

Tax officials, appointment and dismissal of, 192

Technological innovations, readiness to accept, 288

Technological lag, 44

Tepoztlan, Mexico, 276

Tetanus infection, 155

Thieves, fear of, 269

Tinsmiths, 49

Town band, focus of rivalry, 133

Towns, contrast between villages and, 274-89; fieldworker accepted by average urbanite, 207; of Bahia after dwindling of gold, 15; of Brazil are conspicuously urban, 278; social cleavage between villages and, 140-46; village satellites, 28, 36

Trade, settlements based on, encourage development of urbanism, 281

UDN (Uniao Democratica Nacional), see National Democratic Union

United States, changing frontiers, 5

Urban, term, 3

Urban centers, see Towns

Urban complex, 272-73

Urban discontents, 174-78

Urban ethos, of Minas Velhas, 279 ff.; strength of, in town sub-cultures of Brazil, 288

Urbanism, effect of industrialization upon, 282; in Brazil, 3; settlements based on trade and commerce encourage development of, 281

Urbanite, isolation from countryside, 272-73

Urbanization, 284; statistics of urban concentration as index of national trends, 285

Urban-rural differentiation, 274-89

Uricuri, *fazenda* of Sr. Silva, 80

Vargas, Getulio, 187, 188, 191, 200

Vegetation, Bahia, 8

Vendas (stores), 71 ff.

Viana, Odilon, 209, 210

Vianna, Oliveira, quoted, 3

Vila Nova, 6, 8; commerce and agriculture, 10; flour mill, 85; landlords, 77; seat of a new county, 19, 29; shortage of hired hands, 90

Vila Rica (now Ouro Preto), a national monument, 12; opulence became a memory, 14; sculpture: wealth, 12

Villages, agriculture, 83-90; civic improvements lacking in, 207; familiarity of villagers with countryside, 272; homogeneity, 279; indifference to politics, 206; satellites, 28, 36; social cleavage between town and, 140-46; suspicious of fieldworker's investigations, 207

Wages an incentive to emigration, 90

Wagley, Charles, and Marvin Harris, quoted, 285

Waldemar, Sr., 54, 127; social standing, 138

Wealth, differences in, 97

Werewolf, 248, 249

Wheat, 85

White, distinction between Negro and, 96; relative racial attributes, 120 *tab.;* relative racial rank, 121 *tab.,* 122 *tab.;* social characteristics, 129; superiority of race, 114

Wilderness, why it still flourishes, 273

Women, and the church, 212; in local agriculture, 90; menstruating, 157; self-supporting, 94; sense of oppression, 213; wage-earning role, 172; see also Married life

Work patterns, among villagers, 279; rural, 85

Young, George, quoted, 13, 14

Boas, Franz. *Anthropology and Modern Life.* N108

Boman, Thorleif. *Hebrew Thought Compared With Greek.* N534

Brook, G. L. *A History of the English Language.* N248

Bury, J. B. *The Invasion of Europe by the Barbarians.* N388

Bury, J. B. et al. *The Hellenistic Age.* N544

Carpenter, Rhys. *Discontinuity in Greek Civilization.* N453

Childe, V. Gordon. *New Light on the Most Ancient East.* N469

Clark, John W. *Early English.* N228

Contenau, Georges. *Everyday Life in Babylon and Assyria.* N358

Dodds, E. R. *Pagan and Christian in an Age of Anxiety.* N545

East, W. Gordon. *The Geography Behind History.* N419

Embree, Ainslie, ed. *Alberuni's India.* N568

Field, M. J. *Search for Security: An Ethno-Psychiatric Study of Rural Ghana.* N508

Finley, M. I. *Early Greece: The Bronze and Archaic Ages.* N541

Freud, Sigmund. *Totem and Taboo.* N143

Glotz, Gustave. *Ancient Greece at Work.* N392

Glueck, Nelson. *Rivers in the Desert: A History of the Negev.* N431

Gordon, Cyrus H. *The Ancient Near East.* N275

Gordon, Cyrus H. *The Common Background of Greek and Hebrew Civilizations.* N293

Gordon, Cyrus H. *Ugarit and Minoan Crete.* N426

Gorer, Geoffrey. *Africa Dances.* N173

Gorer, Geoffrey. *The American People.* N262

Gorer, Geoffrey and John Rickman. *The People of Great Russia.* N112

Harris, Marvin. *Town and Country in Brazil.* N573

Hatzfeld, Jean and Andre Aymard. *History of Ancient Greece.* N247

Herskovits, Melville J. *Economic Anthropology.* N309

Jespersen, Otto. *Language: Its Nature, Development and Origin.* N229

Jespersen, Otto. *The Philosophy of Grammar.* N307

Kartini, Raden Adjeng. *Letters of a Javanese Princess.* N207

Krappe, Alexander H. *The Science of Folklore.* N282

Landes, Ruth. *The Ojibwa Woman.* N574

Malinowski, Bronislaw. *The Father in Primitive Psychology.* N332

Mauss, Marcel. *The Gift.* N378

Mosse, Claude. *The Ancient World at Work.* N540

Nilsson, Martin P. *The Mycenaean Origin of Greek Mythology.* N234

Ogilvie, R. M. *The Romans and Their Gods in the Age of Augustus.* N543

Pendlebury, J. D. S. *The Archaeology of Crete.* N276

Powdermaker, Hortense. *Life in Lesu.* N566

Powdermaker, Hortense. *Stranger and Friend: The Way of an Anthropologist.* N410

Reeves, James (Ed.). *The Idiom of the People.* N289

Sarton, George. *A History of Science, I: Ancient Science Through The Golden Age of Greece.* N525

Sarton, George, *A History of Science, II: Hellenistic Science and Culture in the Last Three Centuries B.C.* N526

Shway Yoe. *The Burman.* N212

Warmington, B. H. *Nero: Reality and Legend.* N542

Webster, T. B. L. *From Mycenae to Homer.* N254

Wilcken, Ulrich. *Alexander the Great.* N381

Woolley, C. Leonard. *A Forgotten Kingdom.* N450

Woolley, C. Leonard. *The Sumerians.* N292

Woolley, C. Leonard. *Ur of the Chaldees.* N301